"An updated and transcendent extension of their previous book placing Communication at the core of our understanding of the aging process, the authors provide every aging scholar, practitioner, and individual with an empirically grounded and theoretically rich path to successful aging. Contextualized within the Covid pandemic, I highly recommend this book as the best source for all those managing a positive aging experience."

Jon F. Nussbaum, *Liberal Arts Professor Emeritus of Communication Arts and Sciences and Human Development and Family Studies, Penn State University*

"*Communication for Successful Aging* provides a thoroughly engaging and incredibly concise understanding of the human aging process. It effectively conveys the centrality of communication to a successful old age, illustrating that communication provides both the context for and process by which we get older, using numerous (often very entertaining) examples. The book addresses difficult and understudied topics including, most notably, communication and death. Throughout, it emphasizes practical application: A textbook for a course about communication and aging, but equally a 'how to' guide for anybody who is getting older – which is, of course, all of us!"

Jake Harwood, *Professor of Communication, University of Arizona*

"This volume is a timely resource on aging well for our post-pandemic world. The authors present high quality, up-to-date research on topics such as age stereotyping, intergenerational communication, cultural influences on aging, and empowerment – all delivered in an engaging style that includes real-life examples and illustrative figures. This is a book that holds insights on enhancing the experience of aging for both general and academic audiences."

Mary Lee Hummert, *Professor Emerita, Communication Studies Department, University of Kansas*

Communication for Successful Aging

This essential volume explores the vital role of communication in the aging process and how this varies for different social groups and cultural communities. It reveals how communication can empower people in the process of aging, and that how we communicate about age is critically important to – and is at the heart of – aging successfully.

Giles et al. confront the uncertainty and negativity surrounding "aging" – a process with which we all have to cope – by expertly placing communication at the core of the process. They address the need to avoid negative language, discuss the lifespan as an evolving adventure, and introduce a new theory of successful aging – the communication ecology model of successful aging (CEMSA). They explore the research on key topics including: age stereotypes, age identities, and messages of agism; the role of culture, gender, ethnicity, and being a member of marginalized groups; the ingredients of intergenerational communication; depiction of aging and youth in the media; and how and why talk about death and dying can be instrumental in promoting control over life's demands.

Communication for Successful Aging is essential reading for graduate students of psychology, human development, gerontology, and communication, scholars in the social sciences, and all of us concerned with this complex academic and highly personal topic.

Howard Giles, PhD, DSc, is a Distinguished Research Professor in the Communication Department, University of California, Santa Barbara, and Honorary Professor in the School of Psychology, The University of Queensland, Brisbane, Australia.

Dr. Jessica Gasiorek is an Associate Professor in the Communicology program at the University of Hawai'i at Mānoa, USA.

Dr. Shardé M. Davis is an Assistant Professor in the Department of Communication and Faculty Affiliate of various research institutes at the University of Connecticut, USA.

Jane Giles is a software consultant and author with a background in psychology and education.

Communication for Successful Aging
Empowering Individuals Across the Lifespan

Howard Giles, Jessica Gasiorek, Shardé M. Davis, and Jane Giles

NEW YORK AND LONDON

First published 2022
by Routledge
605 Third Avenue, New York, NY 10158

and by Routledge
2 Park Square, Milton Park, Abingdon, Oxon, OX14 4RN

Routledge is an imprint of the Taylor & Francis Group, an informa business

© 2022 Howard Giles, Jessica Gasiorek, Shardé M. Davis, and Jane Giles

The right of Howard Giles, Jessica Gasiorek, Shardé M. Davis, and Jane Giles to be identified as authors of this work has been asserted by them in accordance with sections 77 and 78 of the Copyright, Designs and Patents Act 1988.

All rights reserved. No part of this book may be reprinted or reproduced or utilised in any form or by any electronic, mechanical, or other means, now known or hereafter invented, including photocopying and recording, or in any information storage or retrieval system, without permission in writing from the publishers.

Trademark notice: Product or corporate names may be trademarks or registered trademarks, and are used only for identification and explanation without intent to infringe.

Library of Congress Cataloging-in-Publication Data
A catalog record for this title has been requested

ISBN: 978-0-367-35327-8 (hbk)
ISBN: 978-0-367-35326-1 (pbk)
ISBN: 978-0-429-33068-1 (ebk)

DOI: 10.4324/9780429330681

Typeset in Bembo
by Deanta Global Publishing Services, Chennai, India

Contents

Authors' Biographies		viii
Preface		x
1	Matters of Communication and Aging	1
2	Messages of Agism and Age Stereotypes	20
3	Age Identities: What Are They and How Do They Emerge?	38
4	The Ingredients of Intergenerational Communication	56
5	The Media, Agism, and Anti-Aging	72
6	Talking About Death – Or Not	90
7	Successful Aging and Communication	108
8	Conclusions and Vistas: Communicating Resilience, Hope, and Empowerment	128
Index		145

Authors' Biographies

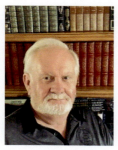

Howard Giles (PhD, DSc, University of Bristol) became Professor (and former-Chair) of Communication at the University of California, Santa Barbara (with affiliated positions in Linguistics and Psychology) in 1989. Before this, he was Chair of Social Psychology and Head of Psychology at the University of Bristol, UK. His research has received many professional awards over the years, including being co-recipient of an (inaugural) Award by the National Communication Association for his career contributions to the study of communication and aging research, which, thereafter, was called the Giles-Nussbaum Distinguished Scholar Award. In 2000, he was the recipient of the Inaugural Career Productivity Award from the International Communication Association. Giles has been the author or editor of many book series and books, including the *Handbook of Intergroup Communication* for Routledge (2012) and the two-volume Oxford Encyclopedia of Intergroup Communication for Oxford University Press (2018). Founding Editor of the *Journal of Language and Social Psychology* and the *Journal of Asian Pacific Communication*, and past Editor of *Human Communication Research*, he has been Past President of the International Communication Association and the International Association of Language and Social Psychology.

Jessica Gasiorek (PhD, University of California, Santa Barbara) is an Associate Professor in the Communicology program at the University of Hawai'i at Mānoa. She studies how people produce and process messages, how people adjust their communication in context, and how people create understanding. She is also interested in the role of communication in people's collective ideas about age and aging, and the implications this has for social dynamics, social evaluations, and people's subjective well-being. She is the recipient of the James J. Bradac Early Career Prize from the International Association of Language and Social Psychology (2015), as well as a Junior Faculty Research Award from the

University of Hawai'i at Mānoa's College of Arts and Humanities (2014). She has served as Chair of the National Communication Association's Communication and Aging Division, and Chair of the International Communication Association's Intergroup Communication Interest Group.

Shardé M. Davis (PhD, University of Iowa) is an Assistant Professor in the Department of Communication at the University of Connecticut. Her research examines the way Black women leverage communication in the sistah circle to invoke collective identity, erect and fortify the boundaries around their homeplace, and backfill the necessary resources to return to white and male dominant spaces in American society. These ideas have been published in over 40 peer-refereed articles and invited book chapters, and are best represented in her theory, *The Strong Black Woman Collective*. Her research was formally recognized with the 2018 American Postdoctoral Fellowship from the American Association of University Women and the 2019 Ford Foundation Postdoctoral Fellowship. Most recently, she created the viral Twitter Hashtag #BlackintheIvory that extended a timely opportunity for Blackademic TRUTHtellers to share personal instances of racism in a virtual space and engage in necessary conversations about anti-Black racism in the academy.

Jane Giles has been an IT Consultant in Santa Barbara, California, since 1989. She earned her BSc (Hons) in Psychology and Postgraduate Certificate of Education at the University of Bristol, UK, and taught high school science in Bristol before moving into the IT business in 1984. She is a *Timeslips* Certified Consultant for Sage Software and provides support to clients in law firms, accounting firms, hospitals, and a variety of other areas, utilizing her training and skills as a teacher. She was the proud recipient of an Honorary Service Award from the PTSA in 2003 for assisting in computerizing the yearbook production at her son's Junior High school. Jane has published with her husband, Howard, on a number of occasions, including work on issues of intercultural communication and bilingualism.

Preface

In 2007, Maria Angels Viladot invited Howard to edit a series of books on the topic of "Communicating With and About Society" for the Spanish Publisher, Editorial Aresta, which specialized in books popularizing scientific knowledge. These books were to be published in English and also translated into Spanish and Catalan. He duly picked up this gauntlet, mostly in gratitude for Maria and Howard's joint publications on intergroup communication in Spain as well as their friendship. An internationally distinguished Editorial Board (including Dana Mastro, Peter Monge, Sik Hing Ng, Miles Patterson, and Linda Putnam) was engaged to assist in procuring and editing what was to be well over a dozen splendid, short volumes. This Series involved a wide range of topics, and three of these tackled issues of aging and communication: sexuality by Jon Nussbaum, Michelle Miller-Day, and Carla Fisher (2008); Alzheimer's Disease by Tony Young, Christopher Manthrop, and David Howells (2010); and agism in the workplace by Bob McCann (2012).[1] Given our own investment in research on many facets of intergenerational communication and aging, plus vivid and intense lived experiences in our families and careers addressing these issues, we decided it was time to write our own contribution to this Series on an array of issues related to successful aging.

The ultimate product[2] was well-received by academics and interested friends and family and resulted in an excellent journal book review by Jon Nussbaum.[3] However, in 2014, Editorial Aresta folded and, hence, so did the Series, and our book consequently fell by the wayside. That said, when colleagues uttered something precatory about others' or even their own aging, Howard would immediately retort: "Read this book, it may help you!" More often than not, not only did he receive feedback that it actually had opened their eyes and, gratifyingly, some also claimed it had even changed their lives to the extent of their looking at aging – and their own attitudes toward and behavior about it – more mindfully and positively.

Subsequently in 2015, together with Craig Fowler, Jessica and Howard published and tested the so-called communicative ecology model of successful aging (CEMSA)[4] that built on and very much extended the last chapter of the Aresta book. This model kick-started an expansive program of empirical work derived from it, and a number of competitive Top Paper convention awards.

Most recently, this 2015 article received the 2020 National Communication Association's Communication and Aging Division's Award for Outstanding Article, which recognizes journal papers that have had a significant impact on the field of communication and aging. Different reviewers for this Award commended the work and its aftermath:

> It's a lens that pushes the field theoretically while being grounded in what is most important – understanding how it can be used to improve the health of society ... Generativity is to be commended – this theory has a long and prolific life ahead of it.

Not unrelatedly, one of Howard's earlier works with colleagues in this theoretical program[5] that introduced the communication predicament of aging model – which is still much-cited and discussed in Chapter 3 of this book – won the same (inaugural) award in 2011.

The original CEMSA study has not only led to an array of follow-up studies with wider health outcomes, many citations, and extensive ResearchGate reads, it also excited interest in the media. For example, a three-page article including the model appeared in *Vibrant Life* magazine. Additionally, a renowned social gerontologist, Susan Krauss Whitbourne, not only had an article about CEMSA in *Psychology Today* (April 5, 2016) but, also, wrote another about the model in *HuffPost* (April 26, 2016). She argued that this "study could eventually lead to a whole new way of building a more age-friendly society for all of us." It was, at this point, that we thought we should definitely not let the 2013 book "die" in its former state. It was also the case that this publisher had sold very few copies worldwide, thereby not yielding the kind of impact we felt it deserved and, which, gratifyingly, Nussbaum had endorsed in his book review:

> This brief, well written, and enjoyable book accomplishes this near impossible task by placing communication at the core of developmental science, by synthesizing decades of theoretical and empirical research, by empowering the reader with a specific path toward successful aging, and by entering into the domain of a must read for all "students" of life.

Hence, we felt that our earlier edition of the book warranted a wider audience with the advantage and sponsorship of a major, international publisher. To our delight, Taylor and Francis processed our book proposal, and it was reviewed by seasoned scholars who strongly recommended publication. Said reviewers insightfully and helpfully reported on it (for whose feedback we are grateful), and a contract was granted.

In preparing this book, we felt the previous text would benefit from being updated, elaborated, and refined, while still maintaining the vibrant, reader-friendly style of the former edition. This volume is more comprehensively referenced and includes a considerable amount of recent work addressing the topics of communication and successful aging. While there was an explosion of empirical research during the 1980s and 1990s on the study of communication and aging that constitutes the proportional heartland of this topic,[6] 35% of cites in this current volume were published after the prior edition was submitted for publication. In integrating these cites into the book, we opted to use numbered superscript endnotes rather than full in-text citations to enhance the flow of the text's narrative. We also retained the format of highlighting potent quotes in grayscale background as well as placing lists of contributing and outcomes factors in bulleted boxes. In addition, we included images and photographs we have collected over time, as well as peppered the narrative with what we hope are poignant and relevant personal anecdotes. In other words, we have attempted (wherever possible) to achieve a kind of conversational tone with readers that we hope helps them see potential pragmatic implications for their own aging.

While there have been many social and technological changes since the former edition, at the point that we decided to revise this book, we (as well as those around us) had no idea how life and lives would suddenly, and globally, change for so long in the light of the COVID-19 pandemic in 2020–2021. There was massive attention to the virus in the nightly TV news and social and other media; the pandemic also affected, at least and arguably, public policies as well as political campaigns attending the presidential elections in the United States. In this, the so-called "elderly" were a communicative focus and framed as an existential threat – inside and outside of long-term care facilities – in light of the precious use of limited ventilators for much younger *versus* older folk. Accordingly, and despite some positive responses for older adults such as special senior early shopping hours, older people in some regions of the United States were considered a very low priority for healthcare during the pandemic. There has also been a diffusion of agism the like of which was never anticipated at the time of writing the first version of this book nearly ten years earlier.[7] That said, the negativity toward older adults is not universal; in Hawai'i, for instance, there has been public emphasis on caring for older adults, and the idea of protecting older community members ("kūpuna") has been an important part of public health messaging in this state.

Like so many, our own lives and work were affected by the pandemic. Taylor and Francis generously understood the pressures and predicaments the COVID-19 placed on us (as well as other authors) and granted us a valued deadline extension. All in all, we are indebted to our colleagues at Taylor and Francis for their forbearance and support and would particularly like to acknowledge the care, assistance, and encouragement of Charlotte (Lottie) Mapp, Helen Pritt, Alison Macfarlane, Nancy Antony, and Shreya Bajpai.

We are thrilled for the opportunity to write this volume as well as extending further our stance on communication and successful aging. Hopefully, it will inspire further research and praxis and not only be relevant to the academy community, but also for all of us who endure the demands, challenges, and exploits of aging!

Howard, Jessica, Shardé, and Jane

Notes

1 Respectively: Nussbaum, J. F., Miller-Day, M., & Fisher, C. (2009). *Communication and intimacy in older adulthood*. Girona, Spain: Editorial Aresta; Young, T., Manthrorp, C., & Howells, D. (2010). *Communication and dementia: New perspectives, New approaches*. Girona: Spain; McCann, R. M. (2012). *Agism at work: The role of communication in a changing world*. Girona, Spain: Editorial Aresta.
2 Giles, H., Davis, S., Gasiorek, J., & Giles, H. (2013). *Successful aging: A communication guide to empowerment*. Girona, Spain: Editorial Aresta.
3 Nussbaum, J. F. (2013). Book review: Successful aging: A communication guide to empowerment. *Journal of Language and Social Psychology, 32*(4), 495–497. https://doi.org/10.1177/0261927X13479351; the quote in the text is p. 496.
4 Fowler, C., Gasiorek, J., & Giles, H. (2015). The role of communication in aging well: Introducing the communicative ecology model of successful aging. *Communication Monographs, 82*(4), 431–457. https://doi.org/10.1080/03637751.2015.1024701
5 Ryan, E. B., Giles, H., Bartolucci, G., & Henwood, K. (1986). Psycholinguistic and social psychological components of communication by and with older adults. *Language & Communication, 6*(1-2), 1–22. https://doi.org/10.1016/0271-5309(86)90002-9
6 Harwood, J. (2007). *Understanding communication and aging: Developing knowledge and awareness*, Chapter 8. Thousand Oaks, CA: Sage; see also his 2nd ed. (2017) with the same title, published by Cognella (San Diego, CA)
7 See Special Issue: Miller, E. A. (Ed.). (2020). Older adults and COVID-19: Implications for aging policy and practice. *Journal of Aging & Social Policy, 32*(4-5), 297–525; for journal online, see: https://www.tandfonline.com/toc/wasp20/32/4-5; Monahan, C., Macdonald, J., Lytle, A., Apriceno, M., & Levy, S. R. (2020). COVID-19 and agism: How positive and negative responses impact older adults and society. *American Psychologist, 75*(7), 887–896. https://doi.org/10.1037/amp0000699; for egregious claims of social, communicative, and physical neglect for older folk in care facilities, see also: Webster, P. (2021). COVID-19 highlights Canada's care home crisis. *World Report, 397*(10270), P183. https://doi.org/10.1016/SO140-6736(21)00083-0

1 Matters of Communication and Aging

There have been over two dozen definitions of what constitutes or defines "successful aging" and its synonyms (e.g., "productive," "robust," "effective," and "positive" aging).[1] We support a lifespan developmental framework that emphasizes that successful aging is a *process* rather than a mere state (see Chapter 7).[2] While successful aging has been an integral and core subject of empirical and theoretical attention in social gerontology and allied social sciences,[3] attention to it in the discipline of communication has been, at best, sporadic.[4] Indeed, a journal review of the first and prior edition of this book (see Preface) stated:[5]

> Several rather popular textbooks have been authored in recent years by communication and aging researchers targeted for undergraduate and graduate students. None of these books, however, focuses upon the critical role communication plays in successful aging with a specific, pragmatic guide to empower aging individuals.

In the current volume, unlike most other analyses, we contend that a *communication*-centric approach is fundamental to understanding the complex dynamics of successful aging. While we appreciate that objective indicators of physical health can affect subjective well-being and vice-versa,[6] we contend that the nature and quality of our communicative practices can shape, and be shaped by, both physical and psychological health, as in Figure 1.1. Furthermore, we argue that managing aging is not so much about how you think, or how old you feel, but rather: *how "old" you communicate and are communicated to and about.*

In what follows in this opening chapter, as a backdrop to the chapters that follow, we briefly introduce data and projections about the demographics of aging; provide an initial backdrop to the role of lifespan communication in the social construction of aging; examine cross-cultural and generational differences in these subjective representations; overview how various disciplines

DOI: 10.4324/9780429330681-1

2   *Matters of Communication and Aging*

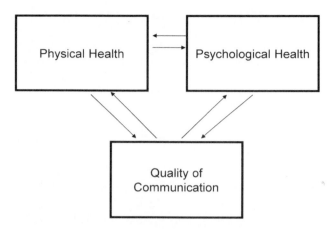

Figure 1.1 Communication and Its Relationships with Objective and Subjective Health

focus on different aspects of aging; and, finally, overview the ensuing chapters and outline the goals of our mission for this book.

The Demographics of Aging

In 1900, the number of over 65-year-olds in the United States was estimated to be three million people. This number had risen to 46 million by 2016, which was about 15% of the population. Figure 1.2 displays the trend over and beyond these years,[7] with the proportion of this age group estimated to be

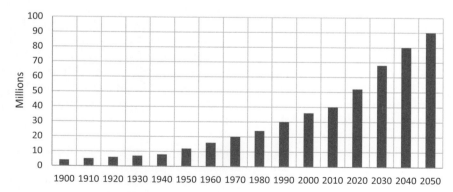

Figure 1.2 Population Age 65 and Older, 1900– and Projected.

Adapted from: https://www.prb.org/the-u-s-population-is-growing-older-and-the-gender-gap-in-life-expectancy-is-narrowing/

21–24% by 2030. While people 85-years-of-age and older were six million in 2014, it is estimated they will be about 20 million by 2060.

Each day, 10,000 Americans turn 65, a figure which has prompted the dubious metaphor of a "silver tsunami."[8] Interestingly, as the so-called "age pyramid" has flattened over the decades, those over 65 are going to be somewhat comparable in number to those in their mid-20s in 2030. Put another way, older adults are not going to be so much of a numerical minority in the future and will be comparable in demographic vitality to their younger counterparts.[9]

More globally, due in large part to increased fertility and lower mortality rates, each nation in the world, in its own ways, will reflect the trend in Figure 1.2. That said, the very large numbers of deaths due to COVID-19 may have a real bearing on this pattern continuing in the way projected. Nonetheless, this trend could be exacerbated by 2050, where one in six in the Hispanic world will be 65 and older; in Europe and North America, it will likely be one in four persons. Centenarians – those 100 years and older – are also expected to increase rapidly in number, with 7.4 per 100,000 globally in 2015, rising to an estimate of 23.6 per 100,000 estimated for 2050. Encouragingly, the potential for continued societal contributions and productivity by people of this age group is well-represented in Tom Moore (shown here), a Briton who raised US$56 million for charity to assist medical workers during the 2020 pandemic and was awarded a knighthood by the Queen.

Hence:[10]

> population aging is poised to become one of the most significant social transformations of the 21st century, with implications for nearly all sectors of society, including labor and financial markets, the demand for goods and services, such as housing, transportation and social protection, as well as family structure and intergenerational ties.

Relatedly, in his address launching the United Nation's "International Year of Older Persons" in 1989,[11] the then Secretary-General, Kofi Anan, talked about "the silent revolution." By this, he was referring to the ever-increasing (yet little talked about) numbers of elderly people in society in tandem with their ever-extending lifespans as among *the* most pressing societal issues needing to be addressed in the upcoming decades. Arguably, it seems that the *silence* has remained more or less until this day. While that message of silence may imply older people are in less need of being accommodated than other age groups, the thrust of this book is that there is a dire need, across societies, to communicate about the aging process and its dynamic forces.

Kofi Anan aptly caricatured the lifespan now as, "less of a sprint, and more like a marathon." Indeed, many of today's elderly never thought they would live much longer than their parents – and many of these have been unprepared to manage these elastic years. As Leon Trotsky famously once wrote in his 1935 *Diary in Exile*, "Old age is the most unexpected of all things that happen to a man [sic]." The focus of this book then is a fascinating topic – life and death if you like (see Chapter 6) – because it is an inevitable experience and process shared by everyone. As the old adage has it: "Two certainties in life are death and taxes!"

Disciplinary Perspectives on Aging

Although the topic of aging may seem like a small research arena to some, this is certainly not the case, and there are many ways in which it has been approached by scholars in various academic fields. In very general terms, past researchers have taken physiological, psychological, or sociological approaches[12] when studying and interpreting aging. The first (physiological) focuses on somatic changes as people get older, such as age-related illness (e.g., certain cancers), decline in mental capabilities, and deterioration of the physical body. The second (psychological) approach examines, for example, how older people can fare better when they maintain high levels of physical activity and cognitive functioning, and what effects challenging hobbies and receiving social support from their family, friends, and other social networks have on memory and quality of life. A third, sociological, approach to aging is important because it examines the ability of larger-scale social institutions to cope with the ever-increasing population of older adults. For example, sociologists study the ways in which longevity could precipitate financial breakdown in government assistance programs, like pension funds, because there are more people in need of supplemental income than there is money to distribute.

Each of these established areas of study uniquely provides distinctively different insights into the aging process. As Henri Frédéric Amiel, the Swiss philosopher and poet, once said: "To know how to grow old is the masterwork of wisdom, and one of the most difficult chapters in the great art of living." We share that stance and argue that one critical element in Amiel's mystery alluded

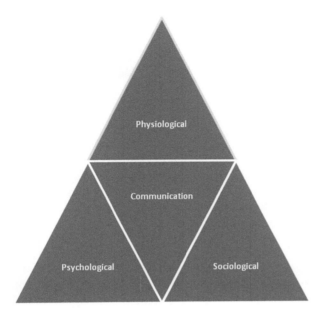

Figure 1.3 A Caricature of Communication and Its Relationship to Other Disciplines

to at the start of this chapter – and one that has not received sufficient public nor academic attention – is how we manage the aging process *communicatively*.

Heuristically, and is seen in Figure 1.3, communication complements and is integral to the three general approaches and systems outlined previously, namely, the physiological (e.g., in terms of health diagnoses and regimes conveyed), psychological (e.g., in terms of how others perceive you as well as yourselves), and sociological (e.g., in terms of how public and media voices influence the construction and maintenance of age-related institutions).

We now turn more specifically to an array of social gerontological theories that address aging. One of the first well-cited theories was *disengagement theory* with its various postulates and others' extensions of it.[13] This framework – and one, these days, not afforded much theoretical weight – suggests (as its title implies) that older people disengage in a seemingly natural way from involving themselves in, and contributing to, society, and this can be passively encouraged by younger segments of society. It was contended that disengagement eases the process of impending demise for older people in later life. In contrast, *activity theory*[14] suggests that socially engaged older adults (e.g., those with hobbies and responsibilities) are happier and survive longer.[15]

Continuity theory focuses on paying attention to the value of internal stability and sustaining enduring and unique characteristics across the lifespan while *identity balance theory* stresses the need for redefining aspects of the self to accommodate necessary and ongoing changes in the world around us.[16] Relatedly, the *selective optimization with compensation theory* emphasizes the need for individuals to energetically strive to be congruent with their ideal self, sidestep any discrepant conceptions of a feared (or even dreaded) self, and compensate for any deficiencies (physical and psychology) along this path.[17] In considering experiences of aging, it is also important to underscore that changes in language and communication deficits across the adult lifespan are generally small,[18] and in any case, when these do emerge, people can adjust for, and offset, them.[19] For example, the authors of a review of the literature, which underscored the latter, stated that: "taking time, making pauses, repeating, and restarting are strategies used for successful word retrieval; comments and jokes are employed to confront the face-threatening potential of these – perceived – deficits." Put another way, eluctable decline is not an inevitable given in the aging process.

The last theory in this section is *socioemotional selectivity theory*, which proposes different developmental trajectories to the extent that in later life, individuals become less interested in garnering knowledge about the world around them and in meeting new people. Instead, the theory suggests, people become increasingly invested in maintaining close personal relationships and social networks that can provide solidarity and protect them from dwelling on social comparisons that could threaten their self-esteem.[20] These social resources allow for the exchange of life narratives and reminisces with empathic age peers that can buffer against feelings of self-demise. An important, and empirically, supported aspect of this theory is that it is not *age* per se that brings on this selective socioemotional focus but, rather, feeling or knowing that one is getting closer to death and its finality (see Chapter 6).

Although the foregoing models were not developed within the discipline of communication, they offer useful perspectives that can be integrated into a communication-centered approach. Collectively, these theories suggest that it is important for a person to:

- Be physiologically and physically healthy;
- Believe that they are as young or old as they feel;
- Contend that aging is partly in "the mind";
- Compensate for skills and abilities not optimally available;
- Sustain a unique, fairly life-consistent notion of selfhood that assimilates emergent change;
- Be active and socially engaged with positively comparative others;
- Have (and even promote or create) social institutions that are sympathetic toward and protective of elderhood and other defining aspects of one's personal and social identities.

That said, if we communicate in ways that cause others dear (or relevant) to us to believe that we are "past it," these others will likely communicate in ways that take this into account and turn it into reality. Consequently, if we are then talked down to in the simplest of terms – and this occurs all too frequently (see Chapter 4) – it will take a very strong person indeed *not* to be susceptible to buying into a "looking-glass philosophy": that is, seeing ourselves as others see us. Indeed, we would also argue that some people even collude in their own demise by taking on aged characteristics and stereotypes earlier in the lifespan in ways that can accelerate mental and physiological decline.[21]

Aging as a Lifespan Social and Communicative Construction

Communication reflects, but also actively shapes, the ways in which people view and experience aging across the lifespan,[22] and the mental associations they have with growing older. People often, mostly unintentionally, use their communications to convey our understanding and notions of what "old age" is, and what it means is variously defined by scholars.[23]

All of us, if we are fortunate enough, grow old and progress through the lifespan, sometimes in similar ways and yet, at other times, with vastly different trajectories. As such, and unbeknown to many younger people, older adults are a very heterogeneous collection of individuals as simply evident in the various ways they embrace digital media. Indeed, their health and functionalities are often typically much better than prevailing negative age stereotypes suggest (see Chapter 2). We were all children once, grew up in our own times and subcultures to become adults, and most of us (we hope, see image) will eventually become older adults.

Across our lifespans, we all experience physical and mental alterations of the body, shifts in family roles, and changes in the status of our work and personal lives that can sometimes feel intrusive or unwelcome. Added to this,

age-based discrimination against older people is a highly prevalent and widespread phenomenon across many cultures even now in the 2020s (see Chapter 2). Interestingly, it has been found that the larger the percentage of older people in a society, the more negative attitudes toward older people are prevalent there.[24] Furthermore, and given the ever-increasing size of older populations, it may be that negativity will only escalate in its pervasiveness over the next decade or so, given the lack of social and public policies enacted to address it. Alarming as this may be, there are also estimates that the health cost repercussions of experienced social discrimination toward those over 60 years of age in the United States amount to US$63 billion per annum.[25] Indeed, scholars suggest that age discrimination is the most pervasive form of social prejudice in Western societies, with extensive agism also directed at young people as well as middle-aged people in the workplace.[26] Speculatively, it could be that those being the recipients of widespread and cruel age discrimination in their childhood and adolescence could account for a sizable proportion of those promoting agist messages to elders in adulthood; this would be akin to young males who were physically abused early in life becoming abusers in adulthood themselves.[27]

Unfortunately, as one American study[28] with college-aged students showed, this lifespan course can be construed as dismal in many ways. In this investigation, students were asked to rate the status of individuals of different ages in society. Status increased from five years until about 30 and declined progressively from then on until 90 (see Figure 1.4 and the attending gender differences where the decline is sharper for females). Obviously, gender differences

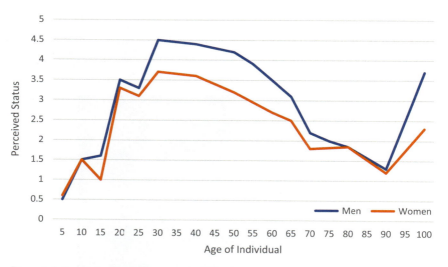

Figure 1.4 Status Attributions across the Lifespan.

Adapted from: https://academic.oup.com/geronj/article/40/4/506/593679

are a child of their time, and we might predict far fewer differences in the middle portion of the graph since this study was conducted – as might be predicted by the impact of the #MeToo movement.[29]

Indeed, one more recent study showed more positive reactions to elder *women* than men by young informants, although the former were attributed with more anxiety about their age than the latter.[30] We would argue that possessing such a cognitive map so early in young adulthood (i.e., between late teens and early 20-year-olds) bodes poorly for healthy aging over the subsequent years, perhaps in part as a self-fulfilling prophecy. Added to that, there is the risk that people then actively "live out" and perpetuate this pattern and its agist associations in their everyday discourse. With that said, we note that there can be a discrepancy between how older people construe their peers' social status in general and their own position in particular. Perhaps protectively, elders themselves are sometimes more positive about their own personal age status than that of *other* older folk around their same age.[31]

Relatedly, as people become older, they tend to see themselves as physically (and perhaps cognitively) younger than those of the same age. Such a process is poignantly alluded to, and portrayed, in this internet tale:

- While waiting for my first appointment in the reception room of a new dentist, I noticed his certificate which bore his full name.
- Suddenly, I remembered that a tall, handsome boy with the same name had been in my high school class some 40 years ago.
- Upon seeing him, however, I quickly discarded any such thought. This balding, gray-haired man with the deeply lined face was too old to have been my classmate.
- After he had examined my teeth, I asked him if he had attended the local high school.
- "Yes," he replied.
- "When did you graduate?" I asked.
- He answered, "In 1957."
- "Why, you were in my class!" I exclaimed.
- He looked at me closely, and then asked ...
- "*What did you teach?*"

The implication here is that our patient would have been taken aback, if not utterly devastated, to learn not only that was she about the same age as the dentist but, seemingly looked a lot older to him than she envisaged herself to be! In actuality, there seems to be a common (yet very wide) set of physiognomic and vocal cues that people invoke to assess someone else's age (e.g., wrinkles, skin color uniformity, and voice perturbations), and depictions of happy faces, tellingly, seem to be *under*estimated in terms of their age.[32] In turn, how old elder individuals believe they look can often depend on comparing themselves with either their former selves or other older people they encounter; this seems to be a common interactive experience.[33] The outcome of such an intra-generational process is that older people, as above, see themselves much more favorably and younger than others in their age group. Interestingly, too, it was found in a six-year longitudinal study in Berlin that across the ages of 70–104 years old, people consistently *felt thirteen* years younger than their actual ages.[34] Indeed, feelings of subjective age can vary during the course of a day, due to whom you meet, where you are, and how you are feeling.[35] We are reminded at this point of what the novelist and poet, Thomas Hardy, once said: "measurement of life should be proportioned rather to the *intensity of the experience* than to its actual length."

It is interesting to speculate about how individuals develop their views about the nature and value of points across lifespan; in Chapter 5, we examine mass media messages as one possible source of ideas about these topics. Whatever their sources, such conceptions can be socialized into young children at an early age. For instance, one of us vividly recalls the plethora of times his mother and father recanted, "Old age is a tragedy!" in his formative years and then beyond in directives such as, "Don't ever get old, son!" Such statements and their possibly lasting impacts can be understood in terms of the construct of "memorable messages" that have been defined as those "remembered for extremely long periods of time and which people perceive as a major influence on the course of their lives."[36]

One recent study[37] elicited memorable messages about age from a fairly large sample of older adults (average age of 64 years). The theme to emerge for the largest number of respondents (44% of the sample) reflected the same kinds of physical and cognitive declines mentioned previously; one participant, for example, recalled the message: "When you get older like me, you suffer from CRS (Can't Remember [sic] Sh*t)."[38] However, there was significant variation – mirroring the notion of older heterogeneity introduced previously – in the valence of the kinds of memorable messages different individuals recalled. The second-largest category of recalled messages (32% of the sample) in this study did *not* have a negative tone but, rather, involved age as being unimportant or not necessarily bad with the right outlook; another participant, for example, recalled:

> My husband looked forward to retirement so very much. He always said it would be his time to do anything he wanted to do. He said it so much and in fact has enjoyed this time for this reason, he has the freedom to do what he wants.

These abiding recollections are significant factors in shaping the process of successful-unsuccessful aging that is examined in Chapter 8.

Cross-Cultural and Generational Differences in Agism and Age Boundaries

The experience of aging can be quite different across cultures due, in large part, to significant global variations in cultural beliefs, values, and traditions.[39] (We note that often, work in this area is criticized for being studied mostly in Western-oriented settings.[40]) Traditionally in collectivistic cultures, the progression to later stages of the lifespan is almost a sacred period in that such people are venerated and highly respected by their family and the community.[41] For people subscribing to non-Western norms and values, the notion of successful aging might not resonate with their lived experiences, because "successful" implies that there are individual winners and losers, with winners attaining success through their own talent. Here, *familism* – the ideology of prioritizing family needs over individual needs – might be more relevant for understanding how older adults in such cultures age well.[42] For these older adults, remaining in tight-knit relationships with spouses, children, grandchildren, and other family members might be especially important in enhancing aging efficacy and in assessments that one is aging well.

Although one might expect attitudes toward aging and older adults to be more positive in collectivistic cultures, research shows this is not necessarily the case (see also, Chapter 2). In fact, *less* favorable attitudes and communicative dispositions toward elderly folk (along some dimensions) have been found among highly educated students in Asian countries compared with Anglophone countries.[43] Even within European countries, it has been found that individualistic communities' attitudes were actually more favorable toward older people (in their 70s) – and less favorable toward younger people (in their 20s) – than in more collectivistic settings. Yet, significant variation was also found from country to country:[44]

> People over 70 were most strongly perceived as competent and warm in Hungary and Ireland. The lowest mean was estimated in several eastern European countries (e.g., Romania, Croatia, Czech Republic, and Slovakia). Perceived age-related discrimination was highest in east European countries (e.g., Czech Republic, Romania, Russia, Slovakia, and Ukraine). The lowest level of perceived age discrimination existed in a mixture of countries from southern, northern, and central Europe (e.g., Portugal, Cyprus, Denmark, Norway, and Switzerland).

Correspondingly, the experience of aging can be different between generations within the *same* nation.[45] People who were elderly during World War II have vastly different experiences than those who were elderly during the 1960s. Both those groups underwent different social and technological climates and had different cultures and histories from those elderly today. Likewise, the values held and behaviors displayed by older patriotic Russians who lived through the Communist era can be vividly contrasted with those born after the Soviet Union collapsed, and who are enjoying a free market economy and embracing a more internationalist culture. The many ways in which generational differences can be manifest in communicative behavior were visible was when one of us went one day to a coffee cart on campus. The unwitting and helpful faculty member gave the exact money for a coffee to the student server, who then giggled. The coffee buyer asked what was so funny. The reply was, "Oh it's just weird how older men bother to give exact change."

Numerous celebrities, such as movie star Kirk Douglas (now deceased) at 95 years old, claim that age is no more than a mere number. Certainly, what *is* young, middle aged, and elderly varies considerably in the minds and perceptions of different people and in different places and at different times, and this is important to emphasize as we start this book. In an attempt to tease out these complexities and in a series of studies across the world,[46] young adults were asked at what age in years they believed the beginnings and ends of young adulthood and middle age, and the start of elderliness occurred. As Table 1.1 indicates, there is great variation across cultures, and some readers might be surprised to find that the onset of "being elderly" – at least for young people – emerges at such an *early* age in the lifespan. In some studies, it was found that it starts even earlier in Australia and that, for women more generally, it was judged as beginning earlier than for men.

It is also interesting to observe in Table 1.1 that in the United States (also in Iran, albeit less so), there is a gap of years between the end of young adulthood and the start of middle age. In almost all cases (and especially in Mongolia and South Africa), there are gaps between the end of middle age and elderliness. It is as though there is, in certain societies, perhaps a period of uncertainty where people do not know where they are in lifespan phases; during these periods, it is also possible people are uncertain as to what to make of this (see Chapter 7).

It should be acknowledged that carving up the lifespan into three distinct periods (with onset and ending) as in Table 1.1 is only one way to proceed analytically. Individuals, in any one particular society and at different times in life, will differ greatly in terms of how they construe phases of the lifespan (retrospectively and prospective) and break them up into

Table 1.1 Age Boundaries across Selected Nations

	USA	India	South Africa	Ghana	Bulgaria	Mongolia	Iran
Young adulthood begins *in years*	17	18	18	20	16	18	17
Young adulthood ends	28	33	30	31	32	31	32
Middle age begins	33	33	29	31	33	29	35
Middle age ends	59	51	45	45	55	45	56
Elderly age begins	61	53	51	50	56	51	59

meaningful chunks (e.g., school, athletic, marital, career, and grandparenting phases). In one study,[47] we found college-aged students carved up the lifespan into chunks in a range of different ways, with very different valences attending them. Regarding the future, these informants also varied in the number, nature, and valence of phases anticipated, the amount of certainty they expressed as attending them, and the projected endpoints of their lives.

In sum, further work on the *subjective* representations of lifespan phases is fertile ground for new insights about aging – and the way we communicate about them. In this book, we shall be focusing much of our attention on "older adults." However, we will also be taking more of a lifespan perspective later (see Chapter 4) by exploring how individuals' reactions to aging from early adulthood, and even way earlier, can lay the seeds for how they adjust to elderliness in later life.

Overview and Goals of this Book

We openly acknowledge that we cannot address all topics relating to communication and aging, as well as all topics that are relevant to successful aging. For instance, we do not discuss elder abuse, a topic that has received much recent media attention as in the dramatic rise in complaints of elder abuse in the United States (most relating to COVID-19 scams) in the first part of 2020, and also in stories of older people being physically and socially neglected in Canadian care facilities.[48] Communication issues obviously figure squarely in how this comes about and how its forms are responded to, as we have written about elsewhere.[49] However, we will deal with issues that confront most of us as we age, and our position on the factors that promote and impede successful aging will be introduced in Chapter 7. But in order to get to that point or, rather, to fully appreciate its value, we first need to establish some building blocks with respect to understanding research and theory in Chapters 2–6 on:

- The messages of age stereotypes and agist attitudes (Chapter 2)
- The imposition and construction of age identities in talk, and the ways we cope with these (Chapter 3)
- The communicative ingredients of how younger and older people talk to each other, and the consequences of this for both "sides" (Chapter 4)
- The media's portrayal of age and related anti-aging dilemmas (Chapter 5)
- The values, challenges, and settings of talking about different death and dying trajectories (Chapter 6)

In the epilogue to this book (Chapter 8), we will highlight that age and the intra- and interpersonal and intergroup communication phenomena and processes we spoke to in previous chapters are contextualized in the larger scheme of societal forces with which an older person has to grapple across the lifespan. More specifically, we discuss how racial tensions (e.g., against Asian-Americans during the pandemic) and the institutional oppression of, and hatred for, an array of social groups in society by some make aging challenging in unique ways for different sectors of society. Along with applied implications arising from the preceding chapters, we will also articulate priorities and questions that future research needs to address, in ways that ally with the topics of previous chapters, as longevity continues to expand.

The goals of this volume *include* an understanding of:

- Research and theory in aging intergenerational and lifespan communication, and the ways in which age as a social variable (*and process*) intersects with relevant others (e.g., gender, culture);
- The ways aging necessarily impacts *all* areas of social endeavor and policies (e.g., interpersonal, intercultural, family, health, media, and organizational) and likewise readers' own current and future intellectual and everyday endeavors;
- The ways in which aging is a social and *communicative* construction and attending this can be pernicious forms of agism as well as a difficulty in managing being a recipient of them;
- How in communicating in, and about, the twilight years, we need to appreciate these processes, contextually, from a lifespan perspective;
- An opportunity for readers to develop a more individual appreciation of the ways in which aging has, does, and inevitably will impact readers' own communicative lives with a view to older adulthood being, ultimately and ideally, mostly a positive experience.

Concluding Thoughts

Ashleigh Brilliant, in one of his poignant cartoons, wrote that "It's hard to believe how old I am ... but harder to believe how old I may become!" Life moves on at an alarming pace for most of us at certain junctures; people inevitably talk about how the years are getting "shorter" and, if teachers, how their students appear to be getting younger. As we discussed previously, many people arrive at a point in their lifespans when they hear a comment from someone that makes them suddenly realize that others see them as being "older" – without their being prepared to be in, let alone manage, this situation fraught with uncertainty. If a younger person says, "You look and act just like my father," this can be a wake-up call that others may be seeing you in older terms than you had conceived of yourself (see Chapter 3). As alluded to previously, many people will in all likelihood have already laid down the seeds of vulnerability through their own, supposedly harmless, agist acts toward others over the years (e.g., age-bruising birthday cards) and then find the experience of being older themselves overwhelming to deal with.

To conclude this chapter, we reference (and reword) what the famous actress Bette Davis once said: "Old age is no place for weaklings!" We believe that part of what makes old age so difficult is our fear and lack of ability to deal with the communicative dynamics of growing and being older. Relatedly, some of the *paradoxes* (and sometimes contradictions) of messages about aging are highlighted in Chapter 5. We portend that it is never too early in adulthood to come to grips with understanding some of the complexities of communication and aging and in ways that can turn Amiel's "mystery" into a more exciting and challenging *adventure*. In this sense, we support the activist Maggie Kuhn's contention: "The best age is the age you are!"

Notes

1 Depp, C. A., & Jeste, D. V. (2006). Definitions and predictors of successful aging: A comprehensive review of larger quantitative studies. *American Journal of Geriatric Psychiatry, 14*(1), 6–20. https://doi.org/10.1097/01.JGP.0000192501.03069.bc; see also: Docking R. E., & Stock, J. (Eds.). (2019). *International handbook of positive aging*. Abingdon, UK: Routledge.

2 Bieman-Copland, S., Ryan, E. B., & Cassano, J. (1998). Responding to the challenge of late life: Strategies for maintaining and enhancing competence. In D. Pushkar, W. M. Bokowski, A. E., Schwartzman, D. M. Stack, & D. R. White (2002). (Eds.), *Improving competence across the lifespan: Building interventions based on theory and research* (pp. 141–157). New York, NY: Plenum.

3 See, for example: Pruchno, R. (2015). Successful aging: Contentious past, productive future. *The Gerontologist, 55*(1), 1–4. https://doi.org/10.1093/geront/gnv002; Castel, A. D. (2018). *Better with age: The psychology of successful aging*. New York, NY: Oxford University Press; Levitin, J. L. (2020). *Successful aging: A neuroscientist explores the power and potential of our lives*. New York, NY: Dutton; Lamb, S. (2014). Permanent personhood or meaningful decline? Toward a critical anthropology of successful aging. *Journal of Aging Studies, 29*, 41–52. https://doi.org/10.1016/j.jaging.2013.12.006; Lamb, S. (Ed.). (2017). *Successful again as a contemporary obsession*. New Brunswick, NJ: Rutgers University Press.

4 See, however: Nussbaum, J. F. (1985). Successful aging: A communicative model. *Communication Quarterly, 33*(4), 262–269. https://doi.org/10.1080/01463378509369606; Nussbaum, J. F., & Fisher, C. L. (2011). Successful aging and communication wellness: A process of transition and continuity. In Y. Matsumoto (Ed.), *Faces of aging: The lived experiences of the elderly in Japan* (pp. 263–272). Stanford, CA: Stanford University Press; Hummert, M. L., & Nussbaum, J. F. (Eds.). (2001). *Aging, communication, and health: Linking research and practice for successful aging* (pp. 23–42). Mahwah, NJ: Lawrence Erlbaum; Harwood, J. (2017); see also: *Understanding communication and aging: Developing knowledge and awareness*, 2nd ed. San Diego, CA: Cognella.

5 Nussbaum, J. F. (2013). Book review: Successful aging: A communication guide to empowerment. *Journal of Language and Social Psychology, 32*(4), 495–497. https://doi.org/10.1177/0261927X13479351

6 Garatachea, N., Molinero, O., Martinez-Garcia, R., Jimenez-Jimenez, R., Gonzalez-Gallego, J., & Marquez, S. (2009). Feelings of well-being in elderly people: Relationship to physical activity and physical function. *Archives of Gerontology and Geriatrics, 48*, 306–312. https://doi.org/10.1016/j.archger.2008.02.010

7 *Older Americans 2016: Key indicators of wellbeing*. Washington, DC: Federal Interagency Forum on Age-Related Statistics. Washington, DC.

8   See: Barusch, A. (2013). The aging tsunami: Time for a new metaphor? *Journal of Gerontological Social Work, 56*(3), 181–184. https://doi.org/10.1080/01634372.2013.787348
9   See: Giles, H., Noels, K., Ota, H., Ng, S. H., Gallois, C., Ryan, E. B., Williams, A., Lim, T-S., Somera, L., Tao, H., & Sachdev, I. (2000). Age vitality across eleven nations. *Journal of Multilingual & Multicultural Development, 21*(4), 308–323. https://doi.org/10.1080/01434630008666407
10 See: U.N. Report, Retrieved from: https://www.un.org/en/sections/issues-depth/ageing/
11 Annan, K. (1999). Address at the ceremony launching the international year of older persons (1999). *Journal of Gerontology, 54B*(1), 5–6. https://doi.org/10.1093/geronb/54b.1.p5
12 Respectively, see, for example: Timiras, P. S. (2007). *Physiological bases of aging and geriatrics*, 4th ed. New York, NY: Routledge; Schaie, K. W., & Willis, S. (Eds.). (2016). *Handbook of the psychology of aging* (8th ed.). New York: NY: Elsevier; Harris, D. K. (2007). *Sociology of aging* (3rd ed.). Lanham, MD: Rowman & Littlefield.
13 See, for example: Cumming, E., & Henry, W. E. (1961). *Growing old*. New York, NY: Basic; Bandura, A. (2015). *Moral disengagement: How people do harm and live with themselves*. New York, NY: Worth.
14 See, for example: Stowe, J. D., & Cooney, T. M. (2015). Examining Rowe and Kahn's concept of successful aging: Importance of taking a life course perspective. *The Gerontologist, 55*(1), 43–50. https://doi.org/10.1093/geront/gnu055
15 See also: Havighurst, R. J. (1961). Successful ageing. *The Gerontologist, 1*(1), 8–13. https://doi.org/10.1093/geront/1.1.8; see also: V. L. Bengtson, D. Gans, N. Putney, & M. Silverstein (2009). (Eds.), *Handbook of theories of aging* (2nd ed.). New York, NY: Springer.
16 See, for example, and respectively: Diggs J. (2008). The continuity theory of aging. In S. J. Loue & M. Sajatovic (Eds.), *Encyclopedia of aging and public health*. Boston, MA: Springer. https://doi.org/10.1007/978-0-387-33754-8_10; Sneed, J. R., & Whitbourne, S. K. (2003). Identity processing and self-consciousness in middle and later adulthood. *The Journals of Gerontology: Series B, 58*(6), P313–P319. https://doi.org/10.1093/geronb/58.6.P313
17 See, for example: Teshale, S. M., & Lachman, M. E. (2016). Managing daily happiness: The relationship between selection, optimization and compensation strategies and well-being in adulthood. *Psychology and Aging, 31*(7), 687–692. https://doi.org/10.1037/pag0000132
18 See: Marini, A., Boewe, A., Caltagirone, C., & Carlomagno, S. (2005). Age-related differences in the production of textual descriptions. *Journal of Psycholinguistic Research, 34*(5), 439–463. https://doi.org/10.1007/s10936-005-6203-z
19 See p. 222: Gerstenberg, A. (2020). Pragmatic development in the (middle and) later stages of life. In K. P. Schneider & E. Ifantidou (Eds.), *Developmental and clinical pragmatics* (pp. 209–234). Berlin, Germany: De Gruyter Mouton; relatedly also: Baltes, P. B. (1997). On the incomplete architecture of human ontogeny: Selection, optimization and compensation as foundation of developmental theory. *American Psychologist, 52*(4), 366–380. https://doi.org/10.1037/0003-066X.52.4.366
20 For example, see: Carstensen, L. L., Fung, H. H., & Charles, S. T. (2003). Socioemotional selectivity theory and the regulation of emotion in the second half of life. *Motivation and Emotion, 27*, 103–123. https://doi.org/10.1023/A:1024569803230
21 This is akin to the process of self-stereotyping in self-categorization theory, see: Turner, J. C., & Reynolds, K. J. (2012). Self-categorization theory. In P. A. M. Van Lange, A. W. Kruglanski, & E. T. Higgins (Eds.), *The handbook of theories of social psychology* (Vol. 2, pp. 399–417). Thousand Oaks, CA: Sage.
22 See Nussbaum, J. F. (Ed.). (2014). *The handbook of lifespan communication*. New York, NY: Peter Lang; see also: Patrick, J. H., Hayslip, B., & Hollis-Sawyer, L. (2020). *Adult development and aging: Growth, longevity and challenges*. New York, NY: Norton.

23 There are different perspectives as to when "old age" begins, with chronological age being only one of the indicators. Indeed, classifying elders as "young-old" versus "old-old" (with various other nomenclatures available) is commonplace in the literature, and even that varies. For instance, one researcher figured it was 60–74 years of age versus 75–90, whereas another indicated it used the age boundaries of 70–77 and 78–100. See, respectively: Kemper, S. (1992). Adults' sentence fragments: Who, what, when, where, and why. *Communication Research, 19*(4), 444–458. https://doi.org/10.1177/009365092019004003; Gold, D. P., & Arbuckle, T. Y. (1995). A longitudinal study of off-target verbosity. *Journal of Gerontology: Psychological, Sciences, 50B* (6), 307–315. https://doi.org/10.1093/geronb/50B.6.P307

24 Marques, S., Mariano, J., Mendonça, J., De Tavernier, W., Hess. M., Naegele, F. P., & Martins, D. (2020). Determinants of ageism against older adults: A systematic review. *International Journal of Environmental Research and Public Health*. Advance Online: https://10.3390/ijerph17072560; see also: Palmore, E. B., Brach, L., & Harris, D. (2016). *Encyclopedia of ageism*. New York, NY: Routledge.

25 Levy, B. R., Slade, M., Chang, E-S., Kannoth, S., & Wang, S.Y. (2020). Ageism amplifies cost and prevalence of health conditions. *The Gerontologist, 60*(1), 174–181. https://doi.org/10.1093/geront/gny131

26 See, respectively: Bratt, C., Abrams, D., & Swift, H. J. (2020). Supporting the old but neglecting the young? The two faces of ageism. *Developmental Psychology, 56*(5), 1029–1039. http://dx.doi.org/10.1037/dev0000903; McCann, R. M. (2018). Aging and organizational communication. In H. Giles & J. Harwood (Eds.), *The Oxford encyclopedia of intergroup communication* (Vol. 1, pp. 21–38). New York, NY: Oxford University Press; see also, for the macro- and micro-origins of ageism: Bodnerag, E. (2009). On the origins of ageism in older and younger adults. *International Psychogeriatrics, 26*(6), 1003–1014. https://doi.org/10.1017/S104161020999055X; Ayalon L., & Tesch-Römer C. (2018). Introduction to the section: Ageism – Concept and origins. In L. Ayalon & C. Tesch-Römer (Eds.), *Contemporary perspectives on ageism* (pp. 1–10). Cham, Switzerland: Springer Nature; de la Fuente-Núñez, V., Cohn-Schwartz, E., Roy, S., & Ayalon, L. (2021). Scoping review on ageism against younger populations. *International Environmental Research and Public Health, 18*(8), 3988. https://doi.org/10.3390/ijerph18083988

27 See, for example: Ohlert, J., Seidler, C., Rau, T., Fegert, J., & Allroggen, M. (2017). Comparison of psychopathological symptoms in adolescents who experienced sexual violence as a victim and/or as a perpetrator. *Journal of Child Sex Abuse, 26*(4), 373–387. https://doi.org/10.1080/10538712.2017.1283652

28 See: Baker, P. M. (1985). The status of age: Preliminary results. *Journal of Gerontology, 40*(4), 506–508. https://doi.org/10.1093/geronj/40.4.506; see also, and compare: Robins, R. W., Trzesniewski, K. H., Gosling, S. D., & Potter, J. (2002). Global self-esteem across the life span. *Psychology and Aging, 17*(3), 423–434. https://doi.org/10.1037/0882-7974.17.3.423. In this study, self-esteem increased from 25 to 65 years of age and, thereafter, plummeted from 65.

29 See relatedly: North, A. (2019). 7 positive changes that have come from the #MeToo movement. Retrieved from: https://www.vox.com/identities/2019/10/4/20852639/me-too-movement-sexual-harassment-law-2019

30 See: Barrett, A. E., & von Rohr, C. (2008). Gendered perceptions of aging: An examination of college students. *International Journal of Aging and Human Development, 67*(4), 359–386. https://doi.org/10.2190/AG.67.4.d; relatedly, see: North, A. (2019). 7 positive changes that have come from the #MeToo movement. Retrieved from: https://www.vox.com/identities/2019/10/4/20852639/me-too-movement-sexual-harassment-law-2019.

31 Robertson, D. A., & Weiss, D. (2018). Rising above it: Status ambivalence in older adults. *Gerontology, 64*(6), 576–588. https://doi.org/10.1159/000488389

32 There seems to be a common set of physiognomic and vocal cues people use to assess someone else's age, see: Nkengne A., Stamatas G. N., & Bertin C. (2017). Facial skin attributes and age perception. In M. Farage, K. Miller, & H. Maibach (Eds.), *Textbook*

of aging skin (pp. 1689–1700). Berlin, Germany: Springer-Verlag; Mulac, A., & Giles, H. (1996). "You're only as old as you sound": Parameters of elderly age attributions. *Health Communication, 8*(3), 199–215. https://doi.org/10.1207/s15327027hc0803_2; see also: Voelkle, M. C., Ebner, N. C., Lindenberger, U., & Riediger, M. (2012). Let me guess how old you are: Effects of age, gender, and facial expression on perceptions of age. *Psychology and Aging, 27*(2), 265–277. https://doi.org/10.1037/a0025065

33 Paoletti, I. (1998). *Being an older woman: A study in the social production of identity.* Mahwah, NJ: Lawrence Erlbaum.

34 Kleinspehn-Ammerlahn A., Kotter-Grühn D., & Smith J. (2008). Self-perceptions of aging: Do subjective age and satisfaction with aging change during old age? *The Journals of Gerontology B: Psychological Sciences & Social Sciences, 63*(6), P377–85. https://doi.org/10.1093/geronb/63.6.P377

35 Weiss, D., & Weiss, M. (2019). Why people feel younger: Motivational and social-cognitive mechanisms of the subjective age bias and its implications for work and organizations. *Work, Aging and Retirement, 5*(4), 273–280. https://doi.org/10.1093/workar/waz016

36 See p. 27: Knapp, M. L., Stohl, C., & Reardon, K. K. (1981). "Memorable" messages. *Journal of Communication, 31*(6), 27–41. https://doi.org/10.1111/j.1460-2466.1981.tb00448.x; see also: Holladay, S. J. (2002). "Have fun while you can," "You're only as old as you feel," and "Don't ever get old": An examination of memorable messages about aging. *Journal of Communication, 52*(4), 681–697. https://doi.org/10.1111/j.1460-2466.2002.tb02568.x

37 See: Bernhold, Q. S., & Giles, H. (2019). Older adults' recalled memorable messages about aging and their associations with successful aging. *Human Communication Research, 45*(4), 474–507. https://doi.org/10.1093/hcr/hqz011

38 Some, perhaps more creatively and less age-deprecatingly, can declare that they are "having a CRAFT moment" (that is, "I can't remember a fxxxing thing").

39 Sokolovsky, J. (Ed.). (2020). *The cultural context of aging: Worldwide perspectives* (4th ed.). Santa Barbara, CA: Prager; see book review: Oxlund, B. (2021). Retrieved from: https://anthropologyandgerontology.com/book-review-oxlund/

40 Liang, J., & Luo, B. (2012). Toward a discourse shift in social gerontology: From successful aging to harmonious aging. *Journal of Aging Studies, 26*(5), 327–334. https://doi.org/10.1016/j.jaging.2012.03.001

41 Ackerman, L. S., & Chopik, W. J. (2020). Cross-cultural comparisons in implicit and explicit age bias. *Personality and Social Psychology Bulletin.* Advance Online: https://10.1177/0146167220950070

42 Campos, B., Ullman, J. B., Aguilera, A., & Dunkel Schetter, C. (2014). Familism and psychological health: The intervening role of closeness and social support. *Cultural Diversity & Ethnic Minority Psychology, 20*(2), 191–201.
https://doi.org/10.1037/a0034094; Feng, Q., & Straughan, P. T. (2017). What does successful aging mean? Lay perception of successful aging among elderly Singaporeans. *Journals of Gerontology Series B Psychological Sciences & Social Sciences, 72*(2), 204–213. https://doi.org/10.1093/geronb/gbw151

43 North, M. S., & Fiske, S. T. (2015). Modern attitudes toward older adults in the aging world: A cross-cultural meta-analysis. *Psychological Bulletin, 141*(5), 993–1021. https://doi.org/10.1037/a0039469; see also: Giles, H., McCann, R., Ota, H., & Noels, K. (2002). Challenging intergenerational stereotypes across Eastern and Western cultures. In M. S. Kaplan, N. Z. Henkin, & A. T. Kusano (Eds.), *Linking lifetimes: A global view of intergenerational exchange* (pp. 13–28). Honolulu, HI: University Press of America, Inc.; Vauclair, C-M., Hanke K., Li-Li Huang, L-L., & Abrams, D. (2016). Are Asian cultures really less ageist than Western ones? It depends on the questions asked. *International Journal of Psychology, 52*(2), 136–144. https://doi.org/10.1002/ijop.12292

44 See p. 358: Seddig, D., Maskileyson, D., & Davidov, E. (2020). The comparability of measures in the ageism module of the fourth round of the European Social Survey,

2008–2009. *Survey Research Methods, 14*(4), 351–364. https://doi.org/10.18148/srm/2020.v14i4.7369; Bratt, C., Abrams, D., Swift, H. J., Vauclair, C.-M., & Marques, S. (2018). Perceived age discrimination across age in Europe: From an ageing society to a society for all ages. *Developmental Psychology, 54*(1), 167–180. http://dx.doi.org/10.1037/dev0000398

45 For a critique of the concept of "generations" and its relationship to storytelling, see: Papacharissi, Z. (2016). Technologies, generations, and structures of storytelling. In J. F. Nussbaum (Ed.), *Communication across the lifespan* (pp. 27–34). New York, NY: Peter Lang.

46 See, for example: Giles, H., Khajavy, H., & Choi, C. W. (2012). Intergenerational communication satisfaction and age boundaries: Comparative Middle Eastern data. *Journal of Cross-Cultural Gerontology, 27*(4), 357–371. https://doi.org/10.1007/s10823-012-9179-9; for perceptions of the onset of "old age" among last surviving, illiterate hunter-gatherers in Northern Tanzania, see: Butovskaya, M., Żelaźniewicz, A., & Sorokowski, P. (2020). Difference in perception of onset of old age in traditional (Hadza) and modern (Polish) societies. *International Journal of Environment Research & Public Health, 17*(7079). https//:10.3390/ijerph17197079

47 Giles, H., & Harwood, J. (1997). Managing intergroup communication: Lifespan issues and consequences. In S. Eliasson & E. Jahr (Eds.), *Language and its ecology: Essays in memory of Einar Haugen* (pp. 105–130). Berlin, Germany: Mouton de Gruyter; see also: Giles, H., & Reid, S. (2005). Ageism across the lifespan: Towards a self-categorization model of ageing. *Journal of Social Issues, 61*(2), 389–404. https://doi.org/10.1111/j.1540-4560.2005.00412.x

48 Respectively, see: May 2020, the FBI had received over 300,000 complaints that nearly equaled the number for the whole of 2019. Retrieved from: https://patch.com/california/paloalto/s/hhtje/elder-abuse-rose-santa-clara-county-countystaffing-dropped; Newton, P. (2021). Families want change after neglect in Canadian care homes proved deadly during the pandemic. *CNN*, March 8. Retrieved from: https://www.cnn.com/2021/02/28/americas/canada-care-homes-pandemic/index.html

49 See, for example: Lin, M-C., Giles, H., & Soliz, J. (2016). Problematic intergenerational communication and caregiving in the family: Elder abuse and neglect. In L. N. Olson & M. A. Fine (Eds.), *The darker side of family communication: The harmful, the morally suspect, and the socially inappropriate* (pp. 155–173). New York, NY: Peter Lang; see also: Lin, M.-C. (2020). Communication neglect, caregiver anger and hostility, and perceptions of older care receivers' cognitive status and problem behaviors in explaining elder abuse. *Journal of Elder Abuse & Neglect*. Advance Online: https://10.1080/08946566.2020.1741054

2 Messages of Agism and Age Stereotypes

It is not uncommon for people in Western societies to have negative attitudes about getting older. Paired with this, people often have unfavorable views of older adults in general. Along with gender and race, *age* is one of the first things people register when encountering strangers.[1] When there is a general social consensus about the characteristics of a group – in this case, older adults – those characteristics constitute people's *stereotypes* of that group. Thus, when people attribute characteristics they associate with older people to members of that group, they are engaging in *age stereotyping* (even if they recognize some individual differences). When age stereotypes are linked to negative attitudes, they may be quite harmful, as they can shape older people's expectations of later life as well as younger people's behaviors toward older adults.

When people treat someone differently than others because of their age, this is *agism*.[2] When older adults are dismissed, ignored, taken less seriously, or otherwise denied opportunities because of their age, it is agism. While most people's immediate association with that term is negative (thinking of, for example, discrimination), agism can be positive as well. Thus, when older adults receive certain privileges (for example, "senior discounts," tax advantages, eligibility for certain housing), this too is agism.[3] Although people often think of agism as something only older people experience, agism can occur to individuals at any point in the lifespan.[4] For instance, it is also agism when young people are unjustly discriminated against solely based on their chronological years, or their appearance (for example, being "baby-faced"[5]). Indeed, recent research indicates that in Europe, younger adults report experiencing greater age-based discrimination than do older adults, though the nature of differences varies by national context.[6]

In this chapter, we explore the nature of age stereotypes and agism, with particular attention to their consequences for communication between age groups. In many ways, this is the foundation from which the other chapters in this volume follow and is the basis for much of our thinking about successful aging, which we discuss at the end of this book.

DOI: 10.4324/9780429330681-2

The Prevalence of Agism

Agism can be both implicit and explicit, and many of its implicit forms are so pervasive that people may not even realize they are subscribing to, and perpetuating, agist ideas. For example, many common sayings or beliefs about getting older reflect negative ideas about older adults. These sayings include:

> - "You can't teach an old dog new tricks"
> - "El loro viejo no aprende a hablar" (Spanish: "An old parrot cannot learn to speak")
> - "I vecchi non imparano cose nuove" (Italian: "Old people do not learn new things")
> - Intergenerational communication is like "playing music to a cow" (Cantonese)

Researchers have identified such beliefs as "myths of aging" – widely held ideas about getting older that are not necessarily true. We would argue that they are also agist in nature. These myths imply that older people are (inevitably) physically and mentally declining, which is *not* consistent with what we know about aging. These agist beliefs are highly prevalent in both interpersonal interaction and the media (see Chapter 5), and their ubiquity means that older people constantly receive messages from members of their local community, larger society, and even their family that their age group is devalued. The emotional spillover of this is that, as British novelist Anthony Powell put it in his book *Dance to the Music of Time*, "Growing old is like being increasingly penalized for a crime you haven't committed."

Age prejudice and discriminatory acts against older people can manifest in both direct and indirect ways. Directly, policies that deny older adults opportunities or hold them to different standards than adults in other age groups are discriminatory. Examples of such policies include mandatory retirement in certain professions (e.g., those for air traffic controllers or commercial airline pilots and judges in many American states[7]) or more stringent requirements for renewing driver's licenses (e.g., vision checks or more frequent renewals).[8] Age discrimination is visible indirectly in the medical field. Geriatrics is often viewed as an unattractive field,[9] and there are proportionally fewer doctors in this specialty relative to the number of patients in this age group. Most medical students do not want to do their residencies and fellowships in this specialty, likely because geriatricians are lower paid compared with many other medical specialties and they are also considered the lowest on the physicians' totem pole of status. Additionally, geriatric specializations are less common than many other specialties in medical schools, meaning there are fewer opportunities for student training.

A lack of geriatric specialists has significant implications for older people. First, there are fewer physicians who are properly trained to take care of a growing population of people who are living longer. Second, older people also tend to have a number of chronic ailments to present at once. When medical professionals do not have the experience to treat multiple conditions, the result can be misdiagnoses, confusion for older patients, and medical prescriptions that may not be appropriate or necessary.[10]

More generally, agism on the part of medical doctors – which can occur across different specialties – can lead to older adults receiving lower quality care. One study had 85 doctors "examine" 72 fictional patients with possible angina via a web survey; the targeted age range of the patients was 45–92 years. Patients over 65 were less likely to be referred to a cardiologist, given an angiogram, or given a stress test than patients under 65. This older group was also less likely to be recommended for operations to open up blocked coronary arteries and less likely to be prescribed statins to reduce cholesterol.[11] While we do not and cannot know the doctors' motivations behind these decisions, it is possible that older adults' position in the lifespan may have led doctors to think such treatment was less "worthwhile." Regardless of the motivation behind it, such differences in treatment could have major implications for patients' health, quality of life, and even mortality.

Although there are professions where there seem to be no age limits – US Supreme Court Justices would be one example – the workplace is another arena where agism is widespread. Older employees often face age-based discrimination because employers fear that older people will not perform as adequately or as quickly as their young counterparts, although research does not necessarily support this belief.[12] Although older workers are often valued for their low turnover rates, reliability, loyalty, and more developed work ethic, employers and fellow employees also see them as declining physically and mentally, and as resistant to new technologies and less able to adapt to (related) change.[13] (Here again, we note that empirical evidence does not necessarily support these beliefs).[14] In the United States, age discrimination lawsuits have been on the increase in recent years, but it is very difficult to prove someone has not been hired, promoted, or let go specifically by an employer solely because of their age. Consequently, age discrimination is difficult to address, which can allow it to persist. This will almost certainly become a bigger problem as an increasing number of workers age, and workers need to stay in their jobs longer in difficult economic times.

The need for people to conform and expectations for them to "look their age" is another site of potential age discrimination (see Chapter 5), and one that often starts early in life. For example, most children are encouraged to dress "appropriately" for their age. Similarly, in later life, older adults can be evaluated negatively (by younger people) for attempting to look younger than their years[15] (as reflected in the derogatory adage, "mutton dressed as lamb"). Expectations like these are pervasive, and generally rooted in people's age stereotypes, which can be prescriptive (suggesting what a group member "should" do) in addition to being descriptive (describing what a group member is). When people do not look their age, they can often be asked to furnish proof before they are granted age-related privileges (such as purchasing alcohol or tobacco or receiving special discounts).

The manifestations of agism we have described so far draw heavily on examples from the West (i.e., the United States and Western Europe), which may leave readers wondering about how age is regarded in other cultural contexts. Some cultures are reputed to have a deep respect, sometimes bordering on reverence, for elderly people (see Chapter 1), because older adults are seen as wise and more experienced. For example, people from certain East Asian societies have historically upheld a Confucian value of *filial piety*, which requires that older family members – and elder people in general – be venerated for their wisdom, piousness, and grace.[16] According to this value, sons and daughters should not move away to distant places while their parents are still living. Indeed, on a questionnaire devised to measure filial piety, there are such items as: "There is no crime worse than being unfilial," "The great debt you have to repay your parents is as boundless as the sky," and "No matter how parents conduct themselves, sons and daughters must respect them." Western respondents often find such sentiments strange and foreign to their experience. Yet these values highlight the hierarchal structure of these traditional Asian cultures where a different and deferential way of speaking is expected, and used, with older people.

Since the 1960s, however, research has found that there has been an erosion of filial piety in East Asia. This is likely largely due to many factors, including children acquiring higher levels of education, the break-up of many intergenerational households and their family structure, young people's use of more advanced forms of technology on a daily basis, the greatly expanding numbers of older adults in the East compared to the West, and younger adults being more financially independent and advancing in the business world. Such changes, which are part of modernization and Westernization, have placed young adults in a higher social position than they had previously experienced.[17] With these shifts, younger adults have come to hold forms of power that their elders used to, and/or now do not, and expectations around respect have been shifting. Increasingly, respect is seen as something that is earned, rather than given based on one's age.

Scholars had initially proposed that attitudes toward older adults, and communication with older adults, should be more positive in East Asia given the cultural values of filial piety. However, this has not been borne out in research. Communication scholars have conducted a series of studies across the length of South and East Asia (e.g., China, Mongolia, Japan, the Vietnams) comparing age stereotypes and the intergenerational climates reported in these cultures to Western settings (e.g., Canada, Australia, and the United States). Although some cross-cultural differences emerged, and more respect was superficially accorded to older people in the East, researchers generally found that the climate for intergenerational communication, and stereotypes of older adults, were as negative or more negative in Eastern cultural contexts, compared with Western ones. [18]

Studies have also been conducted in South and West Africa and still found, even in these cultures where there were purportedly traditional values of filial piety, that the intergenerational communication climate was more favorable in the West.[19] Most recently, researchers turned to the Middle East, looking at aging in Iran.[20] Over the centuries, elderly people in Iran have been considered as sources of knowledge, wisdom, and valued experience for other generations, especially for youth. Iranian scholars have written that in their culture, "the elderly are treated very respectfully and they are privileged by a high position among the family members and are supported by their family for all their needs."[21] In the Quran, it is declared that Muslims should respect older people and treat them as valuable members of society, and these sentiments find expression in Persian poetry and literature. Moreover, when an elder enters a room, others stand up, the best seats are offered to them, and they are offered drinks and food before anyone else. In public places such as the metro and on the bus, young people are expected to be polite and offer their seats to elderly passengers when there are no empty ones. Nonetheless, there was no evidence of a better intergenerational climate in Iran than in the United States.

In a recent meta-analysis of studies on this topic around the globe, researchers found that derogation of older people was actually worst in East Asia, and that cultural values of individualism were associated with more positive views toward older adults. Perhaps tellingly, their analysis also found that the increase in proportion of older adults in national populations predicted negative attitudes toward older people in those countries.[22] These findings also cohere with other work that found the proportion of older adults in a population to be correlated with the extent to which a country's citizens believe aging is a problem.[23] Thus, it is quite possible that the current cultural differences in attitudes toward older adults have both cultural and pragmatic roots. That is, in East Asia, the combination of (collectivistic) cultural expectations that demand care (and attendant resources) for older members of society and a rising number of older adults that expect that care may foster resentment for and antipathy toward older people.

Age Stereotyping

These widespread negative attitudes toward older people and aging, and the age expectations attending them, are not just manifest in healthcare settings and the workplace. Studies with young adults have also shown that the social status attributed to different ages goes up from adolescence – where it is at a low point – to its zenith at 30 years of age. Thereafter, and as we saw in Chapter 1, social status plummets (and especially for women) to the 90s decade.[24] In a meta-analysis of attitudes toward younger and older adults, attitudes toward older adults were found to be consistently more negative, with some of the biggest differences between young and old seen in age stereotypes.[25] Many people consider older adults, in general, to be incompetent, dependent, slow, grouchy, and lacking in warmth, among other unpleasant traits. Drawing on language used in publicly available texts, there is also evidence that these stereotypes have become progressively more negative over the last 200 years.[26] There is also evidence that these stereotypes are established early in life:[27] for instance, one study found that six-year-old children draw older people in seemingly unkind ways, or portray them as feeble (for example, needing a cane or walking stick).[28]

Some of these negative traits appear to creep into views people have of middle-aged adults. (Here, we briefly note that — as discussed in Chapter 1 — the boundaries of "middle age" are not clear cut, with different sources offering different definitions). In one study, for instance, middle-aged adults were seen as significantly lower in vitality (e.g., attractiveness, strength, health, flexibility) than younger adults — though that same study also found that older adults were, in turn, seen as lower in vitality than middle-aged adults.[29] In another study, it was also found that the more younger adults reported identifying middle-aged people in terms of their age, the more likely they were to perceive differences in communication between younger and middle-aged adults.[30]

Negative stereotypes about middle age are also widespread in Western popular culture, both present and past. For instance, birthday cards often feature "jokes" that depict middle age in negative ways. A birthday card designed as a flier for a movie about "The Middle-Aged Zone" included phrases like, "An eerie time warp between youth and old age," and below, "See them awaken to the horrifying reality that is middle age!" However (and in line with research findings on age stereotypes), older adulthood is viewed as even worse than middle age. As Doris Day, the famous American movie actress, once put it: "The really frightening thing about middle age is that you know you'll grow out of it."

With all this said, it is also important to highlight that in addition to widespread negative age stereotypes, there are also a number of *positive* stereotypes. Examples of such traits generated in studies include being wise, knowledgeable, self-accepting, trustworthy, kind, and family oriented.[31] Middle-aged and older workers are also attributed many positive characteristics in the workplace.[32] Thus, when people (and particularly younger people, who are the primary participants in many studies on this subject) think of older adults, it is not all doom, gloom, and decline. Notably, however, positive stereotyping of older people (e.g., labeling older adults as kind, generous, and wise) has been documented to occur more in Western contexts than in East Asian contexts.

Social psychologists have proposed that we can think of stereotypes as essentially falling along two dimensions: *warmth* (e.g., being kind, nice, pleasant) and *competence* (e.g., being smart, capable, independent).[33] While not all traits that people associate with older adults align perfectly with one of these two dimensions, most can be associated with one or the other. In studies that examine how people view different social groups, older adults are consistently found to be characterized by *mixed* stereotypes – that is, stereotypes are both positive and negative (as opposed to predominantly positive or predominantly negative) on these two dimensions. Specifically, older adults are generally stereotyped as high on warmth, but low on competence.[34] In short, overall, people tend to see old people as kind and warm, but incompetent (and closely related, low in social status).

Age Subtypes

Digging a little deeper into the complexities of age stereotyping, research has suggested that people believe there are *subtype*s of elders above and beyond the general stereotypes discussed previously. Mary Lee Hummert has shown that people can reliably distinguish between at least seven subtypes when thinking about older people they know and looking at photographs of older people who are strangers to them.[35] These subtypes, both positive and negative, are depicted in Table 2.1, together with some exemplar traits associated with them.

Interestingly, when shown photographs of older people, respondents generally place those who are smiling into one of the positive subtypes, and those who are not smiling into the negative subtypes.[36] In fact, other studies have shown that attributed ages of happy-looking faces were underestimated by students, whereas the ages of those with neutrally displayed emotions (that is, those neither smiling nor frowning) were judged most accurately. Here, context is also important: the negative subtypes were most prevalent when the occasions for eliciting age stereotypes were associated with leisure and civic commitment settings, and the positive subtypes were triggered more when family and religious circumstances were highlighted.[37]

It should be noted that the stereotypes we review here are based on data from participants that are predominantly white, American, and heterosexual and therefore reflect people's ideas about older adults belonging to these social groups. Other racial and ethnic groups have other, distinct archetypes for older adults (as well as other figures of authority) within their cultures, such as the "Matriarch" or "Mammy" archetypes for American Black women.[38] Similarly, there are distinct stereotypes of older men and women who identify as gay or

Table 2.1 Subtypes of Older Adults and Exemplar Traits

Valence	Subtype	Exemplar traits
Positive	"Golden Ager"	Happy, alert, sociable
Positive	"John Wayne Conservative"	Patriotic, proud, nostalgic
Positive	"Perfect Grandparent"	Kind, loving, family oriented
Negative	"Severely Impaired"	Slow-thinking, incompetent, feeble
Negative	"Despondent"	Depressed, hopeless, lonely
Negative	"Recluse"	Quiet, timid, naive
Negative	"Shrew/Curmudgeon"	Ill-tempered, stubborn, selfish

lesbian,[39] and members of these communities report adapting their behavior in ways to avoid conforming to those stereotypes when they view them as unfavorable or undesirable.

Why Stereotype?

Why do people engage in stereotyping of older adults (or really, any social group)? Psychologists have argued that stereotypes serve an important social function: they help us predict what people are going to do.[40] When we do not know someone and encounter them for the first time, we need to figure out how to react or respond to that person. Recognizing an individual as a member of a group we are familiar with – for example, classifying someone in terms of age (or gender, or ethnicity) – and then generalizing what we know about that group to that individual helps us figure out how to interact with them.

More specifically, researchers have argued that when we encounter a new person, we essentially try to answer two questions about that individual. First, what are this person's intentions? (Are they friendly, or are they threatening?) Second, what is this person capable of doing? (Can they actually carry out their intentions, positive or negative?) Evaluations of warmth address the first question (i.e., positive or negative intentions), while evaluations of competence address the second question (i.e., ability to carry out intentions).[41] Thus, stereotypes help us predict the behavior of people we do not (yet) know. This, in turn, helps us figure out how to interact with those new people.

Having established at least one explanation for why people engage in stereotyping, a next question would logically be: Why is it that, when we stereotype, we come up with the particular characteristics or qualities for older adults that we do? Considering age stereotypes specifically, we might also ask why these stereotypes tend to be more negative than positive, overall. Several possible answers to this question have been put forward.[42]

One explanation is that stereotypes reflect (and contribute to reinforcing) people's perceptions of the social status and competitive threat posed by groups in a given society. When a group has high status (e.g., having power, resources, money, influence), they are stereotyped as being high in competence. When a group is seen as a competitive threat (e.g., for limited resources), they are seen as low in warmth. Thus, when people observe older adults requiring assistance, or not occupying positions of power or influence to the same extent as younger adults, they stereotype older adults as low in competence. Similarly, when people perceive older adults to be cooperative or passive, they stereotype them as high in warmth. Consistent with this explanation, one study that examined stereotypes of older adults' competence across 11 countries found that stereotypes correlated with older adults' participation in the workforce and unpaid volunteer work: in countries where more older adults worked or actively volunteered, they were stereotyped as more competent.[43]

Related to this argument, some have argued that negative attitudes toward older adults may reflect the perception that they are a threat to limited resources.[44] In line with this, it has been found that as the share of older adults in the general population of a country increases (and they presumably demand more resources), members of that country are more likely to consider aging to be a problem.[45] This view (see also Chapter 5) would suggest that negative stereotypes of older people gain currency in society when there are more limited economic opportunities and resources (for example, during a recession). Negative stereotypes provide a warrant for excluding older adults from working too long. In this view, when times demand they are needed in the workplace (such as in an economic upswing after a recession), we would expect negative attitudes to dissipate somewhat.

Another view, rooted in *terror management theory*, suggests that negative stereotypes exist because whenever younger people even *see* older people – and especially those who are frail and infirm – their overriding impression is that they are relatively near to death. This reminder of death, called "mortality salience," can lead younger people to think about their own deaths.[46] Relatedly, young people in a study were shown pictures of younger and older people, and the latter were quite healthy-looking. The participants were then given a different task to undertake to assist with (what they were told was) a different study. They were asked to complete a couple of dozen word fragments, eight of which constituted a "death accessibility" measure. For example, GRA_E can be completed as GRAVE, GRAPE, or GRATE. Those participants seeing older people completed such fragments with more death-related words than did participants seeing younger people, suggesting that when people have contact with those much older, they actually "see" death and mortality[47] (see Chapter 6). In this sense, older people may be a threatening reminder to young (as well as older) people of their own inevitable mortality. Terror management theory contends that disturbing feelings provoked by the thought of death can lead to unfavorable views toward older people, who prompt such thoughts.

Of course, age stereotypes, like all stereotypes, are generalizations, and they offer us simplified pictures of our world. Placing an older person into a mere social category as being a "Golden Ager" might be somewhat more positive than that of a "Recluse," but it still implicitly suggests that the person engages in a rather restricted set of roles and behaviors. It is important to appreciate that people of all ages – but particularly, older adults – are more complex and varied than such stereotypes would suggest (as pointed out in Chapter 1). Additionally, even more positive stereotypes can have negative consequences if they are used or experienced in ways that are limiting for the individual(s) being stereotyped.

Consequences of Stereotyping

Stereotypes about older adults – and really, any group – are not problematic in and of themselves. In many cases, they have a kernel of truth at their core and reflect how the majority of members of a group operate in a given society.

However, stereotypes can and do become problematic when they are inaccurate (which is sometimes the case), and when they are applied to an individual person regardless of that person's idiosyncratic characteristics.

Stereotypes about old age are particularly liable to affect our communication, as described in the *age stereotypes in interaction model* (see Chapter 3).[48] Studies have found that people anticipate more negative interactions with more negative subtypes of older adults (e.g., "Despondent"), compared with more positive subtypes (e.g., "Perfect Grandparent"), and that people with more negative attitudes toward older adults expect older adults to complain more and accommodate them less.[49] People have also been found to construct messages differently according to their stereotypes, with people engaging in more patronizing talk (see Chapter 4) to older adults that are more negatively stereotyped.[50] Researchers have also found that which subtype people associate with a person influences how they evaluate that person's communication capacities. One study has shown that as one moves "down" from being attributed a "Golden Ager" to a "John Wayne Conservative" to a "Shrew/Curmudgeon" to a "Despondent," adults of all ages see people as possessing, at each stage, less conversational prowess, hearing ability, and more memory decline.[51]

People can also have stereotypes of older adults that specifically address communication skills or abilities. For instance, it has been shown that people hold negative beliefs about 75-year-olds' language skills. Specifically, in terms of so-called receptive skills and expressive skills, people tend to expect that a 75-year-old speaker is represented in skills listed in Table 2.2.[52]

Age stereotypes can also influence how people interpret what others say. In one study, for instance, researchers found that even when older people made what could otherwise be regarded as so-called "neutral" remarks, these were interpreted differently — and less favorably — when said by older versus younger adults, because of agist schemas. For instance, the phrase, "I don't know what to think," was interpreted as someone weighing up the complexities of matters at hand when it was said by a young adult. However, when an older adult said the very same thing, it was taken to mean the situation was "too much" for him or her.[53] In another study, it was also found that people's stereotypes also affected what kinds of questions they would ask the person they were speaking with. The researchers asked people to tell them what kinds of questions those people would ask someone who had been in an automobile accident in which no one was hurt. If the person in the accident was a 22-year-old, then people

Table 2.2 Receptive and Expressive Skills Expected from 75-Year-Old Adults

Receptive skills	*Expressive skills*
Be hard to understand as they speak softly	Use fewer difficult words
Lose track of who said what in conversation	Have trouble with facts
Ask for repetition	Find it hard to speak if pressed for time
Be frustrated when they can't hear	Appear less sincere when talking

reported that they would begin by asking about speeding and alcohol – a form of *youth* agism itself. However, when the person in the accident was a 72-year-old, they would begin asking questions about the person's sensory and even mental competences. Interestingly, and in the vein of asking at what age do these stereotypes start kicking in, the researchers found this agist information-seeking bias with respect to sight and intellect began when the "driver" was just 32 years of age.[54]

Age Excuses

Stereotypes – and particularly, negative stereotypes – can also influence how older people communicate. In an effort to combat others' potential attributions of memory decline when people forget something, they typically offer an excuse of some kind. Ellen Ryan and her colleagues have shown that people can adopt one of four kinds of excuses for failing to remember something; these are outlined in Table 2.3.[55]

Table 2.3 Types of Excuses for Memory Failure

Excuse	Example
Age	"Getting old does that to your memory"
Ability	"I've never been able to remember names"
Effort	"I've never been one to bother remembering phone numbers"
Situation	"There is so much going on in this small room, it's impossible to remember anything"

It appears as though older people tend to use age excuses, not fully understanding the range of their repercussions. Ryan and colleagues showed that while there are immediate advantages to relieving awkward situations by adopting age excuses, as they are considered more believable than others, they nonetheless can have quite negative consequences. Younger people are particularly sensitive to them because such excuses frustrate them, perhaps because they do not know how to respond. Additionally, people who offer age excuses are perceived as significantly older than those making one of the other three types of excuses. And from what we have seen already, being seen as older has negative consequences in its own right.

One of our students encountered such an age excuser – and wrote to us the following:

> I have a dear professor who is a mentor and friend whom I work very closely with on a daily basis for the past two years. She, as I found out is 57. Now, almost every day I hear her say something regarding her age (i.e. "I cannot lift that I'm getting too old," "My eyes are just failing me," "You

> would not know that was something of my generation"). On average she uses the age excuse in conversations with her younger students.
>
> Being a student myself, I hear these other students talk about how *mean* and how hard it is to talk to her because she is *old*. They apply any basic problem that could happen to anyone and blame it on her because of her age (that is, "I'm scared of her, she's so old and intimidating" or "She only didn't like it because it's too hip for her to understand").
>
> I find this amazing of how an excuse can trigger such a negative attitude. I know this professor very well and she is very enthusiastic, determined, and a lot of fun to talk to. I realized that I am closest to her because I talk to her like I do any one of my other friends. I don't refine my language because of her age like the others (that is, scared to say cuss words, act over polite, etc.).
>
> In conclusion to my story, I told my professor to "knock it off" every time I hear her use her age as an excuse; and every time I do, she smiles at me.

Although we emphasize the potentially negative consequences of stereotypes here, it should be emphasized that such effects are not preordained. People who are the object of negative stereotypes can and do develop resilience to these negative depictions of their social groups;[56] we address the relationship between resilience and successful aging in greater detail in Chapter 8.

Self-Stereotyping

When a person applies age stereotypes to themselves, whether in the form of excuses or otherwise, it is called *self*-stereotyping. Self-stereotyping can include both thinking that an age stereotype applies to oneself and enacting characteristics associated with being older. Below is an extract from a novel called *Staring at the Sun*, by Julian Barnes, that speaks to how people can come to internalize the stereotypes that others have of being older.

> You grew first not in your own eyes, but in other people's eyes. Then slowly, you agreed with their opinion of you. It wasn't that you couldn't walk as far as you used to, it was that other people didn't expect you to. And if they didn't, then it needed vain obstinacy to persist!

Self-stereotyping often occurs in situations where age is made salient – that is, when age is somehow brought to mind. In laboratory studies, this is often achieved by subliminal presentations of cues related to age; in everyday life, age can be made salient in a range of different ways, which we discuss in greater depth in Chapter 3. When the cues people encounter call to mind negative stereotypes of older adulthood, self-stereotyping can result in a host of negative consequences.[57] Studies have shown that when older people self-stereotype, they report less aptitude for activities of daily living (e.g., shopping and preparing meals), and anticipate less willingness to live when confronted with various scenarios that suggest that they could have threatening illnesses.[58]

Furthermore, when people were asked the extent to which they agreed with various agist statements like "As you get older, you are less useful" and then were re-examined 23 years later, the people who did not endorse such sentiments had significantly longer lifespans. In fact, and controlling for many other factors, they lived on average 7.5 more years![59] Recent work suggests that inflammation may be a mediator between people's perceptions of aging and longevity. In one study of over 4000 adults aged 50 and older, people with more positive self-perceptions of aging were found to have lower levels of inflammation (measured by C-reactive protein levels), which were, in turn, associated with lower mortality over a six-year period.[60] Other negative associations with the internalization of negative stereotypes include greater impairments in memory and recovery from illness.[61]

In sum, internalizing and embodying the negative stereotypes that many older people today have – that is, self-stereotyping – can lead to serious consequences for people's activities, physical health, and even survival. Stereotyping can, therefore, be a pernicious cycle and self-fulfilling prophecy (see Chapter 7). To avoid being caught in it, it is important to do our best to avoid contributing to it ourselves. This highlights the importance of embracing and communicating positive ideas about growing older, and not "buying into" negative stereotypes we may encounter elsewhere (e.g., from friends, family, or the mass media). Indeed, there are some great examples of older adults who actively and publicly defy negative views of their age group. The Red Hatters are a collective of women who meet in flamboyant purple garb and red hats in public to have fun and dispel the myth that older women are not vibrant. Another example is the Buranovo Babushkas, a group of 70- to 80-year-old widows who became a TV sensation in Russia when they competed in the 2011 Eurovision Song Contest.

Concluding Thoughts

Age stereotypes surround us: they are evident in conversations with friends and family, as well as in healthcare and workplace settings. Children are socialized into these beliefs early in life and continue to play them out during their adolescence and adulthood. The effects of negative stereotypes are not trivial and deserve to be taken seriously: having negative expectations about older people's communicative and other social competencies has a demonstrable effect not only on the health of intergenerational relations but also in creating self-fulfilling prophecies for later in our own lives. Endorsing negative views of aging can limit our ability to actively function, lead satisfying lives, and enjoy high-quality relationships over the long haul. In Chapter 3, we look at the diverse ways in which one's age can become prominent in communicating with others, with important social and health implications.

Notes

1. North, M. S., & Fiske, S. T. (2012). An inconvenienced youth? Ageism and its potential intergenerational roots. *Psychological Bulletin, 138*(5), 982–997. https://doi.org/10.1037/a0027843
2. Palmore, E. (1999). *Ageism: positive and negative* (2nd ed.). New York, NY: Springer; see also: Palmore, E. (2015). Ageism comes of age. *The Journals of Gerontology: Series B, 70*(6), 873–875. https://doi.org/10.1093/geronb/gbv079
3. North, M. S., & Fiske, S. T. (2012). An inconvenienced youth? Ageism and its potential intergenerational roots. *Psychological Bulletin, 138*(5), 982–997. https://doi.org/10.1037/a0027843
4. de la Fuente-Núñez, V., Cohn-Schwartz, E., Roy, S., & Ayalon, L. (2021). Scoping review on ageism against younger populations. *International Journal of Environmental Research and Public Health, 18*, 3988. https://doi.org/10.3390/ijerph18083988
5. Zebrowitz, L. A., & Franklin Jr. F. G. (2014). The Attractiveness Halo effect and the Babyface Stereotype in older and younger adults: Similarities, own-age accentuation, and older adult positivity effects. *Experimental Aging Research, 40*(3), 375–393. https://doi.org/10.1080/0361073X.2014.897151
6. Bratt, C., Abrams, D., & Swift, H. J. (2020). Supporting the old but neglecting the young? The two faces of ageism. *Developmental Psychology, 56*(5), 1029–1039. http://dx.doi.org/10.1037/dev0000903; Bratt, C., Abrams, D., Swift, H. J., Vauclair, C.-M., & Marques, S. (2018). Perceived age discrimination across age in Europe: From an ageing society to a society for all ages. *Developmental Psychology, 54*(1), 167–180. http://dx.doi.org/10.1037/dev0000398
7. Grandjean, B., & Grell, C. (2019). Why no mandatory retirement age exists for physicians: Important lessons for employers. *Missouri Medicine, 116*(5), 357–360. Retrieved from: https://www.ncbi.nlm.nih.gov/pmc/articles/PMC6797044/
8. Centers for Disease Control and Prevention. (2015, December 2). *In-person license renewal.* Retrieved from: https://www.cdc.gov/motorvehiclesafety/calculator/factsheet/licenserenewal.html
9. Castellucci, M. (2018, February 27). *Geriatrics still failing to attract new doctors.* Modern Healthcare. Retrieved from: https://www.modernhealthcare.com/article/20180227/NEWS/180229926/geriatrics-still-failing-to-attract-new-doctors
10. Aronson, L. (2019). *Elderhood: Redefining aging, transforming medicine, reimagining life.* New York, NY: Bloomsbury.
11. Harries, C., Forrest, D., Harvey, N., McClelland, A., & Bowling, A. (2007). Which doctors are influenced by a patient's age? A multi-method study of angina treatment in general practice, cardiology and gerontology. *BMJ Quality & Safety, 16*(1), 23–27. http://dx.doi.org/10.1136/qshc.2006.018036; see also: Bowling, A. (2007). Honor your father and mother: Ageism in medicine. *British Journal of General Practice, 57*(538), 347–348.
12. North, M. S., & Fiske, S. T. (2015). Intergenerational resource tensions in the workplace and beyond: Individual, interpersonal, institutional, international. *Research in Organizational Behavior, 35*, 159–179. https://doi.org/10.1016/j.riob.2015.10.003; North, M. S. (2019). A GATE to understanding "older" workers: Generation, age, tenure, experience. *Academy of Management Annals, 13*(2), 414–443. https://doi.org/10.5465/annals.2017.0125

13 Finkelstein, L. M., Ryan, K. M., & King, E. B. (2013). What do the young (old) people think of me? Content and accuracy of age-based meta-stereotypes. *European Journal of Work and Organizational Psychology, 22*(6), 633–657. https://doi.org/10.1080/1359432X.2012.673279

14 Ng, T. W., & Feldman, D. C. (2012). Evaluating six common stereotypes about older workers with meta-analytical data. *Personnel Psychology, 65*(4), 821–858. https://doi.org/10.1111/peps.12003

15 Schoemann, A. M., & Branscombe, N. R. (2011). Looking young for your age: Perceptions of anti-aging actions. *European Journal of Social Psychology, 41*(1), 86–95. https://doi.org/10.1002/ejsp.738; Zebrowitz, L. A., & Montepare, J. M. (2000). Too young, too old: Stigmatizing adolescents and the elderly. In T. Heatherton, R. Kleck, J. G. Hull, & M. Hebl (Eds.), *The social psychology of stigma* (pp. 334–373). New York, NY: Guilford.

16 Ho, D. Y. F. (1994). Filial piety, authoritarian moralism, and cognitive conservatism in Chinese societies. *Genetic, Social, and General Psychology Monographs, 120*(3), 347–365.

17 McCann, R.M., Giles, H., & Ota. (2017). Aging and communication across cultures. In L. Chen (Ed.), *The handbook of intercultural communication* (pp. 289–306). Berlin, Germany: Mouton de Gruyter; see also: Shea, J., Moore, K., & Zhang, H. (2020). *Beyond filial piety: Rethinking aging and caretaking in contemporary East Asian society.* New York, NY: Berghan.

18 McCann, R.M., Giles, H., & Ota. (2017). Aging and communication across cultures. In L. Chen (Ed.), *The handbook of intercultural communication* (pp. 289–306). Berlin, Germany: Mouton de Gruyter; Giles, H., McCann, R. M., Ota, H., & Noels, K. A. (2002). Challenging intergenerational stereotypes across Eastern and Western cultures. In M. S. Kaplan, N. Z. Henkin, & A. T. Kusano (Eds.), *Linking lifetimes: A global view of intergenerational exchange* (pp. 13–28). Honolulu, HI: University Press of America, Inc.; Ota, H., Giles, H., & Somera, L. P. (2007). Beliefs about intra- and intergenerational communication in Japan, the Philippines, and the United States: Implication for older adults' subjective well-being. *Communication Studies, 58*(2), 173–188. https://doi.org/10.1080/10510970701341139

19 Giles, H., Makoni, S., & Dailey, R. M. (2005). Intergenerational communication beliefs across the lifespan: Comparative data from West and South Africa. *Journal of Cross-Cultural Gerontology, 20*(September), 191–211. https://doi.org/10.1007/s10823-006-9003-5

20 Giles, H., Khajavy, H., & Choi, C. W. (2012). Intergenerational communication satisfaction and age boundaries: Comparative Middle Eastern data. *Journal of Cross-Cultural Gerontology, 27*(December), 357–371. https://doi.org/10.1007/s10823-012-9179-9

21 Tajvar, M., Arab, M., & Montazeri, A. (2008). Determinants of health-related quality of life in elderly in Tehran, Iran. *BMC Public Health, 8*(1), Article 323. https://doi.org/10.1186/1471-2458-8-323

22 North, M. S., & Fiske, S. T. (2015). Modern attitudes toward older adults in the aging world: A cross-cultural meta-analysis. *Psychological Bulletin, 141*(5), 993–1021. https://doi.org/10.1037/a0039469

23 Pew Research Center. (2014). *Attitudes about aging: A global perspective.* Retrieved from: https://www.pewresearch.org/global/wp-content/uploads/sites/2/2014/01/Pew-Research-Center-Global-Aging-Report-FINAL-January-30-20141.pdf

24 Baker, P. M. (1985). The status of age: Preliminary results. *Journal of Gerontology, 40*(4), 506–508. https://doi.org/10.1093/geronj/40.4.506

25 Kite, M. E., Stockdale, G. D., Whitley Jr, B. E., & Johnson, B. T. (2005). Attitudes toward younger and older adults: An updated meta-analytic review. *Journal of Social Issues, 61*(2), 241–266. https://doi.org/10.1111/j.1540-4560.2005.00404.x

26 Ng, R., Allore, H. G., Trentalange, M., Monin, J. K., & Levy, B. R. (2015). Increasing negativity of age stereotypes across 200 years: Evidence from a database of 400 million words. *PLOS ONE, 10*, e0117086. https://doi.org/10.1371/journal.pone.0117086

27 Mendonça, J., Marques, S., & Abrams, D. (2018). Children's attitudes toward older people: Current and future directions. In L. Ayalon & C. Tesch-Römer (Eds.), *Contemporary*

perspectives on ageism (pp. 517–548). International perspectives on aging, Vol. 19. Berlin, Germany: Springer (eBook). https://doi.org/10.1007/978-3-319-73820-8_30

28 Falchikov, N. (1990). Youthful ideas about old age: An analysis of children's drawings. *International Journal of Aging and Human Development, 31*(2), 79–99. https://doi.org/10.2190%2FQ28U-2QAW-24AM-6XA3

29 McCann, R. M, Dailey, R., Giles, H., & Ota, H. (2005). Beliefs about intergenerational communication across the lifespan: Middle age and the roles of age stereotyping and respect norms. *Communication Studies, 56*(4), 293–311. https://doi.org/10.1080/10510970500319286

30 Harwood, J., & Giles, H. (1993). Creating intergenerational distance: Language, communication and middle-age. *Language Sciences, 15*(1), 1–24. https://doi.org/10.1016/0388-0001(93)90003-B

31 Hummert, M. L., Garstka, T. A., Shaner, J. L., & Strahm, S. (1994). Stereotypes of the elderly held by young, middle-aged, and elderly adults. *Journal of Gerontology: Psychological Sciences, 49*(5), P240–P249. https://doi.org/10.1093/geronj/49.5.P240

32 Finkelstein, L. M., Ryan, K. M., & King, E. B. (2013). What do the young (old) people think of me? Content and accuracy of age-based meta-stereotypes. *European Journal of Work and Organizational Psychology, 22*(6), 633–657. https://doi.org/10.1080/1359432X.2012.673279

33 Fiske, S. T., Cuddy, A. J., & Glick, P. (2007). Universal dimensions of social cognition: Warmth and competence. *Trends in Cognitive Sciences, 11*(2), 77–83. https://doi.org/10.1016/j.tics.2006.11.005

34 Fiske, S. T., Cuddy, A. J., Glick, P., & Xu, J. (2002). A model of (often mixed) stereotype content: Competence and warmth respectively follow from perceived status and competition. *Journal of Personality and Social Psychology, 82*(6), 878–902. https://doi.org/10.1037/0022-3514.82.6.878

35 For reviews of age stereotypes subtypes, see: Hummert, M. L. (2010). Age group identities, stereotypes, and communication. In H. Giles, S. A. Reid, & J. Harwood (Eds.), *The dynamics of intergroup communication* (pp. 42–52). New York, NY: Peter Lang; Hummert, M. L. (2019). Intergenerational communication. In J. Harwood, J. Gasiorek, H. Pierson, J. F. NussBaum, & C. Gallois (Eds.), *Language, communication and intergroup relations: A celebration of the scholarship of Howard Giles* (pp. 130–160). New York, NY: Routledge.

36 Hummert, M. L., Garstka, T. A., & Shaner, J. L. (1997). Stereotyping of older adults: The role of target facial cues and perceiver characteristics. *Psychology and Aging, 12*(1), 107–114. https://doi.org/10.1037/0882-7974.12.1.107

37 Voelkle, M. C., Ebner, N. C., Lindenberger, U., & Riediger, M. (2012). Let me guess how old you are: Effects of age, gender, and facial expression on perceptions of age. *Psychology and Aging, 27*(2), 265–277. https://doi.org/10.1037/a0025065

38 Baker, T. A., Buchanan, N. T., Mingo, C. A., Roker, R., & Brown, C. S. (2014). Reconceptualizing successful aging among Black women and the relevance of the strong Black woman archetype. *The Gerontologist, 55*(1), 51–57. https://doi.org/10.1093/geront/gnu105; Brown Givens, S. M., & Monahan, J. L. (2005). Priming mammies, jezebels, and other controlling images: An examination of the influence of mediated stereotypes on perceptions of an African American woman. *Media Psychology, 7*(1), 87–106. https://doi.org/10.1207/S1532785XMEP0701_5

39 Wright, S. L., & Sara Canetto, S. (2009). Stereotypes of older lesbians and gay men. *Educational Gerontology, 35*(5), 424–452. https://doi.org/10.1080/03601270802505640; Hajek, C. (2014). Gay men at midlife: A grounded theory of social identity management through linguistic labeling and intra-and intergenerational talk. *Journal of Language and Social Psychology, 33*(6), 606–631. https://doi.org/10.1177%2F0261927X14545344

40 Frith, C. D., & Frith, U. (2006). How we predict what other people are going to do. *Brain Research, 1079*(1), 36–46. https://doi.org/10.1016/j.brainres.2005.12.126

41 Fiske, S. T., Cuddy, A. J., & Glick, P. (2007). Universal dimensions of social cognition: Warmth and competence. *Trends in Cognitive Sciences, 11*(2), 77–83. https://doi.org/10.1016/j.tics.2006.11.005
42 North, M. S., & Fiske, S. T. (2012). An inconvenienced youth? Ageism and its potential intergenerational roots. *Psychological Bulletin, 138*(5), 982–997. https://doi.org/10.1037/a0027843
43 Bowen, C. E., & Skirbekk, V. (2013). National stereotypes of older people's competence are related to older adults' participation in paid and volunteer work. *Journals of Gerontology, Series B: Psychological Sciences and Social Sciences, 68*(6), 974–983. https://doi.org/10.1093/geronb/gbt101.974983
44 North, M. S., & Fiske, S. T. (2015). Intergenerational resource tensions in the workplace and beyond: Individual, interpersonal, institutional, international. *Research in Organizational Behavior, 35,* 159–179. https://doi.org/10.1016/j.riob.2015.10.003
45 Pew Research Center. (2014). *Attitudes about aging: A global perspective.* Retrieved from: https://www.pewresearch.org/global/wp-content/uploads/sites/2/2014/01/Pew-Research-Center-Global-Aging-Report-FINAL-January-30-20141.pdf
46 Greenberg, J., Schimel, J., & Mertens, A. (2004). Ageism: Denying the face of the future. In T. D. Nelson (Ed.), *Ageism: Stereotyping and prejudice against older persons* (pp. 27–48). Cambridge, MA: MIT Press; Greenberg, J., Pyszczynski, T., & Solomon, S. (2002). A perilous leap from Becker's theorizing to empirical science: Terror management and research. In D. Liechty (Ed.), *Death and denial: Interdisciplinary perspectives on the legacy of Ernest Becker* (pp. 3–16). New York, NY: Praeger.
47 Martens, A., Goldenberg, J. L., & Greenberg, J. (2005). A terror management perspective on ageism. *Journal of Social Issues, 61*(2), 223–239. https://doi.org/10.1111/j.1540-4560.2005.00403.x
48 See: Hummert, M. L. (2019). Intergenerational communication. In J. Harwood, J. Gasiorek, H. Pierson, J. F. NussBaum, & C. Gallois (Eds.), *Language, communication and intergroup relations: A celebration of the scholarship of Howard Giles* (pp. 130–160). New York, NY: Routledge; see also: Hummert, M. L., Garstka, T. A., Ryan, E. B., & Bonnesen, J. L. (2004). The role of age stereotypes in interpersonal communication. In J. F. Nussbaum & J. Coupland (Eds.), *Handbook of communication and aging research* (2nd ed., pp. 91–114). Mahwah, NJ: Lawrence Erlbaum; Hummert, M. L. (2012). Challenges and opportunities for communication between age groups. In H. Giles (Ed.), *The handbook of intergroup communication* (pp. 223–236). New York, NY: Routledge.
49 Harwood, J., & Williams, A. (1998). Expectations for communication with positive and negative subtypes of older adults. *International Journal of Aging and Human Development, 47*(1), 11–33. https://doi.org/10.2190%2FGW3C-5CNM-8DPD-N81E
50 Hummert, M. L., Shaner, J. L., Garstka, T. A., & Henry, C. (1998). Communication with older adults: The influence of age stereotypes, context, and communicator age. *Human Communication Research, 25*(1), 124–151. https://doi.org/10.1111/j.1468-2958.1998.tb00439.x
51 Hummert, M. L., Garstka, T. A., & Shaner, J. L. (1995). Beliefs about language performance: Adults' perceptions about self and elderly targets. *Journal of Language and Social Psychology, 14*(3), 235–259. https://doi.org/10.1177/0261927X95143001
52 Ryan, E. B., Kwong See, S., Meneer, W. B., & Trovato, D. (1992). Age-based perceptions of language performance among young and older adults. *Communication Research, 19*(4), 423–443. https://doi.org/10.1177%2F009365092019004002
53 Giles, H., Henwood, K., Coupland, N., Harriman, J., & Coupland, J. (1992). Language attitudes and cognitive mediation. *Human Communication Research, 18*(4), 500–527. https://doi.org/10.1111/j.1468-2958.1992.tb00570.x
54 Ng, S. H., Moody, J., & Giles, H. (1991). Information-seeking triggered by age. *International Journal of Aging and Human Development, 33*(4), 269–277. https://doi.org/10.2190%2FlUV0-UYQL-7AQV-V6UN

55 Ryan, E. B., Bieman-Copland, S., Kwong See, S. T., Ellis, C. H., & Anas, A. P. (2002). Age excuses: Conversational management of memory failures in older adults. *Journal of Gerontology: Psychological Sciences, 57B*, P256–P267. https://doi.org/10.1093/geronb/57.3.P256

56 See, for example: Grandbois, D. M., & Sanders, G. F. (2012). Resilience and stereotyping: The experiences of Native American elders. *Journal of Transcultural Nursing, 23*(4), 389–396. https://doi.org/10.1177%2F1043659612451614

57 Levy, B. R. (2003). Mind matters: Cognitive and physical effects of aging self-stereotypes. *The Journals of Gerontology Series B: Psychological Sciences and Social Sciences, 58*(4), P203–P211. https://doi.org/10.1037//0022-3514.83.2.261; Levy, B. (2009). Stereotype embodiment: A psychosocial approach to aging. *Current Directions in Psychological Science, 18*(6), 332–336. https://doi.org/10.1111%2Fj.1467-8721.2009.01662.x

58 Levy, B., Ashman, O., & Dror, I. (2000). To be or not to be: The effects of aging stereotypes on the will to live. *OMEGA – Journal of Death and Dying, 40*(3), 409–420. https://doi.org/10.2190%2FY2GE-BVYQ-NF0E-83VR; Moser, C., Spagnoli, J., & Santos-Eggimann, B. (2011). Self-perception of aging and vulnerability to adverse outcomes at the age of 65–70 years. *Journals of Gerontology Series B: Psychological Sciences and Social Sciences, 66*(6), 675–680. https://doi.org/10.1093/geronb/gbr052

59 Levy, B. R., Slade, M. D., Kunkel, S. R., & Kasl, S.V. (2002). Longevity increased by positive self-perceptions of aging. *Journal of Personality and Social Psychology, 83*(2), 261–270. https://doi.org/10.1037/0022-3514.83.2.261

60 Levy, B. R., & Bavishi, A. (2018). Survival advantage mechanism: Inflammation as a mediator of positive self-perceptions of aging on longevity. *The Journals of Gerontology: Series B: Psychological Sciences, 73*(3), 409–412. https://doi.org/10.1093/geronb/gbw035

61 Nelson, T. D. (2016). Promoting healthy aging by confronting ageism. *American Psychologist, 71*(4), 276–282. https://doi.org/10.1037/a0040221

3 Age Identities
What Are They and How Do They Emerge?

In Chapter 2, we introduced age stereotypes or the notion that people have a general social consensus about the characteristics of age groups. Age stereotypes can shape the way people perceive and communicate with older adults in important ways and, more specifically, can be a part of why people mistreat older adults because of their age. In this chapter, we delve deeper into the aging process by exploring the ways age identities are fashioned and the way that people's other social identities can lead to diversity in people's age-related experiences. We also consider how one's (older) age can become salient during interactions and the personal, relational, and health-related consequences that ensue from this.

Age Identity

An individual's *social identity* captures who they are in terms of the social groups to which they belong.[1] Social groups are usually defined by shared physical, social, historical, experiential, and/or psychological characteristics of individuals. For example, people belong to groups according to their race, ethnicity, gender, social class (also known as socioeconomic status), sexual orientation, (dis)abilities, and religion/religious beliefs. Age is also a social group with which people identify.

According to social identity theory (SIT), a psychological theory about how we relate to others in terms of social groups (that has been applied to intergenerational communication),[2] people have an intrinsic motivation to strive for a positive social identity. This means that people care how their social groups are perceived. SIT claims that people like to belong to social groups that give them a sense of satisfaction in belonging to them. Having an identity that is revered and respected is rewarding and affords an individual person positive self-esteem. The theory claims that individuals like to engage in activities that maintain a positive differential between their own social group, also known as their *ingroup*, and relevant social groups to which they do not belong, known as their *outgroups*.

Some suggest that age may be the primary category we use to make sense of ourselves and others. While we have many social identities (as noted previously),

DOI: 10.4324/9780429330681-3

our age group – more specifically, what we *believe* our age group to be – makes up an important part of who we are.[3] As a result, as SIT suggests, we are motivated to act in ways that reflect and cultivate a positive sense of age identity. For example, 20-year-olds might try and emulate what they see as prototypical behavior of a "normal" 20-year-old. In both their thoughts and behavior, they may also privilege other members in their age-related peer group and exclude and discriminate against "outsiders" from another age group, such as older people. As readers of this book may anticipate, such differential processes can be evident in communicative practices, such as emphasizing an ingroup dialect or jargon while patronizing, slurring, or obnoxiously labeling members of an outgroup.[4]

It is critical to note that people's age-related experiences are incredibly diverse because age intersects with other identities (some of which are oppressed and some of which are privileged) to create unique social experiences. The concept of *intersectionality* provides a useful framework to help us make sense of this notion. Intersectionality is often used to examine how the multiple identities of individuals interact and relate to societal inequities and social injustice.[5] According to theories of intersectionality, multiple identities co-exist within an individual. Consequently, people do not simply experience "age" (and, relatedly, agism and age stereotyping); rather, they experience "age" *within* overlapping and interdependent systems of oppression/privilege, disadvantage/advantage, and discrimination/preferential treatment from the other groups to which they belong.[6] In this vein, we might think about how one's age-related experiences differ according to one's social class (e.g., older adults who are poor and working are disadvantaged economically and, thus, have a different experience with aging than those who are wealthy), race (e.g., older Latina women are racially oppressed and, thus, encounter different types of social issues than older white women),[7] and sexuality (e.g., midlife and older gay men have to contend with societal-level issues related to both aging and heterosexism, as well as community-level issues such as the appearance-oriented nature of gay culture relative to older men who identify as heterosexual).[8]

Some groups, such as aging Black lesbians and Black gay men, contend with three or more intersecting oppressions – racism, heterosexism, and agism – that coalesce to create especially unique, and difficult, aging experiences.[9] For example, one study revealed that older Black lesbians have specific types of resources that they need to be healthy and thrive, many of which are related and responsive to their cultural traditions, gendered realities, and stigmatized sexuality.[10] In fact, health is a critical factor to consider in this discussion because research shows that in addition to age-related barriers (see Chapter 1 for a discussion of the status of gerontology in the health field), there are additional identity-related barriers that people from historically oppressed social groups have to contend with in healthcare contexts. For instance, older adults who are transgender- and gender-nonconforming are often denied medical care by doctors and nurses, particularly the type of care that relates to their gender transition (e.g., a doctor refusing to write a prescription for hormone medication). They can also experience health-related mistreatment from medical professionals who develop treatment plans according to their former gender identity.[11] Thus, sexuality, gender, race, and class offer important social frames to consider in the context of aging; these considerations are infrequently acknowledged in the field of communication and aging.

As a social identity, age identity is somewhat different from other identities to the extent that everyone moves through different (and culturally distinctive) age groups over the life course.[12] Boundaries between age groups are somewhat more flexible than boundaries between racial or gender groups (though, we note, this flexibility is limited).[13] As a result, it can be easier to disassociate oneself from an unfavorable age group and associate with another. Older people often do not feel their chronological age; instead, they think of themselves as younger as highlighted in Chapter 1.[14] It is also common for older people to dissociate themselves from others in their chronological age group by referring to their fellow ingroup members as "elderly," but not refer to themselves that way. For instance, one of the authors has a colleague who is nearing retirement. And at the start of the COVID-19 pandemic, the colleague expressed to age-peers some relief that the effects of the virus were rather mild for younger people, and that it was primarily older people who had to worry. The colleague soon realized that at 65+ years old, health organizations classify him as "older," making him a member of the vulnerable population for the virus. The disconnect between how we perceive and categorize others compared with how we feel within ourselves is an interesting and challenging process for people of *all* ages to manage psychologically and emotionally. The ability to negotiate one's membership in a particular age group – albeit psychologically – distinguishes age from other social identities with less permeable boundaries.

Salience of Age Identity

One's age identity can become *salient* in different situations. There are a plethora of ways in which age can be made salient, or imposed on us by others. These can include subjective physical experiences, such as feeling less nimble ("weak bones"), having less stamina, not being able to drink wine or beer to the same extent as one used to, or noting a drop in sexual aptitude. Age can also be made salient through changes in activities, like quitting a recreational sport (such as giving up hockey). Additionally, social experiences can make age salient, such as seeing peers' obituaries and attending their funerals (see Chapter 6), taking on new family roles (e.g., grandparent), or failing to recall people's names in conversation. That said, while these experiences can make age salient, we also caution that attributing certain events, like forgetting names, to age might be based on the well-known age stereotypes and expectancies we discussed in Chapter 2, rather than the reality of aging. Sometimes older adults can even self-stereotype by integrating commonly held stereotypes about old age into their self-concept.[15] As also discussed in Chapters 2 and 4, age salience, age stereotypes, and age excuses feed into and reinforce each other, creating a complex communicative package.

It is important to underscore that the effect of potential triggers of age salience varies considerably between people. What may make age salient for one person – for better or worse – might not operate for another person. Additionally, the same content can affect different people differently. For instance, watching reality shows on a television channel directed at young people may "age" one person yet make another feel younger. Researchers investigated this phenomenon with well over 500 people from three generations: students, their parents, and grandparents.[16] Participants were asked to write about what made them "feel their age," "feel younger," and "feel older" as well as how they felt about these incidents and feelings. Nearly 6000 triggers emerged, and the findings were indeed complex. Interestingly, although perhaps not surprisingly, the experience of "feeling older" was viewed negatively by the middle-aged and oldest samples, but more positively by the youngest sample. "Feeling my age" was distinct from "feeling younger or older" for the youngest group but was considered almost equivalent to "feeling older" for the middle-aged and oldest samples. "Feeling younger" was viewed less positively and reported less frequently by the youngest sample, almost certainly due in large part to the widespread social restrictions – which some in this sample regarded as agist – imposed upon them (e.g., age-based restrictions on purchasing and consuming alcohol). Across the samples, women attributed more positive feelings to "feeling younger," while men attributed more negativity to "feeling older." For the older males, this finding might be partially due to the loss of vitality and the void that many older professional men (who are often highly identified with their work) feel after retirement. The centrality of a work identity and its social meanings for many people should not be underestimated, as this has important implications for these people when work is taken away from them (even if it is by choice). In particular, it is possible that being removed from a regular work environment may reduce positively valenced interpersonal interactions with younger people that can trigger some people to "feel younger."

Age can also become salient when it arises in a conversation, explicitly or implicitly. In another study, researchers recorded older and younger women who were instructed to get acquainted with each other. In this study, younger volunteers prided themselves on having valued relationships with, and frequent occasions to talk to, older people. In this, one might expect that the researchers had the "crème de la crème" of age-sensitive individuals with these younger participants. Nonetheless, some of these younger women opened conversations with questions like: "Is your husband still alive?", "Do you feel lonely these days?", and "Do you get to sleep alright?" Such misconceived ways of starting a conversation can frame the entire dialogue to follow as being constrained by age-related (dis)abilities and experiences, especially when a younger person peppers the conversation with other age-themed remarks such as, "Gosh you manage to do that as well do you!"[17] This kind of discourse, in which age is overtly foregrounded, can put an older person on edge, lead them to feel "out of it" or force them to be defensive. It can also restrict topics of conversation to those involving age-related decrements. If these types of remarks were made by younger women who claimed to feel comfortable and uniquely experienced with older folks, one can only imagine what happens with younger people that typically avoid, or at best are uncertain about, conversing with older people.

An important point to keep in mind is that an older person can appear "old and dependent" in one conversation, yet "energetic, playful, and vibrant" in another. Often, the social context has a significant impact on the differences in one's age-related presentation across interactions and corresponding experiences for the older person. Thus, it is important not to rush to conclusions about people of different generations based on limited interactions, let alone one conversation.

Triggers of Age Identity

Indeed, many occasions and events can make older people "feel their age" or, put another way, many things that can make age become salient to them. The following are six specific situations that can trigger a person's age identity:[18]

- Talking to someone of a different age (or age group)
- Medical professionals using age as the cause of a condition
- Seeing obvious physical changes in others and/or oneself
- Others using honorifics, such as "sir," "señora," or "auntie"
- Being asked to provide age documentation
- Receiving agist birthday cards

As we discussed previously, age can be a potent factor affecting interaction when we meet someone for the first time and when we communicate with others. More generally, there is often a tendency to see intergenerational interactions in "intergroup" terms: that is, people tend to see the other person more as a member of an age category than as a unique individual.[19] As a result of this, when people meet someone of a different age, they often fail to see their individuality, and instead just see their age group. Furthermore, as discussed in Chapter 2, people can also take on the characteristics that they believe are typical of their own age group when they think of themselves in terms of their age.

The first trigger listed, "talking to someone of a different age," can quickly make one's age salient. It is worth noting that to younger people, what is considered an "elderly person" might come as a surprise for those who are middle-aged (see Chapter 1). Indeed, when asked for estimates of the amount of contact young people have with elderly people, including family members and chosen kin, they report that it is between 8 and 12% of their daily interactions.[20] As these numbers suggest, young people, and particularly those in the United States, generally have little contact with older people. When people from different age groups do interact, age often becomes very salient, probably for both parties.[21] In addition, older people typically refer to their age in intergenerational encounters, either explicitly in years or in more indirect ways, such as "I remember when …" This practice can make age differentials vivid, particularly since younger people typically do not voice their age in conversation.[22]

Albeit discussed in Chapter 2, all of this can build to a point at which someone may make blatant and direct agist statements. One of us recalls meeting a colleague after 20 years of not seeing each other and getting greeted with the exclamation, "Oh my god, you look … OLD!" This (now ex-)friend then had the audacity to repeat this sentiment a few more times with even more vocal feeling. Having recovered from this, the author then encountered an immigration officer at the airport who looked at his passport and said, "I see it's your birthday today!" which prompted a smile. Yet it was followed up by this officer declaring in a sing-song voice, "You're over the hill … you're over the hill." Another example of such interactions is the case of the elderly American school bus monitor, Karen Klein, who was repeatedly ridiculed to tears by teenagers on her bus.[23] The teenagers' parents, who subsequently saw a video of the event, were clearly shocked and had no ready explanations in TV interviews for their children's behavior (apart from their acknowledgment that their children needed counseling). Hopefully, such incidents of elder bullying and verbal intergenerational assault by teenagers are rare, but this event does serve as an illustration of the first trigger of age salience listed previously.

The second trigger occurs when physicians – and prior studies show that they do this all-too-often in medical diagnoses[24] – utter something of the ilk, "Well, this is what you can expect *at your age.*" One of us recalls the occasion when they went to the eye doctor about some acute short-sightedness, only to have the optician reply that this was not sudden at all but had been going on and progressively getting worse for years. The optician followed up by saying, "Yes, you're bang on target for your age!" It should be noted that both the first and second triggers involve talk and communication in ways that can lead to problematic outcomes.

Looking back on old photos, family videos, or returning for reunions (Trigger #3) can also make age salient, and that includes one's age and the age of others. Sometimes individuals might feel as though *others* are aging more quickly than themselves, but the accuracy of this perception does not negate the fact that the sands of time are falling for everyone. For a retirement party recently, the invitation to celebrate the event (presumably designed by colleagues) was accompanied by a photo of the retiree at the present time and what she looked like in her 20s. The difference was stunning. We can only conjecture about the effects that it had on the honoree at the time, as well as what effects it had on her peers in attendance who had retirement on the horizon. Indeed, even commonplace comments from those who have not seen a child for a while (e.g., "My how you've grown") can lead either the speaker, or others in the interaction, to consider how they must also have changed in the same span of time. Trigger #3 can then come about in a whole variety of ways, starting early in life. For example, one of our students wrote to us:

> Aging was just made present in my head. I was brushing my teeth, getting ready to go to bed, and there ... in the mirror, a white reflection ... a white hair. I'm only 22! Worrying about such things at this early age, surely cannot be that healthy, or be considered on a trajectory to "successful aging."

Being referred to as "ma'am," "señora," "sir," or other age- and gender-based honorifics for the first time (Trigger #4) can also make one's age salient, particularly when it comes unexpectedly early. Famous filmmaker Ava Duvernay took to Twitter to inform her followers to stop using the Black cultural honorific "Auntie" when referring to her.[25] While many Black Americans were taught to use this reference out of respect, Duvernay questioned, "Am I that old? I don't feel that old." How people respond to honorifics can be a communicative dilemma: What is the best way to react? On the one hand, responding with a quip such as, "Geesh, do I look *that old*?! Don't call me 'sir'" might not garner a desirable response, as the speaker might (verbally or mentally) retort, "I was only trying to be respectful." In a similar vein, an older person being referred to by a clerk as "young man" or "young woman" can be personally flattering to some, but cause indignation in others, even when the intent is positive. One woman we came across, personally, was the recipient of this type of remark, and responded in this fashion:

> Don't call me a young woman; it's not a compliment or courtesy, but rather a discourtesy. Being old is a hard-won achievement, not something to be brushed aside, treated as an infirmity or ugliness, or apologized for by a "young woman."

One can imagine that this might not have been a wake-up call for the person that said this but may have reinforced some of the negative age stereotypes discussed in Chapter 2, such as being grumpy, grouchy, or obstinate. In short, there is a delicate line to walk when interactively addressing this trigger; one may try to be part of the solution yet end up fueling the problem.

Trigger #5, age documentation, refers to occasions when people are asked to provide personal identification – a driver's license, passport, university ID, or the like – for some service, such as buying beer or wine, or to receive a discount. The experience of being asked for such documentation can make one's age salient, as age is the reason for the request. What is implied by the request often affects how people respond to it. For instance, receiving a senior discount from a hotel clerk at check-in without any prompting or request for the discount can be, for some, disheartening. Indeed, some older people adamantly refuse to take advantage of such movie, haircut, or "early bird" dinner discounts when they have the chance to avoid being viewed as "old." This would be consistent with what Kenny Rogers, the American singer, once remarked: "Growing older is not upsetting; being *perceived* as old is!"

The last trigger, receiving agist birthday cards, operates in at least two ways. First, simply being reminded of a birthday (by receiving a card, for example) can make one's age salient. Second, the content of birthday cards can make age salient in contentious ways. Many birthday cards are explicitly agist (see Chapter 5), and this is found in cards celebrating birthdays as young as one's 30th. In some cases, it can be challenging to go to a card store and find cards that are *not* agist in character.

Beyond birthday cards specifically, the celebration of birthdays more generally can also make age salient. As an example, a couple of us were told of a surprise birthday party for a friend where attendees had to wear black for what was referred to as "the wake" (as well as for a commemorative group photograph) to signify the "horror" of reaching 60 years of age. This was embraced as great fun and outlandish to those accepting the invitation. However, we caution that events like these can be distressing if this kind of behavior happens decade after decade, or even more often. Anecdotally speaking, the language we use to refer to age across the lifespan is also interesting: We move from, *"You're 4 and A HALF"* to *"GONNA be 16"* to *"You TURN 21"* to *"You ENTER your 30s"* to *"You're PUSHING 40"* to *"You REACH 50"* to *"You MAKE it to 60"* to *"You're ONLY 92."* This was a student of ours reporting on a birthday email she and colleagues had received:

> Subject line: **"Over the hill"**
>
> Please join me in helping poor Marisa today as she tries to navigate her way up and "over the hill." (It's a milestone birthday ☺)
>
> *Happy Birthday Marisa*
>
> The student reported that her sender sent it not only to the birthday girl who turned 40, but to the entire office and nationally to all branch managers within the company ... She told me she had nightmares last night about gray hair and wrinkles, and hearing aids, and ...

The effects here are obvious and, as ever, are not confined to the latter parts of the lifespan. The following are a set of birthday messages that an acquaintance of one of our friends received:

> *From Erin below:* Happy birthday, old man. Hope it's a great day.
> *Eric later:* You're joining the AARP [American Association for Retired People] now, right? Happy b-day. I hope somebody made you a cake this time.
> *Will's comment on Instagram:* Happy birthday, grand pappy.

The lucky recipient of these e-messages was but 25 years old, and the senders are just a few years younger!

In highlighting these issues related to birthdays, we do not intend to be killjoys. We are not advocating that readers avoid celebrating birthdays or stop conjuring enjoyment out of age. Indeed, many claim that it is healthy for a person to be able to (publicly) laugh about themselves and the groups with which they identify. Nonetheless, we do want readers (as well as birthday card manufacturers) to be aware of the potential effects of agist sentiments on receivers and senders. Such triggers might even put older adults at risk of confirming age-related stereotypes known as stereotype threat. Prior research shows that this threat, as well as stereotype embodiment and agism, can serve as barriers to active aging.[26] Indeed, there are various messages that can trigger one's age (and perhaps the negative stereotypes that they invoke), but how do they specifically affect older adults? The nature of communication during an interpersonal encounter can trigger perceptions of age (and even the differences in age between them and another person) and this can have marked effects on both the conversation and the well-being of those involved.

Outcomes of Age Salience

Turning to how age salience affects communication, we move now to a model by one of the authors and colleagues that has been used quite extensively in research on communication and aging.[27] The model aims to explain how age salience, as well as age stereotyping (discussed in Chapter 2), affect intergenerational encounters.[28] Presenting this model will also be a springboard for discussing the ingredients of such encounters more fully in Chapter 4. What can happen when older and younger people meet is schematized in Figure 3.1,[29] which depicts the "communicative predicament model of aging" (CPA). This model sheds light on the powerful role of language in people's aging processes, particularly with respect to older adults' psychological well-being.

As Figure 3.1 indicates, and as already discussed, when a younger person meets an older person – particularly if they are strangers – an "interpersonal" encounter can shift to being "intergroup" in nature.[30] In other words, people can shift to being more likely to see each other in terms of their social groups – older and younger – than as individual people. However, it does not have to be wrinkles, gray or balding hair, or styles of dress that trigger the salience of age; it could be any of the specific triggers that we discussed in the prior section. As another example of the varied ways that age salience can be triggered,

Age Identities 47

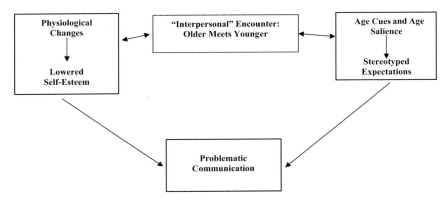

Figure 3.1 The Communicative Predicament Model of Aging[27]

we share the story of an acquaintance who took a bus tour around Britain. At one point, he noticed an "elderly road crossing sign" that is common on the sidewalks there. Seen literally thousands of times a day, it is likely that younger people rarely think about these signs in terms of their social implications – much like seats on the subway or city bus that are reserved "for the physically handicapped *and the elderly*." However, as you can see from the photograph of him, this sign (albeit tongue-in-cheek) likely made age salient for him.

48 *Age Identities*

In short, there is a rich array of ways in which social cues can make age salient, which, in turn, activate stereotyped expectations. If these cues prompt one of the four negative stereotype subtypes mentioned in Chapter 2 (i.e., "Severely Impaired," "Curmudgeon/Shrew," "Recluse," "Despondent"), then this will likely have repercussions for the kind of talk that follows. In particular, problematic communication can arise whereby younger people talk down to the level at which they feel older people are[31] – we discuss details of this in Chapter 4. When this kind of patronizing communication occurs, older people who have internalized negative expectations of age may "instantly age," taking on the characteristics of what they think a prototypical older person should sound like and say (see Chapter 4). As a consequence, communication opportunities are constrained, and neither party will be able to fulfill their potential for good communication.

As Figure 3.1 portrays, this can lead to a vicious cycle whereby the older person actually sustains the younger's view about the validity and reality of age stereotypes, making them more likely to play out the same scenario again when meeting another older person (see Chapter 2). All of this will, unfortunately, have a negative impact on older individuals, who might blame themselves for the lack of conversational flow and interest, and/or incline them to a lower sense of self-worth. The model also suggests that continual interactions routinized like this – together with environmental cues constantly bombarding older adults with agist images (see Chapter 5) – will likely accumulate and cause unfavorable somatic changes. These, in turn, might be transformed into immunological ones that can lower resistance to disease, inhibit recovery, and even accelerate physical demise. According to the model, health degeneration, negative self-perception, lower self-esteem, compromised relationships, mental instability, and lower levels of well-being are all possible negative, health-related outcomes that can ensue from these types of intergenerational encounters.[32]

It is important to note that these negative outcomes are particularly evident among older people from historically oppressed groups, such as those mentioned earlier in the chapter. Health disparities, as group-based differences in health outcomes have been termed, are common in the United States and are a result of systemic issues related to (for example) economic disadvantages, limited access to quality education and culturally sensitive healthcare, and racial discrimination.[33] These issues can make it difficult for older people from historically disenfranchised groups to recover from seemingly innocuous yet troubling intergenerational encounters.

Two criticisms of the CPA model have been that it only depicts what happens when people have negative stereotypes of older adults in interaction and that it does not give older adults agency to intervene and change the negative communicative cycle described in the model. The age stereotypes in interaction model[34] (ASIM) seeks to address these issues, outlining two possible ways in which communication with older adults can unfold. One route is similar to that depicted in the CPA. In the second route, positive stereotypes of older adults set the stage for "normal adult speech," which leads to positive outcomes. The ASIM also depicts the possibility of older adults' responses to the communication they experience changing the trajectory and nature of the conversation.

While the ASIM does highlight the potential for positive stereotypes of older adults to affect communication in positive ways, people's overall views of older adults and older adulthood tend to be negative, which suggests a problem for older adults from all backgrounds. According to SIT, people do not like having a negative social identity, as it disrupts having a positive sense of self, which can be emotionally distressing.[35] The negativity that can be associated with age salience for older people is a topic ripe for intervention. One possible avenue for intervention would be to address the triggers that make age salient. For instance, one might take steps to decrease or delay the onset of triggers associated with physical decline that can invoke "feeling" older. Instead of blaming age, one could consider other potential causes (e.g., reduced fitness) and turn to ways of compensating for these (e.g., joining a gym). Another possible intervention is to reduce the effectiveness of the triggers, though this might involve older adults doing some psychological work to reframe triggers so that they do not correspond to someone "feeling older." Lastly, people across US society can also change the stereotypes or widely held beliefs about age so that (old) age, when made salient, is not viewed so negatively. For instance, family members who are aware of the pernicious effects of age salience, stereotyping, and communication (see CPA model) can assist elders by reimagining their beliefs about old age; the media can follow suit and present less negative (and more positive) images of aging (see Chapter 5).

Negotiation and Management of Age Identity

We now consider how older adults might take up their agency to change how they manage their age identity. SIT suggests some constructive strategies through which people, such as older adults, can address negative feelings associated with their social identity by negotiating their membership in a low-status group.[36] The first, and often the one initially tried, is avoiding any intergroup (or in our case, intergenerational) social comparisons that can cause discomfort, and focusing energy instead on making judicious *intra*-generational comparisons in their favor. For example, rather than dwelling on how energetic, technologically advanced, and sexually active and attractive younger people are, older people could try and avoid contexts where these comparisons would be evident and, instead, make judgments about the relative superiority of themselves compared with other people their own age, such as neighbors, friends, or characters on TV. In this sense, one could focus on having better health, more possessions, and higher-achieving grandchildren than other older folk "on the block" (rather than comparing health, possessions, and achievements to the grandchildren themselves).

A second tactic is to try to change the age group they are associated with; in SIT, this strategy is called "social mobility." For instance, older people can make attempts at looking younger as a means of appearing as if they are part of a younger (and thus more favorably viewed) age group. This can be accomplished by dressing in youthful clothing, undergoing surgical procedures to remove physical signs of aging on different parts of the body, or using more (stereotypically) youthful rhetoric, such as slang or curse words. Recently, we have seen older adults take to social media platforms such as TikTok to participate in the latest dances alongside their children and grandchildren. Some even record themselves doing a solo performance, such as viral the dancer "Granny Coy Bundy," who has demonstrated an agility that is on par with members of Generation Z.[37] Such tactics can easily lead to unintended and undesirable outcomes; fortunately, Granny Coy Bundy has received nothing but praise and admiration.

A third way of coping with a negative age identity is by reframing the situation, a tactic SIT refers to as "social creativity." The idea here is that those who cannot engage in social mobility and/or cannot avoid intergenerational comparisons can accept, embrace, and promote a positive image of their age group by finding unique ways to emphasize the advantages of being older. For example, older people, individually or as couples, may verbalize their experience and time-honored wisdom, emphasize the luxury of having more leisure time to engage in different activities in retirement, or invest in (and perhaps flaunt) the aspects of their lives that they enjoy, such as spending time with family, theater, fine art, or expensive wines. The "Red Hatters" referred to in the previous chapter are an example of this way to address negative age identities, as this group promotes fun and vibrancy among women over the age of 50 years old. Gay men in midlife are another group that engages in social creativity; research has found that they do so by comparing their ingroup to their younger (outgroup) counterparts on dimensions like personality, life conditions, and communication skills to emphasize the relative benefits of aging and, consequently, engender an enhanced sense of self.[38]

Fourth, older people can try to change the way that others view their age group (as a whole), a tactic SIT calls "social competition." In short, this entails "taking on" the age groups that are causing them discontent and challenging those groups' perception and treatment of them. Here, older adults may advocate, sometimes with their increasing demographic edge and political muscle, for their age group's social rights and dignity, and fight to change or even reverse their group's position in society. According to SIT, older adults are likely to adopt this tactic when they come to believe there is some chance of changing their age cohort's status, and when they feel that their devalued situation is illegitimate and unfair, and not simply "normal," "understandable," or a rigid, biologically immutable fact.

In addition to these strategies that specifically address age as a social identity, older adults can also use other means to address the difficulties they may experience associated with their age identity. Practically speaking, older people can leverage emotional resources, such as (social) support and related coping skills, to manage their membership in a stigmatized age group. For instance, one study drew on five years of ethnographic data from elders living alone in New York City and concluded that gossiping with other older adults in local settings (i.e., eateries) constituted a social support network and buffered loneliness.[39] Meeting in the community to gossip (as opposed to attending formal organizations such as senior centers) is not conventionally considered a "resource" or "strategy" for positive experiences aging, but it can be vital for aging adults because it provides a means of being socially involved in, and connected to, their community. Older adults can find other ways to cultivate a large support network, which they can engage to cope with life issues or even seek instrumental or emotional support. Knowing that social isolation is a formidable issue for older adults, many have turned to online spaces (e.g., SeniorNet) to find a community. Research suggests that those who are active in such spaces experienced less life stress.[40]

On a more mundane, day-to-day level, older people can use their communication strategically to manage their elderly identity. For example, older people can disclose their chronological age during everyday conversations with others so that their behavior is contextualized according to their old age.[41] In doing so, older people can potentially deflect judgments that might lend others to see them as impaired, mentally declining, or dependent. This specific communication strategy takes two forms, one "accounting" and one "disjunctive." Elderly people can use an *accounting* tactic when they want to convey that the problems they are experiencing are products of their age and not a flaw of them as an individual person. For instance, if an older man has a hard time getting up from his chair, he might say: "Well don't just stand there, help me! I am old you know." This offers a different perspective on using age excuses, which we introduced in Chapter 2. In this scenario, the man is using this statement to deflect potential judgments or remarks that others could make for his taking too long to get out of the chair, which could serve a protective (and potentially positive) function. However, we caution that there is a fine line to tread here, as it is possible for age-based excuses like this to reinforce negative stereotypes of older people as incapacitated and communicatively problematic.

When older adults mention their age and use a *disjunctive* tactic, they emphasize that the activities or behaviors they engage in are *atypical* for normal people their age. Often, these activities involve physical rigor, such as rock climbing or running a marathon (see Chapter 5), but they can also include other types of behavior, such as staying up late or having a busy social calendar. For instance, a woman could say, "You may not believe it, but I just completed a marathon at the old age of 81." In this case, the person mentions their age in order to show others that they were able to complete the 26.2-mile event in spite of their age. This tactic can be a way of showing that they are "beating the odds," as their atypical behavior goes against long-held assumptions that elderly people have limited social, cognitive, and physical capabilities. While accounting generally maintains age identities, disjunctive tactics can *enhance* older people's age identities by highlighting positive deviations from the elderly stereotype.

Although these last two tactics do draw on (and, thus, potentially reinforce) disadvantages associated with older age, all the strategies outlined earlier can help older people protect their age identity during or after interactions with younger people. With that said, we wish to emphasize that one important feature of SIT is that relations between groups are dynamic. The theory assumes that if a privileged group's identity and vitality are being threatened by lower-status groups trying to "level the playing field," the privileged group will not necessarily lay idle and accept changes to their privileged status.[42] Thus, if and when older people do adopt more widespread socially competitive tactics, we can expect that younger age groups will be just as active – if not more so – in protecting their social advantages. Put another way, if SIT is on the mark, it behooves older people to anticipate that challenging the legitimacy of their group's lower status, and by extension threatening the higher status of other age groups, is unlikely to be passively accepted or ignored.

Concluding Thoughts

In this chapter, we have introduced the concept of age identity and discussed various triggers that make one's (older) age become salient. We turned to the CPA model to consider the consequences (e.g., personal, relational, and health-related) of age salience, particularly during intergenerational encounters. According to the model, age salience can activate stereotyped expectations that will correspond to problematic communication. Fortunately, older adults have quite a bit of agency and can enact various behavioral strategies to manage their older age identity so that it is a more positive experience.

This chapter has also highlighted the way older age is regarded during everyday interactions, particularly intergenerational encounters. In line with the CPA model, research has shown that there is a direct relationship between the extent to which older people feel like they are accommodated by younger generations and both of their self-reported life satisfaction and self-esteem. Put another way, being talked to in ways that undermine your individuality and competence can deplete a person's dignity and feelings of being at ease with the world around them. This can particularly be the case when it occurs regularly, across different contexts and with different people. To prevent such negative outcomes, we should look to the individuality of others, regardless of whether they are younger or older than us. This approach encourages people to move away from the pervasive stereotypes that can lead to negative, problematic interactions and to accommodate the unique, individual characteristics of those they are talking to. Doing so should promote much more healthy, satisfying, and effective communication between people, regardless of their age. We do, however, recognize that enacting such an approach may be easier said than done. In Chapter 4, we address the dynamics, challenges, and potential predicaments of intergenerational conversations.

Notes

1. Tajfel, H. (1981). *Human groups and social categories: Studies in social psychology*. Cambridge, UK: Cambridge University Press.
2. Tajfel, H., & Turner, J. C. (1986). The social identity theory of intergroup behavior. In S. Worchel & W. G. Austin (Eds.), *Psychology of intergroup relations* (2nd ed., pp. 7–24). Chicago, IL: Nelson-Hall.
3. Harwood, J., Giles, H., & Ryan, E. B. (1995). Aging, communication, and intergroup theory: Social identity and intergenerational communication. In J. Nussbaum & J. Coupland (Eds.), *Handbook of communication and aging research* (pp. 133–159). Hillsdale, NJ: Erlbaum; Williams, A., & Garrett, P. (2005). Intergroup perspectives on aging and intergenerational communication. In J. Harwood & H. Giles (Eds.), *Intergroup communication: Multiple perspectives* (pp. 93–116). New York, NY: Lang.
4. Cervone, C., Augoustinos, & Maass, A. (2021). The language of derogation and hate: Functions, consequences and reappropriation. *Journal of Language and Social Psychology*, *40*(1), 80–102. https://doi.org/10.1177/0261927X20967394
5. Crenshaw, K. (1990). Mapping the margins: Intersectionality, identity politics, and violence against women of color. *Stanford Law Review*, *43*(6), 1241–1299. https://doi.org/10.2307/1229039
6. For discussions of the matrix of domination, see Collins, P. H. (2002). *Black feminist thought: Knowledge, consciousness, and the politics of empowerment*. London, UK: Routledge.
7. For example, see: Adamsen, C., Schroeder, S., LeMire, S., & Carter, P. (2018). Education, income, and employment and prevalence of chronic disease among American Indian/Alaska Native elders. *Preventing Chronic Disease*, *15*(3). P. E37. Retrieved from: https://doi.org/10.5888/pcd15.170387; see also: Ferrer, I., Grenier, A., Brotman, S., & Koehn, S. (2017). Understanding the experiences of racialized older people through an intersectional life course perspective. *Journal of Aging Studies*, *41*(April), 10–17. https://doi.org/10.1016/j.jaging.2017.02.001
8. Hajek, C., & Giles, H. (2002). The old man out: An intergroup analysis of intergenerational communication among gay men. *Journal of Communication*, *52*(4), 698–714. https://doi.org/10.1111/j.1460-2466.2002.tb02569.x
9. Woody, I. (2014). Aging out: A qualitative exploration of ageism and heterosexism among aging African American lesbians and gay men. *Journal of Homosexuality*, *61*(1), 145–165. https://doi.org/10.1080/00918369.2013.835603
10. Seelman, K., Adams, M., & Poteat, T. (2017). Interventions for healthy aging among mature Black lesbians: Recommendations gathered through community-based research. *Journal of Women & Aging*, *29*(6), 530–542. https://doi.org/10.1080/08952841.2016.1256733
11. Witten, T. (2016). The intersectional challenges of aging and of being a gender non-conforming adult. *Generations*, *40*(2), 63–70. https://www.jstor.org/stable/10.2307/26556204
12. Giles, H., Coupland, N., Coupland, J., Williams, A., & Nussbaum, J. (1992). Intergenerational talk and communication with older people. *International Journal of Aging and Human Development*, *34*(4), 271–297. https://doi.org/10.2190/TCMU-0U65-XTEH-B950
13. For more information on age boundaries, see Giles, H., & Reid, S. (2005). Ageism across the lifespan: Towards a self-categorization model of aging. *Journal of Social Issues*, *61*(2), 389–404. https://doi.org/10.1111/j.1540-4560.2005.00412.x
14. For more information on subjective aging, see Diehl, M., Wahl, H., Brothers, A., & Miche, M. (2015). Subjective aging and awareness of aging: Toward a new understanding of the aging self. In M. Diehl & H. W. Wahl (Eds.), *Annual review of gerontology and geriatrics* (Vol. 35, pp. 1–28). New York, NY: Springer. https://doi.org/10.1891/0198-8794.35.1; see also: Stephan, Y., Sutin, A., & Terracciano, A. (2018). Determinants and implications of subjective age across adulthood and old age. In C. Ryff & R. F. Krueger (Eds.), *The Oxford handbook of integrative health science* (pp. 87–96). New York, NY: Oxford University Press.

15 For more information about self-stereotyping, see: Coupland, N., Coupland, J., & Giles, H. (1991). *Language, society and the elderly: Discourse, identity and aging.* Oxford, UK: Blackwell.
16 Giles, H., McIlrath, M., Mulac, A., & McCann, R. M. (2010). Expressing age salience: Three generations' reported events, frequencies, and valences. *International Journal of the Sociology of Language, 206*, 73–91. https://doi.org/10.1515/ijsl.2010.049
17 For more information, see Coupland, N., Coupland, J., & Giles, H. (1991). *Language, society and the elderly: Discourse, identity and aging.* Oxford, UK: Blackwell.
18 Giles, H., & Harwood, J. (1997). Managing intergroup communication: Lifespan issues and consequences. In S. Eliasson & E. Jahr (Eds.), *Language and its ecology: Essays in memory of Einar Haugen* (pp. 105–130). Berlin, Germany: Mouton de Gruyter.
19 Barker, V., Giles, H., & Harwood, J. (2004). Intra- and intergroup perspectives on intergenerational communication. In J. F. Nussbaum & J. Coupland (Eds.), *Handbook of communication and aging research* (2nd ed., pp. 139–165). Mahwah, NJ: Erlbaum.
20 These figures are a summary of results from surveys of students in Howie Giles undergraduate courses on communication and aging, conducted each term over many years of teaching.
21 Williams, A., & Giles, H. (1996). Intergenerational conversations: Young adults' retrospective accounts. *Human Communication Research, 23*(2), 220–250. https://doi.org/10.1111/j.1468-2958.1996.tb00393.x
22 Coupland, N., Coupland, J., & Giles, H. (1991), *Language, society and the elderly: Discourse, identity and aging.* Oxford, UK: Blackwell.
23 ABC News. (2012, June 21). Bus monitor, grandmother Karen Klein bullied by students: Caught on tape [video file]. Retrieved from: https://youtu.be/JuCNQFZ-H4E
24 Greene, M., Hoffman, S., Charon, R., & Adelman, R. (1987). Psychosocial concerns in the medical encounter: A comparison of the interactions of doctors with their old and young patients. *The Gerontologist, 27*(2) 164–168. https://doi.org/10.1093/geront/27.2.164
25 Denise, J. (2019, June 4). Is calling random women "auntie" ageist shade or a sign of respect? Either way, Ava DuVernay isn't here for it. *Madame Noire.* Retrieved from: https://madamenoire.com/1076098/is-calling-random-women-auntie-ageist-shade-or-a-sign-of-respect-either-way-ava-duvernay-isnt-here-for-it/
26 Lamont, R. A., Swift, H. J., & Abrams, D. (2015). A review and meta-analysis of age-based stereotype threat: Negative stereotypes, not facts, do the damage. *Psychology and Aging, 30*(1), 180–193. https://doi.org/10.1037/a0038586; Swift, H., Abrams, D., Lamont, R., & Drury, L. (2017). The risks of ageism model: How ageism and negative attitudes toward age can be a barrier to active aging. *Social Issues and Policy Review, 11*(1), 195–231. https://doi.org/10.1111/sipr.12031.
27 Ryan, E., Giles, H., Bartolucci, G., & Henwood, K. (1986). Psycholinguistic and social psychological components of communication by and with the elderly. *Language and Communication, 6*(1–2), 1–24. https://doi.org/10.1016/0271-5309(86)90002-9
28 Giles, H., & Gasiorek, J. (2011). Intergenerational communication practices. In K. W. Schaie & S. Willis (Eds.), *Handbook of the psychology of aging* (7th ed., pp. 231–245). New York, NY: Elsevier.
29 Ryan, E., Giles, H., Bartolucci, G., & Henwood, K. (1986). Psycholinguistic and social psychological components of communication by and with the elderly. *Language and Communication, 6*(1–2), 1–24. https://doi.org/10.1016/0271-5309(86)90002-9
30 Dragojevic, M., & Giles, H. (2014). Language and interpersonal communication: Their intergroup dynamics. In C. R. Berger (Ed.), *Handbook of interpersonal communication* (pp. 29–51). Berlin: De Gruyter Mouton.
31 Ryan, E. B., Hummert, M. L., & Boich, L. H. (1995). Communication predicaments of aging: Patronizing behavior toward older adults. *Journal of Language and Social Psychology, 14*(1–2), 144–166. https://doi.org/10.1177/0261927X95141008

32 Wurm, S., Diehl, M., Kornadt, A. E., Westerhof, G. J., & Wahl, H. W. (2017). How do views on aging affect health outcomes in adulthood and late life? Explanations for an established connection. *Developmental Review*, *46*, 27–43. https://doi.org/10.1016/j.dr.2017.08.002

33 Martinez, I., & Baron, A. (2020). Aging and health in the Latinx population in the USA: Changing demographics, social vulnerabilities, and the aim of quality of life. In I. Martinez & A. Baron (Eds.), *New and Emerging Issues in Latinx Health* (pp. 145–168). Cham, Switzerland: Springer; see also: Hoover, D., Pappadis, M., Housten, A., Krishnan, S., Weller, S., Giordano, S., Bevers, T., Goodwin, J., & Volk, R. (2018). Preferences for communicating about breast cancer screening among racially/ethnically diverse older women. *Health Communication*, *34*(7), 702–706. https://doi.org/10.1080/10410236.2018.1431026; Simons, R., Lei, M., Beach, S., Philibert, R., Cutrona, C., Gibbons, F., & Barr, A. (2016). Economic hardship and biological weathering: The epigenetics of aging in a U.S. sample of black women. *Social Science & Medicine*, *150*, 192–200. https://doi.org/10.1016/j.socscimed.2015.12.001

34 Hummert, M. L. (2019). Intergenerational communication. In J. Gasiorek, H. Pierson, J. F. NussBaum, & C. Gallois (Eds.), *Language, communication, and intergroup relations: A celebration of the scholarship of Howard Giles* (pp. 130–161). London, UK: Routledge; see also: Hummert, M. L., Garstka, T. A., Ryan, E. B., & Bonnesen, J. L. (2004). The role of age stereotypes in interpersonal communication. In J. F. Nussbaum & J. Coupland (Eds.), *Handbook of communication and aging research* (2nd ed., pp. 91–114). Mahwah, NJ: Lawrence Erlbaum.

35 Tajfel, H., & Turner, J. C. (1979). An integrative theory of intergroup conflict. In W. G. Austin & S. Worchel (Eds.), *The social psychology of intergroup relations* (pp. 33–47). Monterey, CA: Brooks Cole.

36 Tajfel, H., & Turner, J. (1986). The social identity theory of intergroup behavior. In S. Worchel & W. G. Austin (Eds.), *Psychology of intergroup relations* (pp. 7–24). Chicago, IL: Nelson-Hall.

37 Toglia, M. (2020, September 29). Meet the TikTok grandma who understands Gen Z better than you do. *Bustle*. Retrieved from: https://www.bustle.com/life/granny-coy-bundy-tiktok-fame-gen-z

38 Hajek, C. (2014). Gay men at midlife: A grounded theory of social identity management through linguistic labeling and intra-and intergenerational talk. *Journal of Language and Social Psychology*, *33*(6), 606–631. https://doi.org/10.1177/0261927X14545344

39 Torres, S. (2019). Aging alone, gossiping together: Older adults' talk as social glue. *The Journals of Gerontology: Series B*, *74*(8), 1474–1482. https://doi.org/10.1093/geronb/gby154

40 Wright, K. (2000). Computer-mediated social support, older adults, and coping. *Journal of Communication*, *50*(3), 100–118. https://doi.org/10.1111/j.1460-2466.2000.tb02855.x

41 Coupland, N., Coupland, J., & Giles, H. (1989). Telling age in later life: Identity and face implications, *Text*, *9*(2), 129–151. https://doi.org/10.1515/text.1.1989.9.2.129

42 Tajfel, H., & Turner, J. (1986). The social identity theory of intergroup behavior. In S. Worchel & W. G. Austin (Eds.), *Psychology of intergroup relations* (pp. 7–24). Chicago, IL: Nelson-Hall.

4 The Ingredients of Intergenerational Communication

For better or for worse – and as we will discuss, it may well be for worse – most Western societies are highly age-segregated. Both younger and older adults mainly spend time outside their homes with members of their own age groups. This typically begins when children enter formal schooling (where classes are divided by age) and continues into adulthood, where people's social and leisure activities often center around people of similar ages to themselves. A study conducted in Canada[1] shows these low rates of intergenerational contact for younger adults and older adults. On a seven-point scale (from 1 = "none" to 7 = "a great deal"), younger adults averaged a score of 3.4 on contact with older adults, compared with a score of 6.4 with their age peers. Similarly, older adults averaged a score of 3.7 for contact with younger adults, compared with a score of 5.5 with their age peers. Interestingly, middle-aged adults – who are sometimes referred to as the "sandwich generation" given their tendency to have to care for others who are both younger *and* older – do seem to have more balanced contact with these two age groups; they reported a score of 5.1 for contact with younger adults and a score of 4.9 for contact with older adults.

In addition to studying quantity of contact between members of different generations, we can also consider its *quality*. In other words, what is the nature and valence of contact between older and younger adults? Often, the picture is not a pretty one: studies have found that younger adults, in general, find conversations between themselves and older people to be quite dissatisfying and that they frequently put the blame on the shoulders of older adults. Even when requested to recall an encounter with an older person that was satisfying, they nonetheless rated it as closer to neutral than positive.[2]

In this chapter, we look at some of the characteristic ways in which younger people often speak to older people, and how older adults talk to younger adults. Before addressing these topics in greater detail, however, it is helpful to introduce two varieties of communication outlined in communication accommodation theory (CAT). This is a theory that explains and predicts how people adjust (or *accommodate*) their communication in different social contexts.[3] While these adjustments often improve the quality of interaction, sometimes they do not; communication that is adjusted in

DOI: 10.4324/9780429330681-4

ways that at least one party in an interaction finds problematic is termed *nonaccommodation*.[4]

One form of nonaccommodation the theory describes is *overaccommodation*. This is when someone adjusts their communication in ways that overshoot or exceed what their conversational partner considers to be appropriate or desirable. Talking to a foreigner, non-native speaker, person of color, or person who is physically challenged using a slow speech rate and simple language, despite the fact that they are capable of understanding complex ideas and participating in sophisticated conversation, is an example of overaccommodation. Often, although not exclusively, we see overaccommodation by younger adults when talking to older adults. In the context of intergenerational interaction, this kind of communication has been termed "elderspeak" or "patronizing talk" and can be experienced as demeaning and condescending.

The second kind of nonaccommodation relevant here, outlined in CAT, is *underaccommodation*. This occurs when someone adjusts their communication in ways that are insufficient or inadequate for their conversational partner's wants or needs. Often, although not exclusively, we see underaccommodation by older adults when talking to younger adults. Older adults' talking about their own illnesses and woes (sometimes termed "painful self-disclosure"[5]) – particularly when their conversational partner has not inquired about or expressed interests in these – is an example of underaccommodation. As this kind of communication often reflects a failure to adequately take their conversational partner's preferences or perspective into account, underaccommodation can be experienced as inconsiderate, egocentric, and/or unhelpful. This general tendency for younger people to overaccommodate older adults who, in turn, tend to underaccommodate them sets the stage for unsatisfying and potentially problematic intergenerational interactions.[6]

Patronizing Talk

Consider the following, a letter written to the US newspaper column, *Dear Dr. Joyce Brothers* (printed August 30, 2000). It is written by 82-year-old "Betty," who is happily living on her own. She seeks help for a matter that she claims is "rather petty": her sons talk down to her.

> Both my grown sons, now in their early 60s, speak to me as if I were one [of] my youngest great-grandchildren. They talk down to me as if I were both deaf and stupid. In my heart, I know they love me and want what is best for me, but in a way, this kind of treatment is humiliating and demeaning. I hate it most when they do it in front of my great-grandchildren, because I have established a nice, friendly relationship with them. They respect me, and I love and respect them. Any solutions to this difficulty of mine?

This is a classic example of what has been termed "elderspeak," or "patronizing talk" directed toward older people. We would argue that this is *not* a "petty" problem. Dr. Brothers acknowledges that this is not an uncommon issue, replying to Betty that, "People frequently treat the elderly in a condescending way without knowing they're doing it." As a solution, Dr. Brothers advises simply, "Talk to them [the sons]." This may seem reasonable, but, of course, the question remains: how, exactly? Shortly, we will discuss how a number of possible ways to respond to this kind of communication can turn out to be counter-productive or have other unintended negative effects.

This letter also highlights an important point about patronizing talk that we will discuss later: it is the implicit message *behind* this sort of talk – that the recipient is incompetent or "past it" – that is most troubling to those who are spoken to this way. In addition to being upset by her own experiences with patronizing talk (finding it "humiliating and demeaning"), Betty also recognizes that others, even those who are very young like her great-grandchildren, understand the implications of this sort of communication.

Research also demonstrates that patronizing talk toward older people is, unfortunately, quite common. It occurs most frequently in institutional settings like nursing homes, hospitals, or adult day cares,[7] but can also occur in community (i.e., non-institutional) settings. One of the first studies investigating this phenomenon, conducted in the early 1980s in a hospital, found that 30% of nurses used this kind of talk to older patients, irrespective of the older patients' actual capabilities. The author of the study called it "secondary baby talk."[8] In the decades since, there have been a host of studies conducted on patronizing talk. Before delving into what those studies have found, however, we think it is helpful to outline some of the classic verbal and nonverbal features of this kind of communication (see Table 4.1).[9]

This list of features in Table 4.1 is not exhaustive, and it is important to emphasize that no single feature listed there "defines" this sort of communication. Patronizing talk can include combinations and permutations of these verbal and nonverbal behaviors, as well as others not listed here.[10] Rather than specific behaviors, what defines communication as patronizing talk is the use of communication forms that are inappropriate for its

Table 4.1 Verbal and Nonverbal Features of Patronizing Talk Directed Toward Older Adults

Verbal	Nonverbal
• Over-inclusive "we" (rather than "me" or "you")	• Loud, slow speech
• Simple words, sentences, and topics	• Little eye contact
• Terms of endearment such as "sweetie," "dearie," "honey"	• Exaggerated smiles
• Exaggerated praise for minor accomplishments	• Excessive touching
	• Rolling eyes
	• Standing too close

recipients – and, in particular, inappropriate in a way that implicitly underestimates recipients' abilities or overestimates their deficits and dependencies. In short, patronizing talk is *overaccommodative* – it is adjusted in a way that overshoots or overcompensates for older adults' needs, based on their perceived capabilities.

In addition to the prototypical communication behaviors outlined previously, another common form of patronizing talk is "third-party talk." In third-party talk, virtually all of the conversation is directed at another person accompanying an older adult (the third party) rather than at the older adult. This often occurs when an older patient is accompanied by a family member to a medical appointment, and physician's questions – including those about the health status of the patient, who is present – are directed to the family member, rather than the older patient.[11] In scenarios involving third-party talk, it can seem as if the older person is somehow invisible or irrelevant (see Chapter 5); this kind of communication can also be seen to suggest that an older person cannot cope with questions about their own condition.

We do wish to emphasize that not all situations involving a third party, particularly in medical settings, are inherently problematic. Indeed, occasions do arise when an older person wants and appreciates a companion (often, a family member) to help or be an advocate for them. In these situations, a third party interacting with a physician or similar figure could be interpreted quite differently, as positive and supportive. However, many instances of third-party talk are not supportive in this way; rather, they are based on age stereotypic views of what older people are thought to be able to handle (see Chapter 2). As in our definition of patronizing talk, the key to distinguishing between (positive) third-party advocacy and (negative) third-party talk lies in the experience and interpretation of the older adult: Is this behavior something they consider appropriate and/or desirable? Or do they view it as an inappropriate overcompensation for deficits they do not actually have? If it is the former, then the communication is accommodative and unproblematic; if it is the latter, it is patronizing talk and is problematic.

Research suggests that patronizing talk is most likely to occur when an older person is not well groomed, looks old-fashioned, and is believed to fall into one of the four negative subtypes discussed in Chapter 2 (i.e., "Severely Impaired," "Despondent," "Recluse," or "Shrew/Curmudgeon"). This may be particularly the case when the patronizer has limited contact or experience with older people.[12] There is also work suggesting that older adults from racial groups that have been historically discriminated against are more likely to experience patronizing talk (e.g., in medical visits[13]) than their white counterparts. There is, however, considerably less research on these groups' experiences than there is on the experiences of white Americans. Previous research also indicates that using patronizing talk reflects poorly on speakers of it. For instance, one study showed that young people who used patronizing talk with older people were viewed unfavorably, even by other younger people. More specifically, such speakers were seen as less warm and more incompetent, less trustworthy, less supportive, more dominating, and more controlling.[14] As our story of Betty attests, older adults are likely to evaluate a patronizing speaker negatively; more often than not, older adults attribute this kind of talk to age stereotyping (which is typically viewed unfavorably).

Generally, and not surprisingly, older people have negative reactions to patronizing talk more generally,[15] as the letter from "Betty" exemplifies. They tend to resent it and be upset by it; in one study of older adults with dementia, being spoken to in a patronizing way was associated with older adults exhibiting behaviors like pulling away, crying, or threatening.[16] Being a recipient of patronizing talk has also been associated with physiological stress responses (i.e., activation of the HPA axis, as indicated by increases in salivary cortisol), and with diminished performance on cognitive tasks. Interestingly, older adults who had more positive attitudes toward aging and more positive intergenerational communication experiences had smaller changes in their performance on cognitive tasks, suggesting that positive experiences and attitudes related to age may buffer some of these negative effects.[17]

If asked directly, most people would readily acknowledge that communication perceived as condescending, demeaning, or patronizing is not a good thing. Most, we also suspect, would want to avoid communicating to people they love and care about in a way that is experienced as such. Given this, we are left asking: Why do (younger) people persist in communicating this way when they talk to older people?

In many cases – as Dr. Brothers notes in her response to Betty above – people do not necessarily know that their communicative choices are being perceived as inappropriate or problematic. Unfortunately, older people generally prefer to respond to patronizing talk by just "letting it go." While this kind of response avoids confrontation or uncomfortable interactions about the communication itself, it also implicitly affirms that this kind of communication is acceptable (because there is no indication to the contrary). In so doing, it also passively confirms the patronizer's agist views, and so encourages further use of patronizing talk. This kind of response also appears to extend to other domains; studies show that older people in the workplace also prefer not to be confrontational when conflicts arise.[18]

Studies have examined and compared various ways in which older people can respond to patronizing talk.[19] In addition to a passive response, one option is a so-called "assertive response" that overtly combats being the recipient of patronizing speech. For instance, an older adult might reply, "Don't talk to me as though I am a child!" This kind of response has advantages. It actively lets the patronizer know that their communication is not appropriate or appreciated, and research indicates that older people who respond like this are seen as more competent than those who are passive. However, it also has drawbacks: assertive responders are also seen as lower in warmth, which can translate to being seen as problematic or grouchy (thus reinforcing other negative stereotypes).[20] Evidence suggests that a less threatening way to address patronizing talk is to couch the retort in a humorous way. An example can be drawn from a study by Ellen Ryan and colleagues[21] in which an older lady, Mrs. Smith, is being patronized by a nursing assistant:

> NURSE: Did we forget again, sweetie? It's time for our crafts!
> MRS. SMITH: I think I'll pass today. I've made more crafts in my lifetime than an over-achieving Girl Guides group at Christmas!

A witty response brings out people's individuality, a trait we know to be so important in intergenerational encounters. In this way, a humorous response helps an older adult be seen as competent, but also *friendly*. While this kind of response does not necessarily provide an overt indication that patronizing talk is not appropriate, it actively challenges the stereotypes of incompetence and dependency that can motivate or underlie it. Humorous or witty responses can be difficult to enact "on the spot," but even anticipating these dynamics and having a ready-made set of options can help older people be ready to respond to patronizing talk in ways that prompt the patronizer to reconsider their communicative choices and condescending stance.

In addition to research studying the effects of different responses to patronizing talk by older adults, there have also been intervention studies with nurses' aides that have aimed to reduce the use of patronizing talk in institutional settings.[22] In such interventions, nurses' aides were first made aware of their use of patronizing talk with elder patients in their care and then given alternative ways of communicating in these interactions. For instance, rather than saying something like, "Good morning, *big guy*. Are we ready for *our* bath?", the nurses were encouraged to rephrase as, "Good morning, Mr. Jones. Are you ready for your bath?" The study showed that after this training, diminutives like "sweetie," and collectives such as "*We* need to get into *our* bath" became significantly less prevalent in the nurses' speech, and the length of their utterances became longer. Such adjustments were generally considered more respectful and less controlling, and it was evident that older residents were aware of this change in staff talk and, thereafter, became more effusive in their own talk. As the authors of this study put it, "Achieving optimal communication environments in NH [nursing homes] may contribute to higher levels of well-being for older adults and to increased satisfaction with NH life."[23] Unfortunately, a second study taking a similar approach found that, two months after the intervention, the positive effects had diminished.[24] This finding both highlights the degree to which this kind of talk can be entrenched, and suggests that such interventions may require periodic follow-up or reinforcement to be successful over time.

Although some studies (like the interventions just described) target particular features of people's speech, we want to emphasize that there are no types of verbal or nonverbal communication that are inherently patronizing and, therefore, inherently problematic. (This includes the list of verbal and nonverbal features we provide as examples of patronizing talk in Table 4.1.) "Patronizing talk" is a label people give to talk that they find to be condescending, and what merits this label is a subjective assessment. In theorizing about patronizing talk, some scholars have argued that it can be thought of as having two motivational dimensions to it: *caring* and *control*. In different circumstances, speakers may have different combinations of these motives (e.g., high caring and low control, or low caring and high control).[25] While studies have not, to our knowledge, explored the extent to which older recipients consciously interpret patronizing talk in these terms, there is evidence that subjective interpretations of the same or similar communication can differ considerably. In particular, those who are frail and dependent can interpret what others might label "patronizing talk" as caring, empathic, and helpful.[26]

Older People Can Be Patronizing Too

Following a discussion of how younger adults can patronize older adults, one of our students said to one of us, "You know *we* get patronized too, don't you? You might give some attention to this!" This student's comment was duly followed up with a research study on patronizing talk from older adults to younger adults.[27] The study found that young adults reported that they felt patronized quite frequently by older people and that this really bothered them. Three categories of this type of talk were identified: *non-listening, youth disapproving,* and *overprotective* talk. Table 4.2 presents examples of each form of old-to-young patronizing talk that emerged from the study.

A hierarchy also emerged for the forms of patronizing talk in combination with non-patronizing talk (see Figure 4.1). *Non-patronizing* was evaluated as least inappropriate and impolite, followed by *overprotective*, which was evaluated as less inappropriate than *non-listening*, which was evaluated as less inappropriate than *youth disapproving*.

However, when it came to negative emotions, such as feeling frustrated, helpless, angry, and resentful, *non-listening* caused the most aggravation. Other research has shown that criticism (which may be interpreted as patronizing) can also be a source of problematic intergenerational communication. In one study, researchers found that over half of the conflicts young people felt they had with older adults were caused by hurtful "older-to-young criticisms" being directed at them.[28]

Table 4.2 Forms and Examples of Older-to-Younger Adult Patronizing Talk

Non-listening	Youth Disapproving	Overprotective
• "Older people never listen to your opinion" • "The elderly don't listen to what you have to say"	• "Young people have it easy these days!" • "You're just beer-drinking dopeheads that don't know any better!"	• "I'm more experienced, trust me!" • "When you get older you'll see this was for the best!"

Least Inappropriate	←──────────→		Most Inappropriate
Non-Patronizing	Overprotective	Non-Listening	Youth Disapproving
		(most aggravating)	

Figure 4.1 Perceived Appropriateness of Forms of Older-to-Younger Adult Patronizing Talk

Reflecting on these findings, we offer a note of caution for older readers when they talk to members of younger generations. Non-listening, disapproving statements about youth, and criticism are all forms of communication that implicitly suggest that older adults "know better" than their younger counterparts (notably, some of the same sentiment that can underlie patronizing talk directed toward older adults). While older people may feel that they have been through the younger years themselves and thus that they "know better" than their less experienced conversational partners, in actual fact, they may *not* have had comparable experiences to those of the younger adults they are speaking with. Cultures can evolve quickly, and the last several decades have seen remarkable changes in the ubiquity of digital technology, social media, and its role in people's social interactions, in particular. Thus, young adults today may well be experiencing very different social demands than previous generations. We suggest that a little more listening and open-mindedness on the part of older adults might be warranted, and could be beneficial for all involved.

In short, while a lot of research has focused on the consequences of younger people overaccommodating (i.e., patronizing) older people, overaccommodation can be a two-way street. If we wish to improve the quality of intergenerational communication as well as the life satisfaction of older (and younger) people, *both* age groups likely need to make an effort to accommodate each other.

Painful Self-Disclosures

We turn now to another form of older-to-younger communication that has been the object of attention in research: *painful self-disclosures*.[29] Research on this topic began in a study conducted in the 1980s that invited older and younger women to get acquainted with each other, as well as with women of their own ages.[30] In these intergenerational interactions, there was a high prevalence of what the authors called "painful self-disclosures": highly personal disclosures on topics such as ill health, ongoing medical problems, hospital stays and operations, sensory decrements, accidents, bereavement, immobility, disengagement, and loneliness.

The "painful" nature of these disclosures refers to their subject matter. Older adults in the study were not necessarily experiencing pain at the time of recounting these incidents, but the experiences discussed had been stressful and difficult for them at some point in the (recent) past. The study's authors found that these painful disclosures were peppered throughout the conversation, and on average accounted for about one-sixth (16%) of the conversational content. Moreover, most of these stories were initiated by the older person completely out of the blue, although sometimes they followed self-disclosures of an older adult's age. These disclosures typically involved a lot of detail, sometimes connecting multiple difficult or painful events. As an illustration, one elderly lady, after having talked about how she arrived at the research study session, said following a five-second silence, "I've got two false hips so I get tired walking on transplants." Without warning, such a painful self-disclosure can feel like a "communicative grenade" to a younger listener.

A letter that one of our graduate students shared – which we have edited for its essence – from his grandfather one Christmas offers another illustration of the phenomenon. Imagine the top border of this letter full of colorful red and green holly bushes, together with the cheerful heading, "Merry Xmas!"

> I missed the joys of celebrating Christmas last year. When I was rushed to the hospital on Oct. 20, 1990 with my 3rd heart attack that year. I certainly did not realize that I was never destined to return to my home on South Ames Way. During a lengthy hospital stay I had my 4th heart attack ... There it was touch and go ... I finally did improve, although it left me scarred a bit – require continual oxygen, loss of 35lbs, weakness and shortness of breath. [...]
>
> When my 100 days of Medicare benefits ran out, they moved me to a private wing which cost me $3500 per month [...]
>
> I enjoyed reading your Christmas cards belatedly, and wish only the best for you and yours this holiday season!

Our student found this letter distressing, could not understand how it could be written, and did not know how to answer it.

Like our student, people often are perplexed about how to respond to painful self-disclosures in conversation. Certainly, there is a dilemma here for the recipient. Does the recipient ask for more details and risk having to then listen to them? Or should they abruptly change the topic, thereby discouraging any further elaborations but also risk coming across as impolite or uncaring? Broadly, these types of responses can be considered *prosocial engagement* and *active disengagement*, respectively. Many people choose a third option, *passive disengagement*, in which they allow the disclosure to continue (without overt encouragement) while they mutter empty conversational fillers such as "oh dear," "hmm," or "ah." Research examining how and when younger people use these different types of responses has found that a number of contextual factors – including the relational situation in which the disclosure occurred, individuals' general tendency to express empathy, the conversational climate in individuals' family, and individuals' emotional reaction to the disclosure – all contributed to determining what type of response they ultimately chose.[31]

Why Painfully Self-Disclose?

When asked why someone would painfully self-disclose, younger people seem to feel that it is because the older person is "losing it." Relatedly, they construe such painful self-disclosers as falling into the negative subtypes of "Shrew/ Curmudgeon" or "Despondent."[32] It is possible that, for younger people, this kind of communication seems quite strange indeed, because the older person breaks three common conventions in younger people's conversational practices: (1) do not disclose immediately; (2) do not disclose negatively; and (3) do not disclose excessively.[33]

There are, however, other reasons for the emergence of painful self-disclosures. First, such a disclosure can be offered because a speaker is seeking sympathy. In other cases, the speaker is saying something that they feel is "newsworthy." If these painful experiences have been the primary events of note in their life recently, they may feel they are notable and important. People of all ages typically share recent events and experiences when they talk with others; in some cases, the content of a painful self-disclosure may be the primary "news" that an older person has to share. Another potential reason is that the intergenerational situation makes age salient (as we discussed in Chapter 3), and as a result, the older adult self-stereotypes as being "old" (see Chapter 2). Given that painful self-disclosures are a behavior associated with being "old" in popular culture, an older adult may enact this behavior as a result of an age-based self-categorization. (We note that this can occur either consciously or unconsciously). In short, for any one (or all) of these reasons, painful self-disclosures may be explicable and rational behavior in a conversation and have nothing to do with mental decline.

In one study exploring this phenomenon, researchers interviewed participants after interactions in which they had made excessive and/or painful self-disclosures in intergenerational interactions. One woman, when asked why she had talked so much, responded that she knew that her younger partner might be a little uncomfortable talking about her own life activities to an older woman who might have a much more closeted life. So as not to put the younger person into this awkward situation, the older woman alleged she talked about her life at some length, some of which was (inevitably) painful.[34] Whether this was a clever and imaginative account constructed after the fact or truly her conscious motive in the moment, we shall never know. However, it does suggest that what some people view as a sign of mental decline and/

or social insensitivity could in fact be the result of an older adult being socially sensitive.

Indeed, older adults likely know that these types of disclosures are associated with perceptions of cognitive decline. As an illustration of this, we include the following transcript – where A is the older person and B the younger person.[35]

> A: You wouldn't believe it – I'm eighty-seven
> B: Wh – eighty-seven, good heavens, you don't look eighty-seven
> A: (gasps and laughs) Well not up *here* (holds hand up to face)
> B: (laughs) I hope I look like you when I'm eighty-seven
> A: Not up here, I'm not (holding hand up against face)
> But it's this (lays hand on leg) Thrombosis!
> B: So how did you get here today?

In one of the authors' courses on communication and aging, this transcript would be read as an illustration of a painful self-disclosure of "thrombosis," and highlight B's abrupt topic shift as a response. Students would be invited to reread the transcript and were asked if anything else occurred to them about the interaction, or about the nature of the older women's disclosures and actions. Across 20 years – in class and among older community audiences – no one recognized that the older woman's references to "up here" were references to her *mind*. That is, she was trying to emphasize to her younger partner that, genuine physical challenges aside, she has a healthy *mind*. One possible interpretation of this interaction is that the older woman is trying to emphasize her mental acuity, even as she offers a type of disclosure that younger people associate with cognitive decline. Sadly, B's reaction indicates that this intended message fell on fallow ground. Interactions like this one highlight both the challenging nature of painful self-disclosures in interaction, as well as the difficulty overcoming (entrenched) age-related stereotypes in intergenerational conversations.

While painful self-disclosures by older adults often occur in intergenerational encounters, they can also happen when older people talk to their age peers. It is also worth noting that although such disclosures as stereotypically associated with older adults, young people can and do painfully self-disclose as well, although they generally do not do so to the same extent as older people. Like older adults, younger people can be motivated by a desire for sympathy, or the intention to share "newsworthy" events in their lives (which happen to be painful in nature). In these ways, younger and older adults are likely more similar than different.

Intergenerational Similarities and Differences

When examining intergenerational interactions (and the topic of aging more generally), it is tempting to focus on differences or contrasts between age groups. However, it is important to remember that most younger adults will eventually become older adults and that many experiences are shared across the lifespan.[36] For instance, although reminiscing is stereotypically thought of as something older people do, in fact, people of *all ages* reminisce. When young adult friends who have not seen each other for a while get together, they often (if not inevitably) talk about their shared past together. People of all ages experience common lived experiences and past fates to good effect. However, these similarities across age groups are not always well-recognized, particularly by younger people. For instance, in one study, young adults were asked to evaluate "typical" older adults and then to evaluate their future selves – that is, how they anticipated they would be when they were older. They imagined their future selves to be significantly different from "typical" older people.[37]

In this chapter, we have seen that both younger and older adults can over-accommodate and underaccommodate each other. Younger people all too often overaccommodate older people, drawing on stereotypes of cognitive and physical decline. However, older adults can also overaccommodate (i.e., patronize) younger people, drawing on stereotypes of inexperience and irresponsibility, giving back as good as they receive. We have also seen that older people underaccommodate younger adults in unhelpful ways, such as painful self-disclosures (which underaccommodate young adults' conversational preferences, in terms of topic). However, younger people can, on occasion, be underaccommodative too.

A final form of younger-to-older underaccommodation we have not yet covered is *deflecting*. Deflecting occurs when something an older person says, such as an expressed emotion, is not legitimized by a younger person. This is well-exemplified in a study in a residential home for older dependent inmates. In one scenario recorded, nurses are bathing an older woman who clearly did not like this activity. The nurses continued saying things like, "isn't that nice?", "that's beautiful!", "there, isn't that nice?", despite the older woman repeatedly groaning and answering "no!" after each such rendition.[38] In another study, one young adult admits that he had been underaccommodating in this way when recounting this conversation with an older person:[39]

> Most of the time, I wouldn't really hear what he said. To me, talking with this kind of older adult did not mean much to me ... I felt like I did not listen to them with my heart. I forgot what this conversation was about right after we finished it. I did not reflect on it or think about it ... instead of trying to find things to talk with him.

Thus, both older and younger adults can over- and underaccommodate each other, though the prototypical forms that these take differs between the two groups.

As a final point of similarity between age groups across the lifespan, we wish to highlight the issue of *listening*. Much time is spent studying and teaching people about talking or speaking effectively. Comparatively less time is spent studying and teaching people effective listening (a point we will revisit when we examine communication about death and dying in Chapter 6). On a number of occasions in the present chapter, we have seen how both parties in the intergenerational enterprise do not listen, and instead rely on their stereotypes of other age groups to guide interaction. Listening is, of course, as much a part of communication as speaking. Reflecting on this, and the lack of listening that often characterizes intergenerational encounters, we can gain some insight into why intergenerational communication can be problematic, and why people might do what they can to avoid it.

Concluding Thoughts

In this chapter, we have explored the range of potential issues that can emerge in intergenerational communication, with particular emphasis on patronizing talk and painful self-disclosures as prominent forms that problematic communication takes. It has been argued that the communicative "gap" between generations is located at the intersection of younger and older people both overaccommodating and underaccommodating each other.[40] In light of this, and the negative outcomes associated with problematic communication, we propose that both groups could learn to be more communicatively respectful and open-minded, and to orient more toward listening and less toward control. While members of both generations stand to benefit from a more positive communicative climate, this may be especially important for younger adults. For younger people, ways of communicating with older adults that are driven by negative stereotypes, such as patronizing talk, provide unfortunate building blocks for their own futures, as they reinforce negative expectations about aging.

Given these concerns, and the role of age stereotypes in problematic interactions, improving age stereotypes may be one means to improve the quality of intergenerational communication. However, and perhaps ironically, one of the most well-established ways to reduce prejudice and improve attitudes and stereotypes about groups is positively valenced *contact*,[41] or interaction, between those groups. Recent research suggests that one possible avenue for doing so could be *imagined* (positive) intergenerational conversations.[42] Imagined conversations may offer a way to have "conversations" – which may be positive and productive for the relationship between groups – in ways that are less anxiety-provoking than traditional face-to-face encounters would be.[43] We see encouraging potential in such proposed interventions and think this is an important area for future work. With that said, even better than working to change entrenched negative stereotypes might be to establish more positive ideas about old age in the first place. In Chapter 5, we will turn to examining one of the major sources of people's age stereotypes: mass media.

Notes

1. Giles, H., Ryan, E. B., & Anas, A. P. (2008). Perceptions of intergenerational communication by young, middle-aged, and older Canadians. *Canadian Journal of Behavioural Science / Revue canadienne des sciences du comportement, 40*(1), 21–30. https://doi.org/10.1037/0008-400x.40.1.21 (p. 24).
2. Giles, H., & Williams, A. (1994). Patronizing the young: Forms and evaluations. *The International Journal of Aging and Human Development, 39*(1), 33–53. https://doi.org/10.2190%2F0LUC-NWMA-K5LX-NUVW; Williams, A., & Giles, H. (1996). Intergenerational conversations: Young adults' retrospective accounts. *Human Communication Research, 23*(2), 220–250. https://doi.org/10.1111/j.1468-2958.1996.tb00393.x
3. Giles, H. (2016). *Communication accommodation theory: Negotiating personal and social identities across contexts*. Cambridge, UK: Cambridge University Press. https://doi.org/10.1017/CBO9781316226537
4. Gasiorek, J. (2016). The "dark side" of CAT: Nonaccommodation. In H. Giles (Ed.), *Communication accommodation theory: Negotiating personal and social identities across contexts* (pp. 85–104). Cambridge, UK: Cambridge University Press. https://doi.org/10.1017/CBO9781316226537.005
5. Coupland, N., Coupland, J., Giles, H., Henwood, K., & Wiemann, J. M. (1988). Elderly self-disclosure: Interactional and intergroup issues. *Language & Communication, 8*(2), 109–133. https://doi.org/10.1016/0271-5309(88)90010-9
6. Giles, H., & Gasiorek, J. (2011). Intergenerational communication practices. In K.W. Schaie & S. Willis (Eds.), *Handbook of the psychology of aging* (7th ed., pp. 233–247). New York, NY: Elsevier. https://doi.org/10.1016/B978-0-12-380882-0.00015-2; Gasiorek, J. (2016). The "dark side" of CAT: Nonaccommodation. In H. Giles (Ed.), *Communication accommodation theory: Negotiating personal and social identities across contexts* (pp. 85–104). Cambridge, UK: Cambridge University Press. https://doi.org/10.1017/CBO9781316226537.005
7. Salari, S. (2006). Infantilization as elder mistreatment: Evidence from five adult day centers. *Journal of Elder Abuse and Neglect, 17*(4), 53–91. https://doi.org/10.1300/J084v17n04_04
8. Caporael, L. R. (1981). The paralanguage of caregiving: Baby talk to the institutionalized aged. *Journal of Personality and Social Psychology, 40*(5), 876–884. https://doi.org/10.1037/0022-3514.40.5.876
9. Ryan, E. B., Hummert, M. L., & Boich, L. H. (1995). Communication predicaments of aging: Patronizing behavior toward older adults. *Journal of Language and Social Psychology, 14*(1–2), 144–166. https://doi.org/10.1177%2F0261927X95141008
10. For a more complete list, see: Ryan, E. B., Hummert, M. L., & Boich, L. H. (1995). Communication predicaments of aging: Patronizing behavior toward older adults. *Journal of Language and Social Psychology, 14*(1–2), 144–166. https://doi.org/10.1177%2F0261927X95141008
11. Giles, H., & Gasiorek, J. (2011). Intergenerational communication practices. In K. W. Schaie & S. Willis (Eds.), *Handbook of the psychology of aging* (7th ed., pp. 233–247). New York, NY: Elsevier. https://doi.org/10.1016/B978-0-12-380882-0.00015-2
12. Hummert, M. L. (1994). Stereotypes of the elderly and patronizing speech style. In M. L. Hummert, J. M. Wiemann, & J. F. Nussbaum (Eds.), *Interpersonal communication in older adulthood: Interdisciplinary theory and research* (pp. 162–185). Newbury Park, CA: Sage.
13. Rhee, T. G., Marottoli, R. A., Van Ness, P. H., & Levy, B. R. (2019). Impact of perceived racism on healthcare access among older minority adults. *American Journal of Preventive Medicine, 56*(4), 580–585. https://doi.org/10.1016/j.amepre.2018.10.010
14. Giles, H., Fox, S. & Smith, E. (1993). Patronizing the elderly: Intergenerational evaluations. *Research on Language and Social Interaction, 26*(2), 129–149. https://doi.org/10.1207/s15327973rlsi2602_1
15. Ryan, E. B., Meredith, S. D., & Shantz, G. D. (1994). Evaluative perceptions of patronizing speech addressed to institutionalized elders in contrasting conversational contexts. *Canadian Journal of Aging, 13*(2), 216–248. https://doi.org/10.1017/S0714980800006048

16 Cunningham, J., & Williams, K. N. (2007). A case study of resistiveness to care and elderspeak. *Research and Theory for Nursing Practice, 21*(1), 45–56. https://doi.org/10.1891/rtnpij-v21i1a006

17 Hehman, J. A., & Bugental, D. B. (2015). Responses to patronizing communication and factors that attenuate those responses. *Psychology and Aging, 30*(3), 552–560. https://doi.org/10.1037/pag0000041

18 Davis, M. H., Kraus, L. A., & Capobianco, S. (2009). Age differences in responses to conflict in the workplace. *International Journal of Aging and Human Development, 68*(4), 339–355. https://doi.org/10.2190%2FAG.68.4.d

19 Harwood, J., & Giles, H. (1996). Reactions to older people being patronized: The roles of response strategies and attributed thoughts. *Journal of Language and Social Psychology, 15*(4), 395–422. https://doi.org/10.1177%2F0261927X960154001

20 Harwood, J., & Giles, H. (1996). Reactions to older people being patronized: The roles of response strategies and attributed thoughts. *Journal of Language and Social Psychology, 15*(4), 395–421. https://doi.org/10.1177%2F0261927X960154001

21 Ryan, E. B., Kennaley, D. E., Pratt, M. W., & Shumovich, M. A. (2000). Evaluations by staff, residents, and community seniors of patronizing speech in the nursing home: Impact of passive, assertive, or humorous responses. *Psychology and Aging, 15*(2), 272–285. https://doi.org/10.1037/0882-7974.15.2.272

22 Williams, K. N., Kemper, S., & Hummert, M. L. (2003). Improving nursing home communication: An intervention to reduce elderspeak. *The Gerontologist, 43*(2), 242–247. https://doi.org/10.1093/geront/43.2.242; Williams, K. N. (2006). Improving outcomes of nursing home interactions. *Research in Nursing and Health, 29*, 121–133. https://doi.org/10.1002/nur.20117

23 Williams, K. N., Kemper, S., & Hummert, M. L. (2003). Improving nursing home communication: An intervention to reduce elderspeak. *The Gerontologist, 43*(2), 242–247. https://doi.org/10.1093/geront/43.2.242; quote at the end of the paragraph from p. 247.

24 Williams, K. N. (2006). Improving outcomes of nursing home interactions. *Research in Nursing and Health, 29*, 121–133. https://doi.org/10.1002/nur.20117

25 Hummert, M. L., & Ryan, E. B. (1996). Toward understanding variations in patronizing talk addressed to older adults: Psycholinguistic features of care and control. *International Journal of Psycholinguistics, 12*(2), 149–169.

26 Ryan, E. B., & Cole, R. (1990). Evaluative perceptions of interpersonal communication with elders. In H. Giles, N. Coupland, & J. Coupland (Eds.), *Communication, health, and the elderly* (pp. 172–190). New York, NY: St. Martin's.

27 Giles, H., & Williams, A. (1994). Patronizing the young: Forms and evaluations. *International Journal of Aging and Human Development, 39*(1), 33–53. https://doi.org/10.2190%2F0LUC-NWMA-K5LX-NUVW

28 Zhang, Y. B., & Lin, M-C. (2009). Conflict initiating factors in intergenerational relationships. *Journal of Language and Social Psychology, 28*(4), 343–363. https://doi.org/10.1177%2F0261927X09341836

29 Barker, V. (2007). Young adults' reactions to grandparent painful self-disclosure: The influence of grandparent sex and overall motivations for communication. *International Journal of Aging and Human Development, 64*(3), 195–215. https://doi.org/10.2190%2FKTNU-0373-20W7-4781

30 Coupland, N., Coupland, J., Giles, H., Henwood, K., & Wiemann, J. (1988). Elderly self-disclosure: Interactional and intergroup issues. *Language and Communication, 8*(2), 109–133. https://doi.org/10.1016/0271-5309(88)90010-9; see also: Coupland, N., Coupland, J., & Giles, H. (1991). *Language, society and the elderly: Discourse, identity and aging.* Oxford, UK: Blackwell.

31 Fowler, C., & Soliz, J. (2013). Communicative responses to the painful self-disclosures of familial and non-familial older adults. *International Journal of Aging and Human Development, 77*(3), 163–188. https://doi.org/10.2190%2FAG.77.3.a

32 Bonnesen, J. L., & Hummert, M. L. (2002). Painful self-disclosures of older adults in relations to aging stereotypes and perceived motivations. *Journal of Language and Social Psychology, 21*(3), 275–301. https://doi.org/10.1177%2F0261927X02021003004

33 Berger, C. R., & Bradac, J. J. (1982). *Language and social knowledge: Uncertainty in interpersonal relations.* London, UK: Arnold.

34 Coupland, N., Coupland, J., & Giles, H. (1991). *Language, society and the elderly: Discourse, identity and aging.* Oxford, UK: Blackwell.

35 Coupland, N., Coupland, J., & Giles, H. (1991). *Language, society and the elderly: Discourse, identity and aging.* Oxford, UK: Blackwell.

36 Nussbaum, J. F. (Ed.). (2014). *The handbook of lifespan communication.* New York, NY: Peter Lang.

37 Giles, H., Fortman, J., Honeycutt, J., & Ota, H. (2003). Future selves and others: A lifespan and cross-cultural perspective. *Communication Reports, 16*(1), 1–22. https://doi.org/10.1080/08934210309384486

38 Grainger, K., Atkinson, K., & Coupland, N. (1990). Responding to the elderly: Troubles-talk in the caring context. In H. Giles, N. Coupland, & J. M. Wiemann (Eds.), *Communication health and the elderly* (pp. 192–212). Manchester, UK: Manchester University Press.

39 Zhang, Y. B., & Lin, M.-C. (2009). Conflict initiating factors in intergenerational relationships. *Journal of Language and Social Psychology, 28*(4), 343–363. https://doi.org/10.1177%2F0261927X09341836

40 Giles, H., & Gasiorek, J. (2011). Intergenerational communication practices. In K. W. Schaie & S. Willis (Eds.), *Handbook of the psychology of aging* (7th ed., pp. 233–247). New York, NY: Elsevier. https://doi.org/10.1016/B978-0-12-380882-0.00015-2

41 Pettigrew, T. F., & Tropp, L. R. (2006). A meta-analytic test of intergroup contact theory. *Journal of Personality and Social Psychology, 90*(5), 751–783. https://doi.org/10.1037/0022-3514.90.5.751; Pettigrew, T. F., & Tropp, L. R. (2008). How does intergroup contact reduce prejudice? Meta-analytic tests of three mediators. *European Journal of Social Psychology, 38*(6), 922–934. https://doi.org/10.1002/ejsp.504; Kranz, D., Thomas, N. M., & Hofer, J. (2021). Changes in age stereotypes in adolescent and older participants of an intergenerational encounter program. *Frontiers in Psychology, 12*, Article 1327. https://doi.org/10.3389/fpsyg.2021.658797

42 Chen, C. Y., Joyce, N., Harwood, J., & Xiang, J. (2017). Stereotype reduction through humor and accommodation during imagined communication with older adults. *Communication Monographs, 84*(1), 94–109. https://doi.org/10.1080/03637751.2016.1149737

43 Harwood, J. (2010). The contact space: A novel framework for intergroup contact research. *Journal of Language and Social Psychology, 29*(2), 147–177. https://doi.org/10.1177%2F0261927X09359520

5 The Media, Agism, and Anti-Aging

The media is a lucrative industry, making billions of dollars each year.[1] Media images have received a lot of attention from researchers because they offer a perceptual contradiction of sorts. They are constructed in a glossy, idealized manner, which often misrepresents reality, and yet they are perceived as "real" depictions of human life by consumers. In some cases, messages people encounter in the mass media can have beneficial effects; for instance, they can raise awareness for important causes like improving personal health habits or taking better care of the global environment. However, messages people encounter in the mass media undoubtedly also do a lot of harm by perpetuating myths and stereotypes about how people should look, who people should date, when sex is inappropriate and even abhorrent, and countless other areas of social life.[2] Although some mass media scholars would posit that individuals have agency to control the images they internalize and can monitor the impact of it on their personal lives, many people still fall victim to their fabricated distortions.

Portrayals of older adults have been examined in the research literature across a wide variety of genres,[3] including the following:

- Disney animated movies
- Magazines
- Network programs
- Prime-time television
- Print advertising
- Saturday morning television
- Teen movies
- Social media

Not surprisingly, people react in different ways. A recent study[4] examined older adults' evaluations of depictions of older adults in ten different forms of media (e.g., social media, magazines, TV shows) and found that 47% of a sample of adults aged 55 and older viewed the depictions as unfavorable, 32%

DOI: 10.4324/9780429330681-5

found them "neutral" (or mixed in tenor), while one-fifth of the sample (21%) viewed them favorably.

With this as a backdrop, in this chapter, we discuss the visibility and valence of older characters in the mass media and the value placed on youthfulness in media messages. Attention is also drawn to the billion-dollar industry of advertising anti-aging surgeries, remedial procedures, and the plethora of rejuvenating creams and other products. We also critically examine the impact of supposedly positive images of older people and programs depicting such characters and look at means of addressing the potentially negative effects of mass media portrayals of older adults.

Agist Images in the Media

As stated, age is omnipresent in mass media content, often in ways people are not aware of. In the Western press, it is a common practice to include people's ages in the body of a news story, even when age is minimally relevant to the story being told: "Woman, 26, tripped over a cat, sprained her ankle, and was hit by a car." This practice subtly sustains our attention to age as a supposedly meaningful dimension of description and identification in everyday life. In an extensive study examining an online corpus (including British and American newspapers, books, and radio broadcasts) of 57 million words, occurrences of the word "elderly" and its collocations (i.e., words that typically co-occur with that word) were examined. The word "elderly" was typically associated with the following words: *infirmed, handicapped, disabled, sick,* and *poor*.[5] For example:

- "projects to help the sick, elderly, and handicapped"
- "healthcare of the elderly and the impoverished"
- "inevitably the elderly and infirm are proving unattractive customers"
- "social safety nets for the elderly and the underprivileged"

Messages in the mass media can also promote and perpetuate age categories that have been constructed by businesses to find or consolidate a niche market. The toy industry is one example: not too long ago, marketing professionals reputedly constructed the label "tween girls" to describe the 8 to 12-year-old girls age bracket. "Twixters" is another target label used for those making the transition into adulthood from their late teens and early 20s;[6] similarly, "Abbies" is a (commercial) label for Baby Boomers. While people might not create these labels for themselves, when people encounter them in the mass media, they often adopt them. In this way, mass media messages can affect how people think about themselves and each other in terms of socially constructed age categories.

One area that has garnered much attention by researchers is the media's representation of various subgroups of people, including Black and Latinx people, undocumented immigrants of color, and working mothers. Naturally enough, scholars of aging have joined this research movement by studying media representations of older people, or perhaps more accurately, the *lack* thereof. Although there are some small differences between media genres, over the decades. studies have consistently shown that those in the age range of 20 to 44 years old are proportionally overrepresented on traditional American television, while those aged over 65 are *under*represented, receiving minimal air time.[7] In fact, over-65-year-olds have been found to be about 5% of characters in traditional prime-time TV shows and are similarly represented in advertisements across a wide variety of magazines. Whether these age trends are represented in current and expansive TV streaming services is, thus far, unclear. Nonetheless, even in the most popular Nielsen-rated television shows, the following profile emerged in 2017:[8]

- Only 9.4 percent of all speaking characters were 60 years of age or over – despite seniors representing 19.9 percent of the U.S. population, according to the 2015 U.S. Census.
- Stereotypical, agist language is prevalent in the shows. Some choice quotes include: "Things just sound creepier when you're old," and "You like the color? It's called 'ancient ivory,' like you."
- Of shows featuring a main senior character, 41 percent contained one or more agist comments. Of those series with agist comments, 62.5 percent had remarks that came from characters speaking to a senior, while 68.8 percent contained self-deprecating dialogue delivered by seniors to themselves.

The picture may be even bleaker for representations of older ethnic minorities and marginalized groups aged 60 and over, although the number of TV sitcoms devoted to strong Black family life (e.g., *Queen Sugar*, *Black-ish*, and *Insecure*) have significantly increased in the last few years.[9]

Issues with traditional age-related representation are not just an American phenomenon. Another study examined 2000 movies in Swedish theaters over a five-year period and found that only nine had senior characters, with no sexual relations apparent. Another recent study showed that in Hong Kong, Japan, and South Korea older people were underrepresented in television adverts.[10] There are also some gender differences and changes over time in age group representation. The frequency of portrayals of white women in their 20s has recently increased; research has also found that male actors in their middle and later years appear more often than female actors of the same age.[11] It is also noteworthy that some members of the entertainment industry have told us they have observed that as media writers age, their work is deemed less desirable for adoption, and their compensation for it is lower.

The social importance of these issues of representation is underscored when we consider that research shows that viewers prefer to select TV programs that (positively) portray members of their own social ingroups.[12] In other words, it has been claimed that people prefer a show where the star reflects their social group (such as their gender or race), compared with an otherwise similar show where the star does not. Age is no exception to this, and both young and older people gravitate to programs in which their age peers are actively engaged as central characters.[13] However, for many older adults, this inclination can be difficult to satisfy because their age group is virtually invisible in a youth-oriented media landscape. If they do not see themselves depicted and, instead, see only representations of younger adults' culture of work accomplishments, attractiveness, beauty, and sexuality, older people may be led to think they are not valued and do not count.

Indeed, one well-cited study[14] showed that the more TV older people watch – and a fair number of this age group do consume many hours of it – the lower they report their self-esteem to be. Although this was an admittedly modest effect (and correlational, meaning we cannot clearly determine what is cause versus effect), it is a notable and sobering finding, particularly when taken alongside other prevailing agist beliefs we have observed. This kind of research and personal experiences in the media industry led older TV star Doris Roberts in an interview about her life and career to say, "[Seniors] do not see themselves portrayed, and when they do, it's in a demeaning manner. They're referred to as 'over the hill,' 'old goats' and 'old farts' etc."

The absence of older characters in many mass media products may make people not wish to negotiate the topic or process of aging openly. When older people *are* found in the media, the quality of their representations can, as we shall see later, be of dubious value. Advertisements, television shows, and movies generally portray the negative aspects of aging, sending a further message that old age is bad and youth is good. Such ideas contribute to and reinforce the damaging age stereotypes we addressed in Chapter 2.

Examples of negative depictions of aging are abundant and well-illustrated in the long-running adult TV cartoon show, *The Simpsons*, which portrays the character "Grandpa" as the outcast of the family. His physical persona is one of a stereotypical old man, consisting of wrinkles, glasses, pale-colored clothing, and a shaky voice. The family treats him poorly and often makes jokes that poke fun at his old age. This is common in comedic portrayals of older adults: such characters are crafted in line with elderly stereotypes and made to be the "butt of the joke" to elicit laughter from the audience. However, in doing so, these depictions reinforce our stereotypes of older people. Because the message is funny, the audience may also be less likely to question the use of age-based stereotypes. With that said, not all comedic portrayals of older adults are negative. Creators of older people of color on TV often devise characters that are old, yet wise and spry. For example, the character, Suga Mama, in the Disney animated TV show, *Proud Family*, fed into stereotypical depictions of older people as teeth-less, gray hairs, wrinkled, and so on. But her character also engaged in various activities and behaviors that are often associated with younger people (e.g., going on a date to a hip-hop concert).[15]

Another time-honored type of TV entertainment is sports, which includes attention to sports personalities and celebrities. Age is very pertinent in most major sports as athlete's professional lifespans are glaringly short; in the United States, the average male career of a National Football League and Major League Baseball player is 5.8 years, and for the National Basketball Association, it is 2.44 years.[16] Often, when an exemplary play is made by a gifted older athlete, it is followed immediately by a commentator's remark about age. When that same athlete performs poorly or under par, a comment about their "being past it" often follows. A fascinating study looked at a large number of *New York Times* articles when the American tennis player, Andre Agassi, reached the last rounds of tournaments during his career.[17] The authors claim that, in 1990, when he was 20 years of age, there were only 11 mentions of his age in sports media, yet when he was 35, it was mentioned in 63 articles, including the headlines. These scholars underscored that "clearly his age was no longer part of the story, but became *the* story." It is also interesting to note that at 24, he was described as "a kid," while at 29 he was classified as a member of the "Geezer brigade," an "ancient mariner," "the elder statesman," and "the wise old gnome of tennis." That is quite a transition in a period of five years.

Negative depictions of aging also appear in mass media products addressing political and economic issues. One example is press articles about the so-called "Boomers' *Burden*." This is fairly widespread media rhetoric in the United States that depicts older generations as soaking up the finite reservoir of Social Security benefits, suggesting (or outright stating) that future generations will consequently have to pay more in the future as a result. Terms such as "generational victimhood" are bandied around in the American media to draw attention to the ways in which younger people will lose out. Mass media outlets also emphasize there is an acute and ongoing "*Battle* of the Ages." For example, the cover of a 2014 *American Association of Retired Persons (AARP) Bulletin* offered an image of direct competition ("war") between generations as with a younger and older person arm wrestling with aggressive looks.

Indeed, similar articles (which authors have noted in passing when in the UK) have reported on this topic using terms and phrases like the "demographic time bomb" and the "aging crisis" that "drives up pensions and health costs." In Canada, there have been media stories about how older women over-rely on younger generations to support them, and corresponding stories of younger generations who have to sacrifice their own careers, social lives, and health as a consequence. The following are some additional examples of headlines and phrasing from American mass media outlets (which, we note, appear despite the estimate that Boomers will pass on $2.4 trillion to their children and grandchildren):

- *New York Times* headline: "Young and old are facing off for jobs"
- *National Journal* article on: "The case against parasitic baby boomers"
- *Reason* magazine online article: "Hey, kids, wake up! ... Old people are doing everything possible to *rob you of your money,* your future, your dignity and your freedom"

If older people accept the premise that is inherent in such reports – that is, that they are a burden to younger generations – then the stories and the accompanied visual depictions are very likely to undermine a sense of a positive elderly identity. Another striking example of negative portrayals of older people, albeit some years ago, came from an opinion column in a UC Santa Barbara student newspaper (*Daily Nexus*, 2/10/2004), the title of which read, "True evil wears liver spots: Grandpa's wrinkled, gnarled face is that of death, kids." An edited excerpt from the column stated (p. 6):

> With all the fuss about terrorism, our leaders are ignoring the fact that there is a growing population of enemies within our own country. Demons so mean that they may bring our country to its very knees. [...]
>
> The people I'm thinking of are so clearly set apart from the rest of us they can't hide their evil ... The group I'm thinking about is, of course, the elderly.

Were there any indignant reactions to this column, published, or otherwise? Sadly, not that we were aware of.

In this book, we have already underscored the notion that children learn their ideas about aging early in life, and that the mass media contributes to this process in a variety of ways. With this in mind, one of our (college) students wrote:

> Disney movies were a prominent part of my childhood. I think my parents ended up hiding *Fantasia* from me because I would watch it over and over. But like every little girl, Disney princess movies were my number one go-to. When you think about the evil characters in these movies ... they are always old, scary, wrinkled characters. Ursula, scary old octopus lady, the old lady in *Snow White* that poisons her, the evil gray-haired stepmother in *Cinderella*, etc. Over and over again as children we have this reinforced stereotype from the media that old = bad (or evil in this case) and young (princess) = good.

Slowly but surely, as we grow older, mass media offers messages about what is expected of us at different life stages (see Chapter 1). For instance, in an article about a marketing consultant, aged 27, the woman recounted: "I wore shimmery eye shadow on a blind date – I thought it was hip. At dinner, the guy says, 'Don't you think that eye shadow is more suited to younger women?' *Never went there again! (With this guy or beyond).*" As viewers and readers, we must be aware of overt and subliminal messages conveyed to us by mass media depictions. It is also important that we not readily accept such depictions, as acceptance may have a profound effect on how we come to view our own limitations as we grow older.

The Media's "Cult of Youth"

Health is one arena commonly linked to age because society and the mass media often make direct links between aging and physical decline, with that association ever-present in ubiquitous advertisements for health-related products targeted at older TV audiences. For instance, it is common to see older people in commercials for pain medicine, as well as for medical, dental, and life insurance. Among the worst offenders here is the beauty industry and their anti-aging, rejuvenating ads, many of which depict particular parts or aspects of women's bodies that are depicted as requiring rather costly "repairs."[18] In one such ad, titled, "I'm 61. But my face is 35," six facial areas were highlighted as "problems." These were:

- Crow's feet
- Forehead wrinkles
- Bags or circles under the eyes
- Smile lines
- Throat and neck looseness
- Fine lines around lips

Calling out specific areas or types of issues may make people susceptible to monitoring or paying more attention to these areas and evaluating themselves or others negatively if these issues are evident. But these problem areas are not confined to the face; according to beauty ads, hands and legs are also potential areas of concern. Highlighting the (absurd) lengths advertisers can go, in one advertisement for slippers, reference was made to the product's "thick anti-age cushioning"; another advertisement promoted "age-defying pillowcases"!

In 2009, a self-help book entitled *How Not to Look Old*[19] quickly became a best-seller in the United States. In an interview about it, the author said:

> Whether we want to admit it or not, in corporate America, we would rather have a cute sexy 30-year-old working for us than a 50-year-old with gray hair who has let herself go and out of it, like a nun ... My book has hit a nerve because I am giving not looking old a spin as if your life depended on it!

Subsequently, we came across a poignant review of the book that stated:

> Agism is one the last frontiers of discrimination where people think that a way around it is not to be seen to age, but we would never say that women should try or act to look more male in order to avoid sexism ... Many people would shun a book if it were titled "How not to be Jewish" or "How not to be Gay" because to cater to discrimination is to capitulate to it. "How not to look old" indicates that popular culture is willing to buy into agism as an acceptable form of prejudice, even against oneself.

It has been estimated that "age-defying" – and sometimes labeled "*de*-aging" – lotions and surgeries are an annual multibillion-dollar business in the United States. Indeed, their worth has been estimated at $58.5 billion in 2020 and is projected to be $88.3 billion by 2026.[20] This suggests that the American public is open to these messages in that aging is a "problem" in need of a "solution," and that people are ready to invest large sums of money to "*look* [and even *sound*] *younger.*" The Guinness World Record for the most cosmetic surgeries was held (in 2011) by a 55-year-old woman who had had 52 surgeries procedures, many with anesthetics, that were worth over $100,000. These included:

- Five facelifts
- Liposuction
- Two eye lifts
- Botox injections
- Hand injections (to deal with "prominent veins and tendons sticking up")
- Jawline surgery
- Lip and cheek implants

Some years ago, in a local City of Santa Barbara newspaper, an article that questioned such pursuits argued:[21]

> For eternity, aging happened. It was as inevitable as the weather. Able to do little in foiling death, people were accepting of life's journey. Today we're in *full throttle combat* in thwarting aging. Defying time is today's martial art, an industry, a second career.

Another article about the famous actress Elizabeth Taylor we came across some years ago was devoted to the claim that she was "nipped, tucked, lifted out of her peer group," with the author of it raising the insightful question, "Is this what 60 looks like? At its best? Or, at its *worst*?"

It has been found that women who are more age-anxious and concerned about appearance in middle age (and older) are more likely than others to buy anti-aging products. In this study, "women also described an interesting paradox whereby they report using these products while remaining critical of media messages and embracing the idea of natural aging."[22] Clearly, some people make dilemmatic choices. Another study investigated how young people react to older people known to undergo these procedures. It was found that such older people were judged as more deceitful and less likable and attractive than those who did not.[23] Interestingly, this effect was strongest among those who endorsed a youthful identity. The researchers believed their findings supported the idea that older women who make efforts to reclaim their youth threaten the distinctiveness of a valued young identity.

One interpretation of this situation is that young people relish their looks and slender body images as a valued aspect of what it means to be young. Because of this, they do not want older people taking away a visible feature that differentiates them from older generations (which is in line with social identity theory; see Chapter 3). It is possible that older people implicitly know this yet are, nonetheless, prepared to take the risk that others will not detect the procedures, and consequently see them as inherently "young." It should be noted that such tactics are no longer the sole prerogative of women; increasingly, men are also opting for such procedures. Although anti-aging research, sentiments, and media advertising have been around for a long time, it is telling that there is very little research to date examining social responses to anti-aging efforts.

All this said, not all facelifts and other "anti-aging" elective surgeries are obvious to third-party observers; some can be medically successful (as well as imperceptible to others), and it is possible that future advances in cosmetic surgery may make this the lucrative norm. If these physical changes decrease the likelihood of being stereotyped in an agist way or being the target of patronizing talk (see Chapters 2 and 4, respectively), then doubtless the outcomes could be deemed advantageous. We believe it is possible to recognize the potential benefits of such procedures, while still subscribing to healthy age ideologies (outlined in Chapter 7). After all, there is a whole range of things people do with their appearance that are more subtle or minor than surgery (dying hair, whitening teeth, selecting clothing, etc.) but still are steps to make themselves appear younger, and that could have similar benefits. Nonetheless, we would advocate for using a label like "life-enhancing" rather than "age-denying," "age-defying," or "age-reversing" when describing such steps taken to appear younger.

More Positive Media Messages?

Some media makers have noted and taken to heart the issues with negative, stereotypical depictions of older people and made efforts to combat them by deliberately constructing more positive images of older adults and programs featuring them. In many of these instances, elderly people are then portrayed as *exceptional* characters and are shown engaging in counter-stereotypical activities. For example, news outlets sometimes report about older people later in their careers taking up marathon running or participating in risky outdoor pursuits, such as skydiving. These portrayals are positive in that they showcase older people engaging in activities that go against stereotypes for their age group as might be the case in the following examples.

82 *The Media, Agism, and Anti-Aging*

The woman shown running in purple is 92-year-old Harriett Thompson who became, on May 31, 2015, the oldest woman to run a marathon (San Diego) in 7 hours, 24 minutes, and 36 seconds; the previous record was 9 hours, 53 minutes, and 16 seconds. The man in the orange turban is Fauja Singh (100 years old) from east London, who finished the 2011 Toronto Marathon in 8 hours, 25 minutes, and 18 seconds – and ahead of five other competitors.

Although these depictions of older adults are positive, they are also presented as violations of expectations, which subtly reinforces the original (more negative) stereotypes people hold. In these stories, the older person is not presented as a typical member of the older age group; instead, they are seen as exceptions. A British TV skit some years ago provided a compelling example of this: an older woman is seen to confront three young men at gunpoint because they were, apparently, about to steal her car. On seeing this and hearing her confidently direct quite profane language at them, the three younger men run away. The next scene sees the woman with her car keys trying to start her (red) car to no avail. She leaves that vehicle and sees another (identical) red car nearby, and immediately starts up the engine. Here, viewers are initially led to believe that they were seeing a very unusual, *a*-stereotypical older woman but, ultimately, the skit's portrayal merely confirms viewers' initial stereotype of an older person not being "together enough" to recognize her own car in a parking garage (to raucous laugh-overs).

Nolan Ryan, an accomplished American baseball player, often had comments in the press reporting him as "still" breaking records at age 45. Indeed, the provocative use of this term is commonly used in discussions of older celebrities to connote an atypical performance for their age: "At 85, *still* provocative," "Bob Hope turns 93 – and he's *still* going strong," and "an older couple *still* enjoying the twilight years." Nolan Ryan himself authored a book called *Miracle Man* in which he ostensibly divulges his secret for a successful life. In this book, and in another newspaper article about a 105-year-old woman who was spending her time looking after "older people." the characters are framed as extraordinarily (and atypically) special. (Interestingly, the people the latter woman took care of were around the age of 60!). Family and observers referred to the 105-year-old caregiver as "unbelievable"; later in this same article, the woman labels what she has done, too, as "unbelievable." While her work is portrayed as positive, literally saying it is *not believable* (which she herself says) leaves readers wondering how, if at all, they can aspire to such lofty heights. As we see here, positive images of older people are present in the media, but the way they are presented often leads them to be discounted as exceptions to the norm and, therefore, less likely to be potential models of positive or successful aging.

Despite the problems highlighted previously, television and magazine advertising can, on occasion, portray older people positively, and as happy and active. This often occurs when older people are depicted in their innocuous, yet socially vital, roles as grandparents. Older people may also be portrayed positively in television shows and movies, but usually the older character is made to behave, as discussed above, in a *non*-stereotypical manner. For example, in the American movie *The Wedding Singer*, there is a scene in which an older woman goes on stage at a wedding and performs a popular rap song, "Rappers Delight." The scene elicits much laughter from the audience because people typically do not associate rap music with older generations. Other examples of positive older characters from American television include the protagonists of *Murder, She Wrote*, *Matlock*, and *Jake and the Fatman*, and in the movies of *The Big Chill* and *Driving Miss Daisy*.

However, such positive media portrayals can backfire. Arguably among the best example of this is the popular American (1985–1992) sitcom, *Golden Girls*, that is still aired regularly on TV in the United States. The creators of this show were known for trying to combat stereotypical images of the elderly by featuring feisty older women as the main characters. Although the initial intention was laudable, and it led to prominent communication and aging scholars praising its virtues, the show was still full of age stereotypes. In a detailed analysis of a random selection of episodes from the show,[24] researchers found that 96% of the jokes were age-related, virtually all contained negative overtones, and with the shows including painful self-disclosures (see Chapter 4). Looking at how college students responded to this show, the researchers found that students thought the actors were not actually old themselves but rather, were made to look old. In other words, young people did not construe the actors as elderly. This finding suggested, that for younger adults, the whole show could be discounted as not being a "true" or a typical representation of the aging process. *Golden Girls* paraphernalia, such as birthday cards, reflected a similar sentiment: "At our age, the days of wine and roses aren't necessarily over … you just have to alternate them with antacid and aspirin." In sum, even something that initially appears to be more positive can end up being another dish contributing to the extensive menu of media agism.

Annulling the Forces of Agism in the Media

This chapter will end with some important provisions. We do not want to claim or imply that all older persons easily fall prey to unfavorable images of their group, or that they have little ability to manage or counteract their negative effects. There is also no intent here to scapegoat the media as the *worst* offender for perpetuating agism. Many older people are not passive consumers of media, and they find programs where portrayals of same-aged characters are *not* demeaning and watch those shows with relish. That said, many older people may not recognize or appreciate the incessant agism embedded in the media content they consume. Making them aware of – or inoculating them against – negative stereotypes on TV may be one way of counteracting these pernicious effects.[25]

However, not everyone who sees mass media portrayals of older adults as negative necessarily experiences negative effects. Somewhat paradoxically, a study referred to earlier[26] found that those who saw media depictions of aging as more *un*favorable than others in the sample were twice as likely to report being both able to manage the aging process well, and to age successfully (see the profile of "engaged agers" in Chapter 7). It may be that those who are highly resilient (see Chapter 8), downplay or dismiss, and/or are not intimidated by such portrayals are the very ones who compensate for these messages (see selective optimization with compensation theory, Chapter 1) by actively embedding themselves in resourceful outlets and social networks in which they can energetically fulfill their goals.

People's own personal circumstances may also affect how they consume, and are affected by, mass media content. For instance, it has been found that older people who are lonely and at a loss for age-related coping mechanisms prefer to watch TV characters who reflect their *own* lifestyles.[27] Shows depicting older characters that are socially active may be threatening to those who feel socially isolated; such isolated older people are also likely to find depictions of same-aged peers who find pleasure in and enjoy their relationships discomforting. However, we would argue that being in close contact with a caring, supportive family and networks of *friends*, as well as having a positive outlook on aging *as growth*, may lessen any malignant, lasting influence the media could have on one's self-worth and life satisfaction (see Chapter 7). This could be because, for these people in more positive circumstances, media images do not represent what they experience in their culture and/or family, and so they are not affected by those portrayals in the same way as someone who does view them as true or accurate.

Not unrelatedly, we are at a time when many movie and entertainment icons are still actively and gratifyingly working into their late 60s, 70s, and beyond, and a mere selection of these are listed here.

Paul McCartney	Helen Mirren	Elton John
Morgan Freeman	Meryl Streep	Clint Eastwood
Jennifer Lewis	Judy Dench	Maggie Smith
Rita Moreno	Tony Bennett	Betty White
Danny Glover	Jackie Chan	Giselle Fernández
Jane Fonda	Anthony Hopkins	David Attenborough

They avidly talk about their enthusiasm not only for continuing their work but for continuing to improve their performances. It may well be that their frequent visibility, together with the prominence of their high caliber products, will make younger people question their views of older people as well as re-imagine, in more positive terms, their own potential as they age. In fact, they may be construed as age role models for some older people (see Chapter 7).

As discussed in Chapter 4, there is a large literature on intergroup contact,[28] including that devoted to intergenerational contact even when it is imaged,[29] looking at the conditions under which it can undermine previously held stereotypes and improve attitudes to another group. (We do note, however, that researchers infrequently focus on encouraging *communication* with that other group). The so-called, *social identity theory of intergroup contact*[30] proposes that for contact to enhance intergenerational harmony, accomplished older people must not be discounted as individual exceptions (as discussed earlier), or even subtyped into a small, exceptional group of older adults. Rather, these people need to be seen as typical, representative group members (here, older adults). Thus, celebrity icons may only have the favorable impact that we claimed for them earlier if they become seen as somewhat *typical* of their age group as well as positive role models. Icons that are known to elect for cosmetic procedures that depict them on screen as obviously less than optimal to the extent that visual repair work is visibly apparent – and well-known exemplars do exist – are unlikely to lead to productive changes in intergenerational attitudes.

Concluding Thoughts

In this chapter, we have examined research on how older adults are depicted in the mass media. In many cases, older people are ignored, invisible, and/or are negatively portrayed. It was argued that this can have unfortunate consequences for older people, as well as how other age groups view them, and in ways that construct an unfortunate template for their own aging trajectories. As one Ambassador to the United Nations put it in a speech entitled, *Reflections on an Agequake*:[31]

> The borders of the TV screen frame not only the image being broadcast, but also the edges of our consciousness. A positive image of older people in the media can help bring them back in the picture in more ways than one.

Even when older folk are portrayed positively in *a*-stereotypical ways, we argued that their status as seemingly rare exceptions boomeranged back in the sense that they solidified traditional depictions of this age group in general.

The ways in which age-related changes (e.g., wrinkles) can be considered distasteful physical deficits, thereby perpetuating the notion that youthfulness is highly valued, was also discussed. The cosmetic store, *The Body Shop*, once had a compelling ad that proclaimed: "Never mind an antidote for aging. Let's find one for agism." In this regard, we leave you with Pat Benata's assertion that:[32]

> People are constantly telling you what's wrong with your looks or your age ... learning how to ignore them is an acquired skill ... Every laugh line, every scar is a badge I wear ... the inner rings of my personal tree trunk that I display proudly for all to see. Nowadays, I don't want a "perfect" face and body; I want to wear the life I've lived.

In this chapter, we also highlighted the heterogeneity of elders' responses to the variety of messages about aging and, where necessary, the means by which individuals can push back against negative messages.

Throughout, we have highlighted the ubiquity of the media in creating and sustaining age stereotypes, which play important roles in topics addressed in other chapters in this book. This is no less evident in Chapter 7, where the chapter shows how people manage messages in the mass media *and* face-to-face is an important contributor to the process of successful aging. But before we arrive at that point, Chapter 6 focuses necessarily and explicitly on the last stage of life, namely death and dying, which is a compelling feature of our model of successful aging.

Notes

1. For trends predicted for the industry for 2021: Retrieved from https://www2.deloitt e.com/us/en/pages/technology-media-and-telecommunications/articles/media-and-entertainment-industry-outlook-trends.html
2. For negative and positive effects of media on self-esteem, see: Smeesters, D., & Mandel, N. (2006). Positive and negative media image effects on the self. *Journal of Consumer Research, 32*(4), 576–582. https://doi.org/10.1086/500489; see also: Akram, W., & Kumar, R. (2017). A study on positive and negative effects of social media on society. *International Journal of Computer Sciences and Engineering, 5*(10), 347–354. Retrieved from: www.ijcseonline.org
3. Robinson, J. D., Skill, T., & Turner, J. W. (2004). Media usage patterns and portrayals of seniors. In J. F. Nussbaum & J. Coupland (Eds.), *Handbook of communication and aging research* (pp. 423–446). Mahwah, NJ: Erlbaum; Makita, M., Mas-Bleda, A., Stuart, E., & Thelwall, M. (2019). Aging, old age and older adults: A social media analysis of dominant topics and discourses. *Aging & Society*. Advance Online: https://doi.org/10.1017/S0144686X19001016; see also: Atkinson, J. L. (forthcoming). *Talking age: Examining the (not so) subtle language of agism across mediated contexts* (provisional title). New York, NY: Peter Lang. The image in the text is edited from this source.
4. Bernhold, Q. S. (2021). The role of media in predicting older adults' own age-related communication and successful aging. *Mass Communication and Society, 24*(1), 1–30. https://doi.org/10.1080/15205436.2020.1743862; Relating to "neutral" and "positive" portrayals of aging in this study, see also: Oró-Piqueras, M., & Marques, S. (2017). Images of old age on YouTube: Destabilizing stereotypes. *Continuum, 31*(2), 257–265. https://doi.org/10.1080/10304312.2016.1265098
5. Maunter, G. (2007). Mining large corpora for social information: The case of elderly. *Language in Society, 36*(1), 51–72. https://doi.org/10.1017/S0047404507070030
6. Byers, C. R. (2017). *The Twixters! Tweens in-between*. Scotts Valley, CA: CreateSpace.
7. Roy, A., & J. Harwood. (2009). Underrepresented, positively portrayed: Older adults in television commercials. *Journal of Applied Communication Research, 25*(1), 39–56. https://doi.org/10.1080/00909889709365464; see also: Loos, E., & Ivan L. (2018). Visual agism in the media. In L. Ayalon & C. Tesch-Römer (Eds.), *Contemporary perspectives on agism*. (pp. 163–176). Cham, Switzerland: Springer. https://doi.org/10.1007/978-3-319-7 3820-8_11
8. See: USC Annenberg-Humana studies suggest relationship between TV age bias and health of seniors (2017). Retrieved from: https://annenberg.usc.edu/news/research/usc-annenberg-humana-studies-suggest-rel ationship-between-tv-age-bias-and-health
9. Towbin, M. A., Haddock, S. A., Zimmerman, T. S., Lund, L. L., & Tanner, L. R. (2004). Images of gender, race, age, and sexual orientation in Disney feature-length animated films. *Journal of Feminist Family Therapy, 15*(4), 19–44. https://doi.org/10.1300/J086v15n04_02; see also: https://www.oprahmag.com/entertainment/tv-movies/g 25693667/best-black-tv-shows/
10. Respectively see: Bildtgård, T. (2000). The sexuality of elderly people on film – Visual limitations. *Journal of Aging and Identity, 5*(3), 169–183. https://doi.org/10.1023/A: 1009565321357; Prieler, M. P., Ivanov, A., & Hagiwara, S. (2017). The representation of older people in Asian television advertisements. *International Journal of Aging & Human Development, 85*(1), 67–89. https://doi.org/10.1177/0091415016677972
11. Kelly, S. (2020). Representation for white women increased in 2019 movies, but intersectional inclusion remains elusive. *Los Angeles Times*. Retrieved from: https://www.lat imes.com/entertainment-arts/movies/story/2020-01-08/women-film-hollywood-ge nder-study
12. Abrams, J., & Giles, H. (2007). Ethnic identity gratifications selection and avoidance by African Americans: A group vitality and social identity gratifications perspective. *Media Psychology, 9*(1), 115–135. https://doi.org/10.1080/15213260709336805

13 Harwood, J. (1997). Viewing age: Lifespan identity and television viewing choices. *Journal of Broadcasting & Electronic Media, 41*(2), 203–213. https://doi.org/10.1080/08838159709364401
14 Korzenny, F., & Neuendorf, K. (1980). Television viewing and self-concept of the elderly. *Journal of Communication, 30*(1), 71–80. https://doi.org/10.1111/j.1460-2466.1980.tb01771.x; for a discussion of the quote below, see: Harwood, J. (2007). *Understanding communication and aging: Developing knowledge and awareness*, Chapter 8. Thousand Oaks, CA: Sage; see also 2nd ed.: San Diego, CA: Cognella.
15 The Disney Wiki. Retrieved from: https://disney.fandom.com/wiki/Suga Mama
16 https://www.quora.com/What-pro-sport-has-the-longest-average-player-longevity-the-NFL-NBA-or-MLB
17 Atkinson, J. L., & Herror, S. K. (2010). From the Chartreuse Kid to the wise old gnome of tennis: Age sereotypes as frames describing Andre Agassi at the U.S. Open. *Journal of Sport and Social Issues, 34*(1), 86–104. https://doi.org/10.1177/0193723509358966; for more details, see also: Atkinson, J. L. (forthcoming). *Talking age: Examining the (not so) subtle language of agism across mediated contexts* (provisional title). Chapter 2. New York, NY: Peter Lang.
18 Virpi, V. (Ed.). (2012). *Representing aging: Images and identities*. London, UK: Palgrave Macmillan; Tortajada, I., Dhaenens, F., & Willem, C. (2018). Gendered aging bodies in popular media culture. *Feminist Media Studies, 18*(1), 1–6. https://doi.org/10.1080/14680777.2018.1410313; see subsequent articles in this special issue, entitled "Gender aging bodies in popular media culture"; see also: Binstock, R. H. (2003). The war on "anti-aging" medicine. *Gerontologist, 43*(1), 4–14. https://doi.org/10.1093/geront/43.1.4; Haber, C. (2001/2). Anti-aging: Why now? A historical framework for understanding the contemporary enthusiasm. *Generations, 25(4),* 9–14. https://www.jstor.org/stable/26555096
19 Krupp, C. (2009). *How not to look old*. New York, NY: Springboard Press; see also: Coupland, J. (2007). Gendered discourses on the 'problem' of aging: Consumerized solutions. *Discourse and Communication, 1*(1), 37–61. https://doi.org/10.1177/1750481307071984
20 Statista. Size of the anti-aging market worldwide from 2020 to 2026. Retrieved from: https://www.statista.com/statistics/509679/value-of-the-global-anti-aging-market/
21 See Heller, K. (2005). Laughing in the face of wrinkles. *Santa Barbara NewsPress*, December 7, A10.
22 See p. 126: Muise, A., & Desmarais, S. (2010). Women's perceptions and use of "Anti-Aging" products. *Sex Roles, 63*(1–2), 126–137 (2010). https://doi.org/10.1007/s11199-010-9791-5; see also: Calasanti, T., King, N., Pietilä, I., & Ojala, H. (2018). Rationales for anti-aging activities in middle age: Aging, health, or appearance? *The Gerontologist, 58*(2), 233–241. https://doi.org/10.1093/geront/gnw111
23 Schoemann, A. M., & Branscombe, N. R. (2011). Looking young for your age: Perceptions of anti-aging actions. *European Journal of Social Psychology, 41*(1), 86–95. https://doi.org/10.1002/ejsp.738
24 Harwood, J., & Giles, H. (1992). "Don't make me laugh": Age representations in a humorous context. *Discourse and Society, 13*(4), 403–436. https://doi.org/10.1177/0957926592003004001
25 See: Donlon, M. M., & Levy, B. R. (2005). Re-vision of older television characters: A stereotype-awareness intervention. *Journal of Social Issues, 61*(2), 307–319. https://doi.org/10.1111/j.1540-4560.2005.00407.x; for a critique of this stance suggesting a more cautious approach to implementations, see: Giles, H., & Reid, A. A. (2005). Agism across the lifespan: Towards a self-categorization model of aging. *Journal of Social Issues, 61*(2), 389–404. https://doi.org/10.1111/j.1540-4560.2005.00412.x; for a potentially applicable general theory of media literacy that could be invoked for our purposes, see: Potter, W. J. (In press). *Media Literacy* (8th ed.). Thousand Oaks, CA: Sage.

26 See again: Bernhold, Q. S. (2021). The role of media in predicting older adults' own age-related communication and successful aging. *Mass Communication and Society, 24*(1), 1–30. https://doi.org/10.1080/15205436.2020.1743862
27 Mares, M., & Cantor, J. (1992). Elderly viewers' responses to televised portrayals of old age: Empathy and mood management versus social comparison. *Communication Research, 19*(4), 459–478. https://doi.org/10.1177/009365092019004004
28 See, for example: Kuehne, V. S. (Ed.). (1999). *Intergenerational programs: Understanding what we have created*. New York, NY: Haworth Press; see also: Fox, S., & Giles, H. (1993). Accommodating intergenerational contact: A critique and theoretical model. *Journal of Aging Studies, 7*(4), 423–445. https://doi.org/10.1016/0890-4065(93)90009-9; Burnes, D., Sheppard, C., Henderson, C. R., Jr., Wassel, M., Cope, R., Barber, C., & Pillemer, K. (2019). Interventions to reduce agism against older adults: A systematic review and meta-analysis. *American Journal of Public Health*. Retrieved from: https://doi.org/10.2105/AJPH.2019.305123
29 Fowler, C., & Harwood J. (2020). Does perceived normativity of intergenerational contact enhance the effects of imagined intergenerational contact? *Group Processes & Intergroup Relations*. https://doi.org/10.1177/1368430220934548
30 Brown, R., & Hewstone, M. (2005). An integrative theory of intergroup contact. In M. P. Zanna (Ed.), *Advances in Experimental Social Psychology, 37* (pp. 255–343). Cambridge, MA: Elsevier Academic Press. https://doi.org/10.1016/S0065-2601(05)37005-5; for a recent model: see Levy, S. R. (2018). Toward reducing agism: PEACE (positive education about aging and contact experiences) model. *The Gerontologist, 58*(2), 226–232. https://doi.org/10.1093/geront/gnw116
31 Alvarez, J. T. (1999). Reflections on an agequake. Retrieved from: Julia_Tavares_Alvarez_Speech_For_The_Ages.pdf; see also: Scialfa, C. T., Pichora-Fuller, K., & Spadafora, P. (2004). Interdisciplinary research education in communication and social interaction among health older adults. *Educational Gerontology, 30*(9), 733–750. https://doi.org/10.1080/03601270490498007
32 Benatar, P. (2019). *Between a heart and a rock place: A memoir*. New York, NY: HarperCollins.

6 Talking About Death – Or Not

This chapter tackles a daunting and sobering topic for many: death. From childhood upwards, people see a myriad of fictional deaths watching television and playing video games. Indeed, in a study examining 65 of the highest-grossing movies, 857 death-related scenes were located, with an average 100-minute movie containing such a scene every eight minutes. It was concluded that such depictions of death were sensational and unrealistic, with realistic grief rarely associated with them. The authors argued that such portrayals encourage denial and the avoidance of authentic death concerns, promoting emotional repression.[1] Ironically, despite all this exposure to death at a distance, it can be exceedingly difficult to engage with the topic when it comes to talking about our own deaths, addressing the seemingly rapid march of time,[2] or planning for the inevitabilities of those close to us who are getting on in years. We propose that assuming some discursive control over the process of death and dying can be enormously empowering, and even uplifting,[3] when we are able to do so. How we manage – or do not manage – this cultural taboo is the topic of this chapter and is arguably an important element of the relationship between communication and successful aging.

At the outset, we note that it is important to recognize that our *culture* shapes not only the meaning of death and how it is or is not talked about, but also what makes for a "good death" for the person who has died, their family and friends, and medical support staff.[4] For instance, a "good" death in a developing country like Uganda,[5] where resources are scarce, occurs when the dying person is being cared for at home, is free from pain and other distressing symptoms, feels no stigma, and is at peace. Ideas about death change throughout a society's history, and cultures differ greatly in ascribing socially constructive meanings to it and its attending communicative practices and routines. In what follows, we provide some examples of these issues in specific cultural contexts.

In Muslim societies, death is a common topic discussed within families.[6] This cultural tradition endorses the view that planning for death may be good (within reason, of course). Both men and women often purchase their burial shroud while they are alive. Loved ones often visit family members' graves and may even crawl down into them to pray and feel the experience of being there. Islamic culture endorses the belief that death is just one stage toward eternal

DOI: 10.4324/9780429330681-6

life. Many Muslims look forward to death because they will join Allah in paradise. Consequently, death may actually be openly celebrated in this culture.

In Mexico (and among Mexican émigrés elsewhere[7]), death is celebrated with a holiday, *Día de los Muertos* (translated in English as "Day of the Dead"). On this occasion, family, loved ones, and others in the local community engage in daylong festivities at the cemetery, as shown in the image here. People bring flowers and candles to their loved one's grave and clean the stones and place symbolic artifacts around it. The celebration lasts through the evening where the candles are lit as another means of honoring the lives of those who have passed on. Skeletons are placed all around cities in commemoration of the holiday.

In Asian cultures, many people are more accepting of death than in the former cultures targeted; however, this does not always translate to open discussion of it. For example, in China, death is viewed as a continuous and integral part of life, and there is comparatively less fear associated with it than in the West. However, Chinese people seldom talk about death or death-related issues,[8] due to a belief that it is bad luck to even speak words with the same phoneme as the Chinese word for "death."

Not unrelatedly, life expectancy is, of course, hugely dependent on place of birth, with the highest, globally, being females in Hong Kong at 88.17 years and, contrastively, lowest among males in the Central African Republic at 52.16 years (according to United Nations data). Life expectancy in Hong Kong is ten years higher compared with females in China generally, thereby underscoring the significant role that regional, socioeconomic, and other (e.g.,

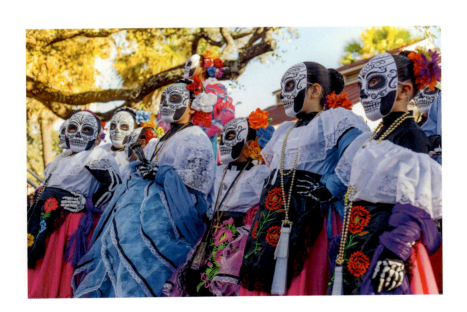

wars and neighborhood) factors play. Interestingly, the United States ranks #46 out of 193 global sites for both sexes, with life expectancy at 76.61 years for males.[9] However, as vividly depicted in a multiple award-winning documentary (2020) directed by Mary Mazzio called, *It's a Beautiful Thing*, death among Black males in West Chicago is common by 20 years. In this community, extraordinary gang violence is one of the main reasons for such a low life expectancy. However, this documentary displays what kinds of uplifting actions and messages of hope those males who survive into middle age can inspire.[10]

The actual physical and social process of laying a person "to rest," and the messages this conveys, also varies considerably across nations, as do the ways mourners dress and present themselves. For instance, on the Polynesian island of Tonga, funerals are expensive occasions for expressing love and respect for the deceased (with tinges of humor).[11] Mourners wear woven "mats" (or *ta'ovala*) that are related to one's relationship with the deceased. For example, should the deceased be the father, then the oldest sister would wear a finely woven ta'ovala that is very colorful, whereas other family members would wear worn-out, even frayed mats (especially the youngest brother) to mark respect. The size of the mat often represents the amount of grief experienced. Interestingly, on the Polynesian island of Bora Bora, there are no public cemeteries, and graves are mostly found in people's front yards. Turning to the Caribbean island of Jamaica, a feature of funeral rituals there is called "Nine Nights."[12] It is believed that a person's soul does not leave the body, or lingers, for nine nights where the deceased remains in the family home and their spirit is appeased by celebratory evenings filled with the singing of hymns, dancing, and the offering of drinks. As they say in Jamaica: "No call a man dead till you bury him."

In the United States and many European countries, there is a reluctance to talk about information and emotions associated with an impending death, even in families that are reputedly open to discussing sensitive topics. Americans over the age of 50 regularly receive information in the mail regarding pre-paid cremation. Those who have never been the recipient of such mail can imagine the sentiments this can provoke. Despite our reluctance to talk or think about it, sometimes we are ominously reminded of our own demise in ways we can either ignore or plan for. Gratifyingly, there has been an outgrowth of interest in talk about death and dying from communication researchers. Drawing on this work, we argue that people's inability to manage death's challenges – at least in Western societies – may seriously impair their ability to adapt to growing ever-older. In this chapter, we discuss what we know of communicating *about* and *at* the end of life, which is an important element in successful aging.

Communicating *About* the End of Life

Both the point in the lifespan at which a person is dying and the cause of their death shape and guide how people communicate about it. For instance, the death of a young child often elicits conversations about potential and "a life that could have been."[13] In contrast, the death of a very elderly person is often discussed in more reflective conversations, as the death of people of advanced age is often considered more "appropriate." Furthermore, deaths due to long-term illness may be talked about very differently than deaths due to sudden illness or accidents.

When a loved one is diagnosed with a terminal illness, family members are generally uncertain of what they should say and communicating about the eventual end-point of that illness – death and dying – is particularly difficult. For instance, as scholars who study communication at the end of life have written, "to deal successfully with communication at the end of life, people must also have a strong aptitude for empathy, authenticity, compassion, responsiveness, adaptability, mindfulness and the ability to be truly in the moment."[14] In talking about death and dying to the terminally ill, scholars emphasize that it is best to convey bad news in such a way that the recipient is assured that they will not be abandoned. In fact, researchers point out that family members' uncertainty about their loved one's illness is often compounded by medical personnel not communicating bad news in as a fine-tuned or sensitive way as family members surmise they should. Indeed, it is relatively uncommon for families to discuss a family member's terminal illness together, and even less common for them, in general, to talk about that family member's death or dying.

The families that do discuss death take many different approaches to these conversations.[15] For instance, they might talk about the possibility of death once, but not return to the topic thereafter. As the illness progresses, family communication about death and dying typically becomes increasingly intermittent.[16] In the final stages of a disease, families sometimes engage in selective communication, discussing only facts about the illness or condition, which may be more comfortable than discussing their emotions.[17] As a consequence of this avoidance, concerns about a family member's death are infrequently discussed, even as death approaches. Medical personnel can compound this problem by failing to share information with families that might alleviate anxieties, such as available provisions for hospice care (that is, care in a facility devoted to caring for the terminally ill in their last few days or weeks).[18]

In one study, physicians were interviewed about issues related to communicating prognosis information to patients with metastatic cancer.[19] The study found that the physicians struggled with the tension between realism and hope. On the one hand, doctors believed that patients wanted to know their prognoses and, to this end, most physicians provided survival estimates to those who requested them. On the other hand, almost half of this physician sample indicated that they do not provide survival estimates to those who do not request them and that this was, in part, to preserve the patients' hope (see Chapter 8). Overall, physicians were more comfortable giving qualitative information, such as telling patients their disease was not curable, than quantitative estimates of survival time.

In a similar vein, and underscoring the extent to which the information-sharing process is a bilateral negotiation, a sample of cancer patients were asked what kinds of prognosis information, if any, *they* would like to receive, whether they requested this information from their physicians, and whether they actually received it.[20] The researchers mailed a survey to these patients asking them how often they desired, requested, and received qualitative prognosis information (whether or not their disease was terminal), and a quantitative estimate (how long they may survive): 80% of patients wanted a qualitative prognosis, but only about half wanted a quantitative prognosis. Of those who wanted a qualitative prognosis, over 90% were given one, whereas only about half of those who wanted a quantitative prognosis were provided it. Furthermore, whereas about 15% of those who wanted a qualitative prognosis did not ask for it, more than 30% of patients who reported wanting a quantitative prognosis failed to ask for it.

Many people do not wish for unrealistic or even false prognoses — nor do they want blunt factual information stripped of empathy and compassion. Most prefer some honest indications of hope for a fulfilling end of life as well as some faint possibility of remission. In this frame, different kinds of hope like inner peace and dignity, as well as perhaps optimism, can evolve over the course of time, as patients also balance other considerations such as the need for dignity, attaining treatment aspirations, or finding inner peace.[21]

Because death can be such a frightening topic for so many people, family members may also worry that by discussing it, they will bring distress to their dying loved one and/or to themselves. Thus, terminally ill patients and their families are likely to avoid talking about death in an effort to prevent distress for each other in what is termed "protective buffering." For instance, one study found that spouses emphasized the psychological needs of their dying loved one, which often meant concealing the spouses' fear that their partner may not survive their disease.

In American culture, this reluctance to openly address death is exacerbated by a much more general tendency to not talk about negative matters. In the face of adversity (e.g., terminal illness), there exists the cultural expectation that one must think positively and not give voice to potential negative outcomes.[22] It has been found that 15% of family members of terminal lung cancer patients admitted that they refused to discuss the possibility that their family member would not make it for fear that such talk would accelerate the patient's death. The influence of this mandate for "positive thinking" may actually impede or prevent important conversations that a person who is dying and their loved ones might benefit from having before death. It is also possible that this topic avoidance contributes to the distance that often emerges between couples or spouses during the end stages of coping with a terminal illness. Thus, it is important to recognize that there may be benefits and costs to talking about death, all of which depend on the situation, including the characteristics of the person who is dying, how, and of what.[23]

As the studies cited show, the outcomes of such discussion can vary among different people; it is important to appreciate the existence of this diversity before deciding to engage this topic with a particular person. That said, we should perhaps not assume that we implicitly *know* whether another person – either someone dying or someone surviving – is ready to talk about death. Negotiating whether this is desirable or appropriate with relevant parties, and perhaps doing so at different junctures over time, can be a useful way to address this issue. Regardless of when and how the topic is broached, we want to emphasize that providing messages that assure the dying individual that he or she will not be abandoned is absolutely necessary, as abandonment and the preservation of dignity are among the most common fears that people who are dying report.[24]

Communication *At* the End of Life

Scholars have argued that one can make death less problematic by downgrading its perceived probability, altering the evaluation of death to be more positive, or combining these strategies.[25] Research has found that viewing death as a high-probability outcome can produce negative emotional experiences that can be overwhelming for many families in a hospice care setting. Concerns about these kinds of experiences may explain why doctors may be reluctant to give a life expectancy prognosis, especially when the prognosis is poor. Dying people and their loved ones frequently have difficulty accepting that death is approaching; this often manifests in people's refusal to discuss the process and the ultimate event, as we discussed in the previous section. According to hospice workers, the most difficult communication issues for both those dying and their loved ones include: "letting go," accepting death, admitting acceptance to each other, and giving the other permission "to let go."[26] Interestingly, people tend not to use the second strategy we noted, framing impending death as positive (i.e., as an escape from suffering, or a journey to a higher spiritual plane). Rather, it is much more common for people to just minimize their thoughts about the probability of death occurring.

Researchers have studied final conversations between survivors and their loved ones who have passed away, and retrospective interviews with survivors have uncovered a number of key themes that are common to final conversations.[27] Although what actually transpired, relative to what participants report retrospectively, is of course debatable, this body of work provides some insight into how people communicate at the end of life. In this work, three prominent themes emerge.

First, and perhaps unsurprisingly, one of the most prominent themes in these conversations is the expression of love. Final conversations represent a communication act wherein unconditional love may be readily exchanged between people because a sense of impending separation removes many of the barriers that normally prevent messages of love and intimacy. Messages of love are often repeated and may be conveyed both verbally and nonverbally. These messages tend to emphasize connectedness and closure in a relationship. Affirmations of love between a dying person and their loved one can further strengthen their existing bond and can consequently aid in the survivor's healing process after the loved one has passed. In circumstances where relationships have been strained, messages of love may be difficult to convey. However, when such messages are delivered under these circumstances, they can serve as a means of reconciliation that help people let go of differences. Nonverbal expressions of love (for example, expressing love by touch and look) are also important, as they are a means to express to the dying loved one that it is okay to "let go."

A second common theme in final conversations at the end of life is a reflection on the evaluative construction of the self, both as an individual and as a partner in a relational dyad. These messages can alter, or bolster and confirm survivors' personal and relational identities, and create the opportunity for both parties to re-examine, re-affirm, and adjust their own self-esteem, self-image, and identity. As we will discuss shortly, people like to reduce uncertainty about what their lives have meant to them and significant others, and this gives rise to dying people crafting or developing a coherent story of their lives, or a *life review*. Family members can also discuss spiritual or religious beliefs in final conversations to help provide meaning to death.[28] These messages can take various forms, including direct affirmations of faith, explicit acknowledgment of a higher power, and the expression of the belief that all family members will be reunited in the next life. Such messages can also serve to validate religious values, which could mean reaffirming long-held beliefs, restoring lapsed beliefs, or shifting belief systems.

Research has found that the validation of one's spirituality or faith can provide comfort for both the dying individual and their loved ones, albeit not so for atheists, of course.[29] In particular, survivors often comment that they found solace in speaking to their loved one about their religious beliefs, and many believed that discussions about faith and the afterlife assuaged their loved one's fear of dying; this is important in Catholic families in Spain and Latin America, and with Buddhist families in Tibetan communities.[30] Communication about faith during the final conversation can also address "rules of conduct" by which survivors should live after the loved one has passed away, and these rules can help survivors to cope with life's challenges during bereavement. Messages about faith, religion, or spiritual beliefs during final conversations can enhance survivors' ability to enact their spirituality and be more vocal or demonstrative in their beliefs.

Third, a final theme for these end-of-life conversations was so-called "routine talk," which encompassed messages on a wide range of topics, many of which centered on family issues and dynamics. These discussions often had a lighthearted quality that preserved a sense of normalcy in spite of the circumstances. Over the course of a terminal illness, such talk can help ease the burden of having to say goodbye, or of constructing the best way to say it.

Some participants in these survivor studies discussed difficult interactions with their dying loved one; such difficult conversations often included criticism, defensiveness, guilt, manipulation, coldness, or contempt. For example, one survivor described a final conversation with her dying alcoholic mother in which she was eventually able to work up the courage to talk about some of the troubling issues in their relationship. Ultimately, this discussion helped the two to reconcile and move the interaction in a more positive direction. The author noted that this interaction reflected the "tendency of individuals that

Table 6.1 Talking to the Dying and Bereaved Person: Recommendations

To the dying person	To the bereaved person
• Say little and listen • Be neutral in family squabbles and issues • Do not be too upbeat • Do not use platitudes • Do not try and tell them how to behave	• Avoid interrupting • Honor the silences • Do not try to express logical feelings for the tragic loss • Do not compare experiences • Listen and be seen to listen

have difficult relationships to 'dance around' many of the issues pertaining to their difficult past relationship while, at the same time, wanting to engage in a more important, but more difficult final conversation."[31]

In sum, final conversations may result in a number of positive psychological and social consequences for both the dying individual and their surviving loved ones. As noted earlier, these conversations can both help those involved better understand their own personal identities, as well as their relationship with each other. Many survivors noted that final conversations confirmed the relationship and its importance to both the survivor and their loved one. These conversations may also help to strengthen that relationship by providing a venue to celebrate their relationship and resolve any issues or problems. Additionally, as discussed previously, addressing difficult topics during final conversations may also help survivors let go of anger toward dying loved ones and allow them to reconcile a troublesome relationship.

During the recent pandemic, the dynamics of end-of-life conversations have been made more complex with the implementation of social distancing and no-gathering mandates. In many care facilities for older people, in which residents are especially susceptible to COVID-19, as well as intensive care units (ICU) at hospitals, visits by family and friends have been banned. For those approaching death, "goodbyes" have been rendered to loved ones over Facetime or Skype – often with the assistance of empathic nurses or healthcare workers. How the nature of these experiences affect survivors, and whether or to what extent these conversations differ from more "traditional" final conversations, will almost certainly be an area of future research.

There have been some guidelines from scholars about the "dos and don'ts" of how to talk to those dying as well as those recently bereaved. We present a summary of these recommendations in Table 6.1.[32]

While we do not wish to be overly prescriptive, as each person and each situation is different and demands their own accommodation, we would like to draw attention to the fact that *listening* is paramount in these interactions (which is consistent with study findings that non-listening in intergenerational interactions is problematic; see Chapter 4). Interestingly, one study asked young people what they should probably *not* say to those bereaved. Their responses included the following[33]:

> - "You must get on with life"
> - "I know exactly what you're going through"
> - "It was really a blessing, you must be relieved"
> - "Don't worry, it is for the best"
> - "Try to keep yourself together"

When those recently bereaved themselves were asked what were the kinds of things that were *actually said* to them, the overlap was startling. Much like knowing that patronizing talk is bothersome but still doing it (see Chapter 4), people often appear to know what they should not say, but still end up saying these things anyway. Tellingly, those bereaved reported being irritated and upset by these utterances, but also said they did not rebuke the sender for expressing them. Perhaps, unfortunately, this lack of confrontation facilitates these kinds of remarks appearing again in other circumstances.

Engendering Feelings of Control Over Death

We argue that having some sense (or not) of being in one's control of death and dying, and communicating about these topics, can have implications for people's health and well-being. A useful communication theory here is *uncertainty reduction theory*.[34] This theory proposes that people need to make sense of the self, relationships, and their surroundings, and that they constantly seek ways to control their lives, make future events more predictable, and find areas by which they can engage in activities that give them a sense of purpose. By seeking and possibly gaining control over a situation, people lessen the ambiguities of life.

Aging is an inherently uncertain experience. As they age, individuals will often say such things as: "I don't know how I am supposed to act; I've never been this old before!" One of us received a birthday card[35] recently that said on the front, "Know how the well-adjusted deal with aging?" On the inside was written, "Neither do I! Happy Birthday." These phrases and sentiments suggest that people have little or no frame of reference for the experiences to come in the next age phase along their lifespan, let alone their final days. Some people may find such uncertainty anxiety-provoking or difficult to cope with. To address these anxieties and concerns, we encourage individuals to talk to people who can help them cope with their lack of control over death and dying, because in doing so, they may gain some command of it.

Although some people express not caring what happens to them once they are dead, other people cope with the idea of their own death and its inevitability by planning their funeral and their legacy to those left behind. Hence, when people try to plan their funerals, they often do so because they want to exercise control over the unknown, which can help quell some of their fears. For example, Helen Gurney Brown, the then 71-year-old editor of *Cosmopolitan* magazine, was described as outlining what she wished to wear:

Talking About Death – Or Not 99

> She later reveals that when she planned her burial she stipulated that she be laid to rest in her newest Pucci creation. A clingy little print chemise with a short hemline dripping flapper fringe. Just my style, she says, It's wispy, colorful and sexy!

Many of our students are horrified by the idea of someone planning their own funeral, seeing it as a rather macabre plan. However, for those who are older, it may make perfect sense to be the Master of Ceremonies of this last event.

A classic example of this control was in the funeral service of Prince Philip – the Duke of Edinburgh and Queen Elizabeth II's Consort. This was a low-key public affair as requested by the Duke, yet he had for years planned it with so-called "military precision," including the details of the service and the custom-made vehicle he himself had designed to carry his coffin. Similarly, a close friend of one of us, knowing he was going to die of an incurable illness at an early stage in his life, videotaped a message to friends and family. He intended for this message to be played publicly for loved ones gathered for his funeral. Not only did this message of expressed gratitude contribute to his own sense of control at the end of his life, but it also made it vividly clear to those who were mourning his loss that he was in command of his destiny. In this videotape, he requested that those assembled leave the ceremony when it ended dancing the conga to the song, "Always look on the bright side of life!" Predictably, this "gift to them" – together with the upbeat eulogies that seemed appropriate to follow – was indeed experienced as a gift and had an enormous benefit of offering comfort and celebrating both who he was and

what he had achieved. As the character Madam C.J. Walker, played by Octavia Spencer, remarked as she was preparing her inheritance and business near to her death in the 2021 movie, *Self Made*, "I can control what I leave behind!"

Tributes to those grieving can provide tremendous group-based solace. An image of an aerial view of the area outside Buckingham Palace is included here, after the sudden and tragic death of Princess Diana in a car crash in 1997; this is an extreme example of such public tributes, but a powerful one. More conventional (and ritualized) funerals, as well as obituaries and events like celebrity TV tributes, can serve multiple, socially important functions, such as:[36]

- Maintaining social order, including reinforcing long-established, accepted rules and procedures, and dress styles
- Helping support beliefs in the afterlife
- Assisting in the process of grieving (and/or maybe stoicism)
- Providing an opportunity to express and cope with personal emotions, connection, love, and respect for the deceased
- Providing a recognized context for the expression of distress, anguish, sorrow, loss, regret, etc.
- Creating distance from overwhelming emotion
- Re-acquainting and networking with others connected to the deceased
- Facilitating the offering of emotional, informative, and physical support to the bereaved

Further, the long-standing informal personal portraits of those buried on tombstones (e.g., in Mediterranean cultures, such as Greece) portray a "life-like" ethos and remembrance. Not unrelatedly, in Săpânța, Romania, the so-called Merry Cemetery (illustrated here) shows a very different, if not joyful, scene

where epitaphs and images on gravestones celebrate, sometimes with wit, and secrets of the departed.

Many of the important social functions funerals serve have been disrupted during the COVID-19 pandemic. Mandates for social distancing have meant that no gatherings have been possible at funerals in many parts of the world, which has derailed the usual and accepted way of honoring and celebrating the dead. With these restrictions in place, at best, funerals can be held virtually; in other cases, celebrations of life have been delayed indefinitely.

Another way in which people can gain control over death and dying is assisted suicide, a highly controversial topic. When the topic is brought up for (legal or other) discussion, many have presumed that people would seek this procedure in alarming numbers if the means were available. In the state of Oregon, lawmakers and government officials have legalized suicide with the assistance of a physician with the Death with Dignity Act. Oregon is, as of the writing of this chapter, the only American state to pass such a law (1997). After the law was passed, the requests for lethal prescriptions increased, but the percentage of individuals that actually *chose to take* the prescription, and therefore end their lives, was significantly smaller. This supports the idea that people want to feel a sense of control over death – that is, to have a prescription that would allow them to end their lives if they chose to – but most people seeking this kind of control do not necessarily truly want to die. Statistics show that less than 1% of deaths in Oregon are due to physician-assisted suicide and, of those, most were well-educated, terminal cancer patients who were tired of battling the disease. During 2019, the estimated rate of deaths under the law was 51.9 per 10,000 total deaths in the state.[37]

Thus, we see that although very few people actually seize the opportunity to take death into their own hands, there is currency to the adage, "my life, my death." In fact, there is evidence that people's will to live, even in bad situations, is actually quite strong. In one study, researchers asked patients how long they would like to live in various hypothetical conditions (e.g., enduring severe pain; in-home-bed confinement).[38] Surprisingly, those who were elderly and frail wanted to live longer than their healthier peers, and under more severe medical circumstances. One potential explanation for this finding is that the frail can value life more because they can more acutely differentiate between it and death.

However, not all of us can control our destinies with dignity,[39] after "the fact" or before it. This is chronicled in a qualitative study where researchers explored the symbolically violent (and non-consensual) *de*-transitioning of trans people after their deaths.[40] For many families, it seems it is only after the restoration of their loved one's gender-assigned-at-birth that the deceased can be considered "mournable." This process is apparent with regard to the life and times of a trans woman named Jennifer Gable who died suddenly in Idaho. The person described in the obituary and laid out in the casket – with hair cut short and dressed in a man's suit – was unmistakably masculine. Jennifer's friends, already shocked by her sudden death, were even more shocked by her family's treatment of her. In Jennifer's obituary, her family emphasized the male-associated aspects of her life, including her dead name, Geoffrey, her heterosexual marriage to a woman, and her love of baseball. "Her father erased her identity," said Meghan Stabler of Human Rights Campaign. Her identity became yet another casualty in an ongoing pattern of physical, emotional, and symbolic violence visited upon transgender people in the United States. In life, the woman had done what was required to be seen as her authentic self, but she could not defend her identity after death. This anecdote offers a sobering example of the potential limits of exerting control over one's death and legacy.

Returning to the notion of giving back control to someone near to death, one of us recalls the number of instances, typically during a holiday dinner, when a relative – a father in this instance – would say, "I probably won't be here next year." Oftentimes, this would be followed up by statements like: "I've put some money away for you when I pass on for your boy's college days," and "I've cleaned the attic so you won't have to be bothered when I move on." How does one respond to such statements? It certainly is an uncomfortable, if not personally threatening, situation to think of one's relative (and especially parents) not being around anymore. Often, people sidestep or deflect the issues this raises, offering responses like: "You've got plenty of life left in you!" However, upon one of us figuring out that our relative's actual message for us was of a different order than we had initially realized, one insightful day another response to these statements was offered: "Thanks, that's enormously kind of you, and obviously you'll be missed terribly when you've gone!" Unlike previous occasions, his eyes lit up! At last, his efforts at making his kids know he was OK about dying, and at being in control not only of his destiny but ours, which were clearly important to him, were recognized and validated. Subsequently, his son also realized that not having to go through his father's possessions, and to decide what to keep and what not to, was in fact a huge and generous gift from his father.

Concluding Thoughts

We started this chapter acknowledging that death can have different social meanings, and socially related causes, across different cultures. However, most of the research we have discussed relates to the Western experience that families often avoid discussing this topic together, even when death is near. As one response to this culture of avoidance, so-called *Death Cafes* have recently emerged in the United States. The locations of these change and are places where members of the community are invited to tea and cookies to informally discuss issues related to death for 90 or so minutes. Of these events and efforts, the Coordinator of the Santa Barbara, California branch has said:

> I really see death as this sacred taboo we're not talking about [...] everything else has come out of the closet, cancer, alcoholism. Death is in the closet because it's in *everyone's* closet. Nobody wants to open it ... There's no getting out of here without it, so we might as well embrace it.

We have seen how conversations about death and dying may have psychological benefits for families, such as facilitating adjustment to the death of their loved one for survivors, and can be construed as "successful dying."[41] In line with this is the proclamation that "Death is the most precious thing that has been given to man."[42] However, we have also noted, talking about death or dying may not be the best recipe for all families. Scholars have underscored the importance of the role of practitioners and hospice care workers in encouraging conversations between patients with a terminal disease and their family members and loved ones about death and dying. These conversations may help individuals begin to accept and understand their impending loss, and subsequently experience improved psychological outcomes during their bereavement period. Such conversations may also help families to resolve any unfinished business, plan for the future, and work through potentially difficult emotions surrounding the impending loss. Families can also benefit from communicated guidance of healthcare and palliative support workers.[43] These workers can often provide insight into the specifics of what kinds of communication may occur at the end of life, and how this communication can function positively for the family.

The process of death and dying can take many turns, have many trajectories, and be exceedingly complex. Nonetheless, it is clear that communication is fundamental to effecting what has been termed a "good death" and, as discussed, serves diverse social and relational functions. We echo the sentiments found in the book *Tuesdays with Morrie*[44] that proclaimed, "Learn how to live, and you'll learn how to die. Learn how to die, and you'll learn how to live!" If we can somehow come to redefine our own dying (and perhaps that of others close to us) as the final *adventure*, some good outcomes may ensue. In the enthusiastic words of Marine Sergeant Rock: "Life's journey is not to arrive at the grave safely with a well-preserved body. But rather to skid in sideways, totally worn out, shouting: 'Holy shit, what a ride!'"

In Chapter 7, we move to the ultimate focus of this book, namely, successful aging, wherein we argue that one of the important elements of this process can be how people manage their own and others' deaths and dying.

Notes

1 Schultz, N. W., & Huet, L. M. (2001). Sensational! Violent! Popular! Death in American movies. *Omega – Journal of Death and Dying, 42*(2), 137–149. https://doi.org/10.2190/6GDX-4W40-5B94-MX0G; see also: Robinson, J. D. (2015). Mass media depictions of the dying process. In J. F. Nussbaum, H Giles, & A. K. Worthington (Eds.), *Communication at the end of life* (pp. 77–90). New York, NY: Peter Lang.

2 Carstensen, L. L. (2006). The influence of a sense of time on human development. *Science, 312*(5782), 1913–1915. https://doi.org/10.1126/science.1127488; see also: Kavedzija, I. (2020). "Introduction" The ends of life: Time and meaning in later years. *Anthropology & Aging, 41*(2), 1–8. https://doi.org/10.5195/aa.2020.320

3 See: Giles, H., Thai, C., & Prestin, A. (2014). End-of-life interactions. In J. F. Nussbaum (Ed.), *The handbook of lifespan communication* (pp. 405–423). New York, NY: Peter Lang.

4 Meier, E. A., Gallegos, J. V., Montross-Thomas, L. P., Depp, C. A., Irwin, S. A., & Jeste, D. V. (2016). Defining a good death (successful dying): Literature review and a call for research and public dialogue. *American Journal of Geriatric Psychiatry, 24*(4), 261–271. https://doi.org/10.1016/j.jagp.2016.01.135; see also: Pitts, M. (2011). Dancing with the spirit: Communicating family norms for positive end-of-life transition. In M. Miller-Day (Ed.), *Family communication, connections, and health transitions* (pp. 377–404). New York, NY: Peter Lang.

5 Kikuli, E. (2006). A good death in Uganda: Survey of needs for palliative care for terminally ill people in urban areas. *British Journal of Medicine, 327*(7408), 192–194. https://doi.org/10.1136/bmj.327.7408.192

6 Sheikh, A. (1998). Death and dying: A Muslim perspective. *Journal of the Royal Society of Medicine, 91*(3), 138–140. https://doi.org/10.1177/014107689809100307

7 Marchi, R. (2013). Hybridity and authenticity in U.S. Day of the Dead Celebrations. *The Journal of American Folklore, 126*(501), 272–301. https://doi.org/10.5406/jamerfolk.126.501.0272

8 Xu, Y. (2007). Death and dying in the Chinese culture: Implications for health care practice. *Home Health Care Management & Practice, 19*(5), 412–414. https://doi.org/10.1177/1084822307301306; Wu, A. M. S., Tang, C. T. S., & Kwok, T. C. Y. (2002). Death anxiety among Chinese elderly people in Hong Kong. *Journal of Aging and Health, 14*(1), 42–56. https://doi.org/10.1177/089826430201400103

9 See: Life expectancy of the world population. Retrieved April 1, 2021, from: https://www.worldometers.info/demographics/life-expectancy/#countries-ranked-by-life-expectancy

10 For readers interested in gang membership from a lifespan perspective and/or its intergroup communication dynamics, see Chapters 5 and 8, respectively: Decker, S. H., & Pyrooz, D. C. (Eds.). (2015). *The handbook of gangs*. Malden, MA: Wiley/Blackwell.

11 Goldade, J. (2018). Cultural spotlight: Tongan funeral traditions. Retrieved from: auwee.wordpress.com/2013/12/03/traditional-tongan-funerals/

12 Simpson, G. E. (1957). The Nine Night ceremony in Jamaica. *The Journal of American Folklore, 70*(278), 329–335. https://doi.org/10.23071.537806

13 Galvin, K. A. (2015). Family communication as a child is dying. In J. F. Nussbaum, H. Giles, & A. K. Worthington (Eds.), *Communication at the end of life* (pp. 139–156). New York, NY: Peter Lang.

14 See p. 5: Keeley, M. P., Giles, Howard, & Nussbaum, J. F. (2015). Introduction: Communicating at, for, and about the end of life. In J. F. Nussbaum, H. Giles, & A. K. Worthington (Eds.), *Communication at the end of life* (pp. 1–10). New York, NY: Peter Lang.

15 Hinton, J. (1998). An assessment of open communication between people with terminal cancer, caring relatives, and others during home care. *Journal of Palliative Care, 14*(3), 15–23. https://doi.org/10.1177/082585979801400305

16 McDonald, D. D., Deloge, J., Joslin, N., Petow, W. A., Severson, J. S., Votino, R., Shea, M. D., Drenga, J. M. L., Brennan, M. T., Moran, A. B., & Del Signore, E. (2003). Communicating end-of-life preferences. *Western Journal of Nursing Research, 25*(6), 652–666. https://doi.org/10.1177/0193945903254062

17 Stone, A. M., Mikucki-Enyart, S., Middleton, A. V., Caughlin, J. P., & Brown, L. (2012). Caring for a parent with lung cancer: Caregivers' perspectives on the role of communication. *Qualitative Health Research, 22*(7), 957–970. https://doi.org/10.1177/1049732312443428

18 Kaplowitz, S. A., Osuch, J. R., Safron, D., & Campo, S. (1999). Physician communication with seriously ill cancer patients: Results of a survey of physicians. In B. DeVries (Ed.), *End of life issues: Interdisciplinary and multidimensional perspectives* (pp. 205–227). New York, NY: Springer.

19 Kaplowitz, S. A., Campo, S., & Chiu, W. T. (2002). Cancer patients' desires for communication of prognosis information. *Health Communication, 14*, 221–241. https://doi.org/10.1207/S15327027HC1402_4

20 Thompson, T. L. (2011). Hope and the act of informed dialogue: A delicate balance of end-of-life. *Journal of Language and Social Psychology, 30*(2), 177–192. https://doi.org/10.1177/0261927X10397150

21 Yingling, J., & Keeley, M. P. (2007). A failure to communicate: Let's get real about improving communication at the end-of-life. *American Journal of Hospice and Palliative Medicine, 24*(2), 95–97. https://doi.org/10.1177/1049909106297244; see also: Zhang, A. Y., & Siminoff, L. A. (2003). Silence and cancer: Why do families and patients fail to communicate? *Health Communication, 15*(4), 415–429. https://doi.org/10.1207/S15327027HC1504_03

22 Caughlin, J. P., Mikucki-Enyart, S., Middleton, A. V., Stone, A., & Brown, L. (2011). Being open without talking about it: A rhetorical/normative approach to understanding topic avoidance in families after a lung cancer diagnosis. *Communication Monographs, 78*(4), 409–436. https://doi.org/10.1080/03637751.2011.618141

23 Back, A. L., Young, J. P., McCown, E., Engelberg, R. A., Vig, E. K., Reinke, L. F., Wenrich, M. D., McGrath, B. B., & Curtis, J. R. (2009). Abandonment at the end of life from patient and clinician perspectives. *Archives of Internal Medicine, 169*(5), 474–479. https://doi.org/10.1001/archinternmed.2008.583

24 See, for example: Emanuel, E. J., Fairclough, D. L., Wolfe, P., & Emanuel, L. L. (2004). Talking with terminally ill patients and their caregivers about death, dying, and bereavement: Is it stressful? Is it helpful? *Archives of Internal Medicine, 164*(18), 1999–2004. https://doi.org/10.1001/archinte.164.18.1999

25 White, Z. M., & Gilstrap, C. M. (2017). "People just don't understand": Challenges communicating home hospice volunteer role experiences to organizational outsiders. *Management Communication Quarterly, 31*(4), 559–583. https://doi.org/10.1177/0893318917696991; see also: Egbert, N. (2015). Hospice care and communication. In J. F. Nussbaum, H. Giles, & A. K. Worthington (Eds.), *Communication at the end of life* (pp. 157–174). New York, NY: Peter Lang.

26 See: Keeley, M. P. (2007). "Turning toward death together": The functions of messages during final conversations in close relationships. *Journal of Social and Personal Relationships, 24*(2), 225–253. https://doi.org/10.1177/0265407507075412; Keeley, M. P., & Koenig Kellas, J. (2005). Constructing life and death through final conversation narratives. In L. M. Harter, P. M. Japp, & C. S. Beck (Eds.), *Narratives, health, and healing: Communication theory, research, and practice* (pp. 365–390). Mahwah, NJ: Erlbaum.

27 Keeley, M. P., & Yingling, J. M. (2007). *Final conversations: Helping the living and the dying talk to each other.* Action, MA: Van de Wyk & Burnham; Foster, E., & Keeley, M. P. (2015). Conversations at the end of life. In J. F. Nussbaum, H. Giles, & A. K. Worthington (Eds.), *Communication at the end of life* (pp. 105–120). New York, NY: Peter Lang.

28 Tullis, J. A. (2015). End of life communication and spirituality. In J. F. Nussbaum, H Giles, & A. K. Worthington (Eds.), *Communication at the end of life* (pp. 61–76). New York, NY: Peter Lang; Moberg, D. O. (2012). *Aging and spirituality: Spiritual dimensions of aging theory, Research, practice, and policy.* New York, NY: Routledge; Crowther, M. R., Parker, M. W., Achenbaum, W. A., Larimore, W. L., & Koenig, H. G. (2002). Rowe and Kahn's Model of successful aging revisited: Positive spirituality – The forgotten factor. *The Gerontologist, 42*(5), 613620. https://doi.org/10.1093/geront/42.5.613.

29 For atheists and the "gift of dying" see: Burley M. (2012). Atheism and the gift of death. *Religious Studies, 48*(4), 533–546. https://doi.org/10.1017/S003441251200011X

30 See: Rueyling, C., & Chen, G.-M. (2003). Buddhist perspectives and human communication. *Intercultural Communication Studies, 12*(40), 65–80. Retrieved from

https://web.uri.edu/iaics/files/04-Rueyling-Chuang-Guo-Ming-Chen.pdf; see also: Gire, J. (2014). How death imitates life: Cultural influences on conceptions of death and dying. *Online Readings in Psychology and Culture, 6*(2). https://doi.org/10.9707/2307-0919.1120

31 See: p. 243: Keeley, M. P. (2007). "Turning toward death together": The functions of messages during final conversations in close relationships. *Journal of Social and Personal Relationships, 24*(2), 225–253. https://doi.org/10.1177/0265407507075412

32 Miller, V. D., & Knapp, M. L. (1986). The *post nuntio* dilemma: Approaches to communicating with the dying. *Annals of the International Communication Association, 9*, 723–738. https://doi.org/10.1080/23808985.1986.11678634

33 Lehman, D. R., Ellard, J. H., & Wortman, C. B. (1986). Social support for the bereaved: Recipients' and providers' perspectives on what is helpful. *Journal of Consulting and Clinical Psychology, 54*(4), 438–446. https://doi.org/10.1037/0022-006X.54.4.438

34 Berger, C. R. (2016). Uncertainty reduction strategies. In C. R. Berger, M. E. Roloff, S. R. Wilson, J. Dillard, J. Caughlin, & D. Solomon (Eds.), *The international encyclopedia of interpersonal communication* (Vol. 3, pp. 821–825). New York: Wiley/Blackwell. https://doi.org/10.1002/9781118540190.wbeic032; see also: Afifi, T. D., & Afifi, W. A. (Eds.). (2009). *Uncertainty, management, and disclosure decisions: Theories and applications.* New York, NY: Taylor & Francis.

35 For age issues relating to birthday cards, see: Robertson, G. (2017). Aging and agism: The impact of stereotypical attitudes on personal health and well-being outcomes and possible personal compensation strategies. *Self & Society, 45*(2), 149–159. https://doi.org/10.1080/03060497.2017.1334986; see also: Kelly, L. E., Knox, V. J., Gekoski, W. L., & Evans, K. M. (1987). Age-related humor as an indicator of attitudes and perceptions. *The Journal of Social Psychology, 127*(3), 245–250. https://doi.org/10.1080/00224545.1987.9713690

36 O'Rourke, T., Spitzberg, B. H., & Hannawa, A. F. (2011). The good funeral: Toward an understanding of funeral participation and satisfaction. *Death Studies, 35*(8), 729–750. https://doi.org/10.1080/07481187.2011.553309; for the role of music fulfilling similar functions, see: Caswell, G. (2011–2012). Beyond words: Some uses of music in the funeral setting. *Omega, 64*(4), 319–334. https://doi.org/10.2190/om.64.4.c

37 Oregon death with dignity: Annual Report released 2020. Retrieved from: https://www.deathwithdignity.org/oregon-death-with-dignity-act-annual-reports/

38 Winter, L., & Parker, B. (2007). Current health and preferences for life-prolonging treatments: An application of prospect theory to end-of-life decision making. *Social Science and Medicine, 65*(8), 1695–1707. https://doi.org/10.1016/j.socscimed.2007.06.012

39 Englehart, K. (2021). *The inevitable: Dispatches on the right to die.* London: Macmillan.

40 Whitestone, S. B., Giles, H., & Linz, D. (2020). Un-mournable lives: The precariousness of transgender identities. *Sociological Inquiry, 90*, 316–338. https://doi.org/10.1111/soin.12357; see also: Weaver, K. K. (2020). Paying your respects: Transgender women and detransitioning after death. *Death Studies, 44*(1), 58–64. https://doi.org/10.1080/07481187.2018.1521886

41 See again: Meier, E. A., Gallegos, J. V., Montross-Thomas, L. P., Depp, C. A., Irwin, S. A., & Jeste, D. V. (2016). Defining a good death (successful dying): Literature review and a call for research and public dialogue. *American Journal of Geriatric Psychiatry, 24*(4), 261–271. https://doi.org/10.1016/j.jagp.2016.01.135

42 p. 104: Weil, S. (2004). *The notebooks of Simone Weil* (Vol. 1). trans. A. Wills. London: Routledge.

43 Whitney, A. (2015). Discourse "on or about dying": Palliative care. In J. F. Nussbaum, H. Giles, & A. K. Worthington (Eds.), *Communication at the end of life* (pp. 27–42). New

York, NY: Peter Lang; Wittenberg-Lyles, E., Goldsmith, J., Ferrell, B., & Ragan, S. L. (2013). *Communication in palliative nursing.* New York, NY: Oxford University Press; see also: Wittenberg, E., Goldsmith, J.V., Ragan, S. L., & Parnell, T. A. (2020). *Communication in palliative nursing: The COMFORT model* (2nd ed.). New York, NY: Oxford University Press.

44 Albom, A. (1997). *Tuesdays with Morrie: An old man, young man, and life's greatest lesson.* New York, NY: Doubleday; see also: Vail, K. E., III, Juhl, J., Arndt, J., Vess, M., Routledge, C., & Rutjens, B. T. (2012). When death is good for life: Considering the positive trajectories of terror management. *Personality and Social Psychology Review, 16*(4), 303–329. https://doi.org/10.1177/1088868312440046

7 Successful Aging and Communication

Throughout this book, we have provided overviews of research within, and ideas arising from, the study of communication and aging that we hope readers will have found to be of interest, both conceptually and practically. In this chapter, we introduce the notion of "successful aging" and pull together ideas we have developed throughout the book to consider their connections to, and implications for, experiences of successful aging. More specifically, we first review how scholars have examined successful aging, then discuss different age ideologies, or sets of attitudes related to aging, which people develop across the lifespan. We then present a theoretical model that depicts how communication relates to successful aging and provide an overview of recent research that has been guided by this model.

In this, our aim is to provide some research-informed suggestions for those seeking to get the most out of their later years. However, we emphasize that what follows is – of course – not some kind of panacea for growing older gracefully. Many factors are responsible for how we age and cope with aging (see Chapter 8), and people can and do have different experiences with these factors (and in different combinations). Accordingly, there is no single "best" or "one-size-fits-all" way to manage aging. However, there is research to suggest that some approaches and courses of action are likely to be more beneficial than others.

Successful Aging: Its Meanings and Components

The notion of "successful aging" has been given many different labels, such as "productive aging," "effective aging," "robust aging," "aging well," and "positive aging." To date, there are at least 29 different scholarly definitions of it;[1] readers of this book likely have their own ideas of what aging "successfully" means to them. In addition to differences in the content of definitions, there have also been critiques of these definitions, as well as differences in how "successful aging" is conceptualized across cultures.[2] In what follows, we discuss some characteristics that are often associated with successful aging and offer a definition that we find useful in the context of our focus on communication.

DOI: 10.4324/9780429330681-7

When people talk about getting older, there is sometimes a tendency to think that longevity is the goal. For us, "successful aging" does not necessarily mean maximizing longevity: indeed, we believe that a person could live quite a long time yet age quite *un*successfully. Similarly, people often think that slowing the pace of time signals a "successful ager." From such a perspective, using Botox, facelifts, silicone injections, and other body-altering operations to remove markers of old age could be linked with successful aging (see Chapter 5). We do not endorse this view of aging; similar to longevity, we contend that one could appear quite "youthful" for one's age but in fact be aging quite *un*successfully.

Many definitions of successful aging include the notion of *physical* well-being, such as freedom from disability[3]. However, when we look at studies that examine the proportion of older adults that fulfill such physical criteria (i.e., freedom from disability), it is typically quite low. When those same older adults are asked to evaluate how successfully they *feel* they were aging, however, many more people report that they are aging successfully.[4] In other words, while physical health is certainly important (as the adage, "If you don't have your health, you have nothing," would suggest), there are clearly other factors that also affect how people experience the process of aging, and how positive or successful they feel that experience is.

Thus, in line with a growing body of scholarly work on this topic, we contend that *successful aging*, broadly defined, is not about being in perfect physical health, or eliminating the traces of aging. Rather, it is about embracing one's age, taking advantage of opportunities, and building healthy relationships with friends and other loved ones in a way that fosters contentment with a person's current stage of life. In this regard, we favor a definition that considers successful aging as a subjective, psychological experience, rather than an objective set of benchmarks that one achieves or a set of metaphorical boxes one "checks." One such definition that we favor is the following:[5]

> Successful aging is a highly individualized and subjective concept and is recognized when an older individual is able to achieve desired goals with dignity and as independently as possible. This means that successful aging is possible for a nursing home resident whose goal is to be able to maintain health and complete basic activities as well as for a recent retiree whose goal is to be an active member in the community.

As this definition suggests, what allows people to feel they are achieving their goals, or content with their life circumstances, is highly individual. There are, however, some factors that frequently have a role in helping people age successfully (in whatever form that takes). One factor is one's finances. Here, we wish to make clear that we are not proposing that money can "buy" positive experiences of aging, or that having ever greater financial resources should map to ever greater success in aging. Rather, being financially secure to the extent needed to cover one's basics needs and wants – such that finances do not present a significant source of stress – tends to help position individuals to age successfully. Conversely, not being financially solvent to this extent may hinder people's ability to age successfully. The importance of finances is reflected in the following quotes from Jane Bryant Quinn, a financial journalist:[6]

> It's daring and challenging to be young and poor, but never to be old and poor. Whatever resources of good health, character, and fortitude you bring to retirement, remember also to bring money!

Another factor we might consider is a person's psychological perspective on their life. In line with the definition that we quoted earlier, a number of scholars have suggested that successful aging is closely linked to subjective (i.e., psychological) well-being and people's satisfaction with life. Examples of psychological experiences and approaches to life associated with satisfaction with life are as follows:[7]

- Taking pleasure from the round of activities that constitute everyday life – a *zest* for life
- Regarding life as meaningful and accepts resolutely that which life has been
- Feeling successful in achieving major goals
- Holding a positive image of oneself
- Maintaining happy and optimistic attitudes and mood

Age Ideologies

In addition to the factors and indices of life satisfaction we have just discussed, we would also like to highlight three *age ideologies* related to successful aging. Age ideologies are sets of attitudes and feelings about aging that people develop across the lifespan. These sets of attitudes are socially constructed and are therefore potentially amenable to change. Thus, even if readers do not currently embrace the ideologies we outline later, they can adopt or move toward adopting these approaches if they so wish.

Motivated acceptance is the first of these age ideologies and refers to a mentality that not only accepts the life stage that a person is at but relishes its unique prospects and potentials. We believe it is healthy and productive to not fight one's current age and life stage (which generally cannot be changed) and instead to try to focus on positive aspects of the present. Indeed, we would counsel teenagers, many of whom cannot wait to be older so they can enjoy some of the advantages of "coming of age," that they might be losing out on the many life gems that being *their current age* provides them. Instead, we would encourage young adults to set and strive for goals, but also to appreciate what their present situation may offer them. Even early in the lifespan, adopting an ideology of motivated acceptance can lay down foundations for people to become comfortable nurturing and nourishing being who they are at any age. Focusing on the positive aspects of each stage in life also positions people to anticipate and expect that subsequent life phases – in all due time – will open up new and exciting experiences.

At the other end of the lifespan, it is not uncommon for older adults to have regrets or to reflect on lost opportunities from some point in their past; these may be particularly acute when an individual feels they have no recourse to redress them anymore.[8] Here, rather than wishing one were further along in the life course (as teenagers might), older people may wish they could return to a previous life stage to "right" these "wrongs." The political novelist Benjamin Disraeli captures this sentiment: "Youth is a blunder; manhood a struggle; old age a regret."

Dwelling on and continually ruminating about past events that cannot be changed, and blaming oneself for the nature or outcome of those events, can lead to bitterness. Regret and bitterness, in turn, have been shown to take a toll on psychological well-being later in life.[9] Further, (repeatedly) talking about such events can foster a communicative climate that is less than optimal for everyone involved. Given these considerations, we suggest it is important to try to let go of regrets about past events that cannot be remedied and instead seek ways to make peace with, or compensate for, prior disappointments. For example, an older person who regrets not having had their own children could decide to help care for others' children, and/or get involved in related pursuits in their local community (see selective optimization and compensation theory, Chapter 1).

Closely related, in the spirit of this ideology, we encourage people to embrace identities that are consonant with their age, but not defined or limited by it. In an interview with the *Boston Globe* in 2000, at the age of 95, the Nobel Prize-winning poet Stanley Kunitz stated, "I never think of myself as having outlived my useful existence. I don't wake up as a nonagenarian. I wake up as a poet. I think that's a big difference." We agree that this *is* an important difference and suggest that this perspective provides a helpful model for ways to live with one's age without being constrained by it. This stance also highlights the importance of seeking out identities or ways of viewing oneself that extend beyond chronological age.

Although we advocate for acceptance of one's age and life stage, we also want to emphasize that this should not be mistaken for complacency or resignation. A prominent scholar of aging offers a similar perspective, noting that when people become too complacent about their current situation, and do not worry at all about the future, this can also be problematic:[10]

> "It's good to have some anxiety about aging if it gets you moving and taking care of yourself, but it's bad if you become incapacitated by it."

In addition to providing motivation to take care of oneself, caring about one's future can also help people stay active and involved in life more generally. When we do, there is value in remaining passionate and engaged in life to the last. As the Welsh poet, Dylan Thomas, advised of the twilight years, "Do not go gentle into that good night. Old age should burn and rave at close of day."

A second age ideology we advocate is termed *studenthood*. This ideology encompasses the values of learning and engaging new ideas across the lifespan. Often, people think about education and knowledge-seeking as the province of the young. However, research suggests that maintaining a heightened sense of curiosity and an active mind is health-promoting. We firmly believe that one *can* teach an "old dog new tricks," and that the dog will be better for it. In the spirit of embracing studenthood, Clint Eastwood, the Hollywood actor and movie director, once said:[11]

> I'd like to be a bigger and more knowledgeable person 10 years from now than I am today. I think that for all of us, as we grow older, we must discipline ourselves to continue expanding, broadening, learning, keeping our minds active and open.

One way of embracing studenthood is continuing to take part in structured education, such as classes, throughout (or later in) the lifespan. In the United States, there are programs that allow for free or discounted college courses for older people in all 50 states. Other options for continuing education can be found in programs and organizations for older people, such as one in Los Angeles (EngAGE), which offers arts, computer, and other topic-based classes to people in their apartment buildings.[12] Older adults can also take classes offered by other local entities, including their city or county, junior/community college, or other community organizations (e.g., music stores or dance studios).[13] There are also an increasing number of (free) online courses being offered, many of which are created by instructors at major universities, offering a growing range of opportunities to learn from the comfort of one's home. This growth in online learning options has been accelerated by the 2020 coronavirus pandemic, and we expect (and hope) that some of these increased offerings are likely here to stay. The ability to take courses from home expands options for lifelong learning considerably, as it allows people whose mobility may be more limited (e.g., by health conditions, being unable or preferring not to drive) to continue to participate in a wide range of learning activities.

The ideology of studenthood also encompasses the notion of seeking to keep abreast of technological developments,[14] such as social media, texting, and personal computing, and to keep up with current events. Doing so can help people to stay engaged and involved in contemporary life and facilitates interactions with conversational partners of all ages. This engagement, in turn, can have positive social and psychological benefits for all parties involved.

We also propose that studenthood encompasses being open-minded and flexible in one's worldview. People of all ages should expect, and be actively prepared for, inevitable and ongoing changes in language use, lifestyles, architecture, and literature, as well as the ongoing evolution of cultures and ways of thinking. We wish to emphasize that being open-minded and prepared for change does not necessarily mean people cannot be critical of changes. Indeed, it is quite possible that people will encounter new styles, practices, or social mores that they are not especially fond of (and this can occur at any point during the lifespan).

Although it is common for members of older generations to question social and cultural changes, we would argue that it generally is not productive or helpful to vocally criticize these changes, particularly when talking with members of younger generations. In this, we remind readers that older adults can be seen as patronizing when they disapprove of youth (see Chapter 4), and by extension, the values and ideas that younger generations are embracing. Rather than rejecting or complaining about changes in the world, we encourage readers to think critically and reflect on them. By the same token, we also encourage them to be thoughtful about the potential outcomes of different ways of communicating about these changes with different audiences and in different contexts, and make informed decisions about how they choose to engage with these issues.

The third and final age ideology we would like to highlight is an appreciation that the lifespan is an *interculturing* process.[15] By this, we mean that as people move along the lifespan they participate in different and distinct "cultures" associated with different ages and life stages. These cultures are formed by developmentally determined aspects of a given phase of the lifespan (e.g., growing into awareness of the world as children; individuating and launching one's own life as teenagers and young adults; starting one's own family or independent life trajectory in middle adulthood) and the historical moments in which they are embedded. As a metaphor for our passage through these cultures across their lives, we suggest thinking of the lifespan as a 400 meter hurdle race. The hurdles stand for the (approximate) age boundaries that we have to "jump over" to enter into the next culture or phase of life. Hopefully, we arrive at the finish line having successfully negotiated each hurdle – in life as in a race, one cannot turn around and try and go over a hurdle again.

Both the inability to "return" to previous cultures, and the way in which these cultures are embedded in particular moments in historical time, became clear to two of the authors when their then pre-teenaged son told them to turn off the popular music TV channel they were watching, and then told them never to turn it on again! He emphasized that this channel was "his" (and his age cohort's), and not theirs. This was quickly followed up by his also admonishing them for using the word "cool." Such media and language were part of what their son and his friends constituted their *culture*, and it was not theirs to "mess with." This culture was given to them by society, big business, and so forth, but their son and his peers, like all consumers of culture, also co-constructed it.

Appreciating this idea of age- and generationally grounded "cultures" can be very important for rearing (or even just talking to) a child or adolescent. The period they are going through is not simply a "passing phase" that will be grown out of. Rather, children and adolescents are participating in cultures with their own unique rules, standards, loyalties, dignity, expectations, and norms for acting and communicating. If we are able to recognize this, it can help us act in ways that may render intergenerational communication less problematic, and perhaps richer. More generally, thinking of life as a sequence of cultures, the complexities of which are only beginning to be understood, may help us better appreciate and cope with moments where we feel a gulf or disconnect between our own experiences and those of people of other ages.

Table 7.1 shows a small selection of the value systems – although different commentators differ in the ways they ascribe them – that people were born into at different points in history, which suggest contrasting cultures in the sense we have described here.[16]

Often, generational cultures are shaped by shared experiences of indelible historic events. The Holocaust, the Franco era, the political and social unrest of the 1960s, September 11th, 2001 (when terrorists piloting hijacked planes destroyed New York's Twin Towers), and an abundance of other difficult or challenging historical times have enduring memories for those that survived them. Quite likely, the coronavirus pandemic of 2020, as well as the swell of protests against systematic racism and racial injustice during the same year, will soon be considered in similar terms. One can anticipate the day when our grandchildren will have no first-hand associations with some of the events we

Table 7.1 Generational Cohorts and Selected Values

Traditionalists ("Silent Generation")	Baby Boomers	Generation X	Millennials (Generation Y)	Generation Z
• Born 1928–1945 • Worked long and hard • Patriotic • Lived through Great Depression	• Born 1946–1964 • Competitive • Materialistic • Deeply connected to careers	• Born 1965–1980 • Self-reliant • Distrustful of institutions • Resourceful	• Born 1981–1995 • Likely to question • Value teamwork and collaboration • Value work-life balance	• Born after 1995 • Progressive • Support activist government • Hold positive views of racial/ethnic diversity

have listed here, or any real empathy when, at their bemusement, members of the generations that lived through them might refer back to them. But it is important to underscore the role of these events in shaping the culture(s) of the generation(s) that experienced them.

While generational differences in culture within a nation or region can be significant, as we have just described, such differences can be even greater for different generations of immigrants. When families move to a new part of the world, they may experience additional cultural adjustments and dilemmas, particularly as younger adults straddle heritage- and host-nation cultures. Indeed, problems (let alone conflicts) and needed adjustments can become acute when children of first-generation immigrants grow up in a local youth culture with very different values and communicative styles than the traditional (and oftentimes religious) ones often still adhered to by their parents.[17]

Today, it can feel as if generational changes are happening at an accelerated rate, spurred by rapid developments in communication technology and the exponential rise in the use of social media (e.g., Facebook, Twitter, Instagram). It is, however, worth noting that previous generations experienced similar developments. For instance, Boomers experienced television in a way that was largely unimaginable in a comparable time in Traditionalists' lives. Video games and personal computers became part of Generation Xers' everyday lives in ways that were largely unimaginable in a comparable time in Boomers' lives. Millennials largely pioneered using mobile phones for (primarily) social uses; as of 2019, more than 90% of this generation owns a smartphone, and more than 85% uses social media.[18] Generation Z, in turn, is the first to grow up with ubiquitous and continuous Internet connectivity and mobile devices as a routine characteristic of everyday life (at least, in the West).

Thinking about age groups as having, and participating in, distinct cultures thus offers an alternative perspective on differences we may experience when we encounter people from other age groups. When someone attributes the strangeness of what another person who is older (or younger) is saying or doing to "age," we note that it actually may have little to do with *age* discrepancies per se. Rather, the apparent strangeness is likely due to the quite different "cultures" into which both sides were socialized. Being open to this possibility may lead to more effective, or at least more empathic, communication between members of different age groups.

A *Communication*-Centered Approach to Successful Aging

Our position, which has, of course, already permeated this book (see the Preface), is that communication practices can create and/or maintain the age ideologies we have just outlined. If one accepts that these ideologies are in fact meaningful contributors to successful aging, as we have proposed, it follows that communication practices are also critical to successful aging.[19] In this section, we lay out seven specific, interrelated communication practices that we argue have the potential to contribute to successful aging. We then summarize a growing body of research that has explored how these forms of communication (individually and in combination) relate to experiences of successful aging, as well as related emotional and cognitive experiences. Through these discussions, we aim to provide insight into the ways in which communication can contribute to successful aging specifically, and to avoiding negative experiences and ideologies related to getting older.

Following from extant research on communication and aging, we highlight the following domains of communication related to age and aging.

1. ***Self-categorizing with respect to age.*** When communicating with others, older adults often refer to themselves in terms of their age, or language that invokes an age category (e.g., "Well, I'm getting *old*, so …" "When you're *my age* you'll …"). One common way that age (problematically) creeps into everyday conversations is through age excuses, which attribute a problem or shortcoming to one's age. As discussed in Chapter 2, age excuses, as well as similar phrases that negatively invoke one's own age, have potentially negative consequences associated with them, as they reinforce stereotypes of aging as a process of decline. We also suggest that, to the extent that one can do so in a socially sensitive manner, readers should try to help make those who are engaging in age-based self-categorization more aware of the issues associated with this kind of messaging and encourage them to communicate in another way. One option, highlighted in the quote from the Nobel Laureate poet cited earlier, is to foster, prioritize, and self-categorize in terms of identities that are not related to their age, and instead are related to other valued aspects of their lives.

2. ***Actively categorizing, teasing, and reacting to others in terms of their age.*** There are many forms this can take; just a few examples include sending agist birthday cards and engaging in patronizing talk based on presumptions or stereotypes related to age (see Chapter 4). As another, one of us recalls an email, this time sent to an entire department at their workplace. It read, "Just in case you weren't sure, Mark is 50!!! Please join me in *torturing* him!" Mark has a strong personality and does not "take fools lightly" (as the saying goes), but this day he left the office looking visibly older than his years, having been duly "tortured" by all and sundry. Repeating agist ideas, even when they are directed at others, also reinforces these negative ideas and beliefs about aging for ourselves, which is not helpful for our own experiences of aging.

   More generally, we encourage readers to try to *personalize* the people they interact with – that is, recognize and respond to that person's unique, individual qualities rather than stereotypes or qualities associated with that person's observed age, and communicatively accommodate to those individual qualities. In Chapters 2 and 3, we discussed the ways in which feeling accommodated by younger people is related to older people's life satisfaction. In addition, and closely related, it is widely observed that much of how we think about ourselves is shaped by the way others treat us. For the sake of others' well-being, we should treat them with the same respect and care we would want to receive ourselves, which includes (but is not limited to) being accommodated to as individuals, regardless of our age.

3. ***Expressing positive emotions and optimism about the aging process, including both the past and the future.*** Expressions of optimism about aging explicitly recognize what is positive about one's situation (past, present, and future). Findings from what has been nicknamed the "Nun Study" provide insight into the potential value of this form of communication. Researchers in the United States tracked a relatively homogeneous sample (for example, in terms of education, beliefs, and lifestyle) of Catholic Nuns in the Midwest over many years. At the time of their initial vows, which is when they were about 22 years of age, researchers requested the nuns to write short autobiographies. These essays were later coded for positive, neutral, and negative words. Several decades later, researchers looked at the relationship between the nun's writing and their mortality rate and found that the more these nuns expressed positive emotional words in their early 20s, the lower their risk of mortality was 50 or 60 years later. Although these analyses were only correlations – and therefore, cannot show causality – they are thought-provoking; they also underscore the importance of looking at aging as a process that occurs across the lifespan. We suggest that conveying positive messages about life early on can help set a foundation for establishing favorable outcomes later in life (and there is almost certainly little harm in being more positive!).

    An important concept related to this third element of age-related communication – and particularly, about the notion of looking to the future with optimism – is *generativity*. This concept refers to thinking about, and engaging in acts that might benefit, the next generation, such as passing on talents and skills. Interestingly, it has been suggested that generativity really only helps bolster psychological well-being if these acts, and *talking about* them, are endorsed as valuable by younger recipients of them.[20] This highlights the importance of one's social environment, and communication within that environment, to experiences of successful aging.

4. ***Managing being the inevitable recipient of agism.*** Despite the most valiant efforts people may make to be positive about their own aging, and to surround themselves with those with similar intentions, it is near-inevitable that they will be on the receiving end of expressions of agism at some point in time. One of us recalls, at a decade-marked birthday, being harangued with comments from a couple of close friends about being older. He quickly retorted that his life had been rich over the past ten years and *they,* for their parts, might be fighting in court in ten years' time over their marriage and children – or not even be alive at all! At first, he felt good about having combated this agist "attack," but then heard one of his friends saying to the other as they were leaving, "Wow! He has a

real problem with his age, doesn't he!" In sum, his efforts were a failed response to agism that may have made matters worse. In contrast, the following (unverified) anecdote was told about Jeanne Calment, a French woman who lived to be 122 years:

> At the party celebrating her 120th birthday, a journalist said, hesitantly: "Well, I guess I'll see you … next year?"
> To which she replied in a flash: "I don't see why not, you look in pretty good health to me!"

Although it may be difficult to emulate Ms. Calment's priceless response in the spur of the moment, her example should inspire people to consider developing a repertoire of (rehearsed) responses to deflect agism when it occurs. Having ready, and deploying, such judicious responses allows people to assert their competence and agency, and avoid implicitly perpetuating both agist beliefs and the notion that it is socially acceptable to express those beliefs. If they are enacted prudently, we believe that responses to agist comments can help those around us question their assumptions. If enough of us were able to prompt such questioning, it might go some modest ways to changing negative stereotypes of older adulthood, and the negative intergenerational communication climate that accompanies those stereotypes (see Chapter 4 for a related discussion of responses to patronizing communication).

5. ***Being literate about agism in the mass media and in "anti-aging" products.*** The unfortunate reality is that most cosmetics companies (and indeed, most advertisements found in the mass media today) spend considerable effort trying to convince consumers that aging is a problem in need of a remedy. To age successfully, it may be advisable to push back against such notions (see, however, Chapter 5 for a discussion of inherent dilemmas).

   One way in which people can do so is to be (or become) aware of the conveyor belt of dubious age-related images and ideas appearing in the media that we discussed in Chapter 5, and to recognize that these do not reflect reality. Taking this a step further, people can also overtly question the appropriateness and accuracy of such content in public forums (e.g., in letters to newspaper editors or magazines), and in everyday conversations with friends and peers. If we do not call these depictions and products into question, they will persist, and the media ecosystem that fosters them will continue to thrive.

6. ***Discussing and communicatively planning our own and others' care and end-of-life needs with family.*** Death is an uncomfortable, even taboo, topic in Western societies, as we have discussed in Chapter 6. Unsurprisingly, people generally do not like thinking (or talking) about their loved ones becoming ill or impaired. While this is understandable, it is also problematic, as a reluctance to broach these topics often results in people avoiding

discussions about family members' wishes related to care and end of life. Indeed, few people in Western societies have explicit conversations about their end-of-life and/or health-related care wishes.

Some have argued that this avoidance is, in large part, because older and younger people do not feel competent or confident in raising such matters (a situation that is, unfortunately, perpetuated by avoiding these topics and/or considering them taboo). We certainly recognize and appreciate that such discussions can be challenging, emotionally and interpersonally. At least one study has suggested that people avoid such conversations because they think they already know what their family member would ultimately like or desire (despite not having discussed the issues).[21] Such thinking is potentially problematic because people's inferences about others' wishes can be partially or wholly incorrect. As discussed in the previous chapter, it has been found that those who *have* discussed these issues experience positive outcomes in both the short- and longer-term.[22] Knowing that one has had the chance to express one's love, emotions, ideals, and lifespan needs (including talking about issues of death and dying) with another leads to stronger bonds, feelings of control, and healthy relational and family identities (see Chapter 6).

7. **Embracing (or at least, remaining open to) new communication technology as a means to stay connected.** As discussed at several points in this book, a common stereotype of older adults is that they are "incompetent" with, or uninterested in, new technology. For those who did not grow up with the constant connectivity that Generation Z takes for granted, or who have lived the majority of their lives without texting or social media, it can be hard to grasp how younger generations can be so reliant on, and consumed by, these technologies. While some older adults enthusiastically engage with each new app or platform that emerges, many others question the need or value of such things (particularly when they have gotten along fine for many years without them).

We are not unbridled evangelists for new technology, but we suggest that it may be in one's best interests to be open to new forms of communication technology as they emerge, for (at least) two reasons. First, as discussed previously, we believe there is value in approaching life with an ideology of ongoing studenthood, and technology is one (of many) domains in which we can continue to learn and explore. Second, and perhaps more importantly, a common concern by and for older adults is that of social isolation; the 2020 coronavirus pandemic has underscored the importance of social connections for people of all ages, and the difficulties associated with isolation. Staying connected to those that we care about is critically important to our well-being, satisfaction with life, and even survival.[23] Indeed, in times of need, these connections can be sources of emotional and instrumental social support. Engaging with and using new technology can allow us to stay connected with people, and in ways, that we might not be able to otherwise.

Although one might wish that others – particularly, members of younger generations – would use the communication channels that one prefers or is accustomed to (e.g., phone), the reality is that people are more likely to communicate in ways that they find habitual and comfortable. If people (and particularly, older adults) can meet their conversational partners in those new technological spaces, they are more likely to maintain and foster those connections. It is also possible people who are initially reluctant to engage could find unexpected benefits of embracing these technologies, such as being in contact more frequently with loved ones (even if those contact points are short bursts of text, rather than a sustained conversation), or being able to see loved ones' faces (through video conferencing or video-calling applications).

Steps from Communication to Successful Aging

A growing body of research has been examining the associations between these forms of communication – both individually and in combination – and experiences related to successful aging. Specifically, researchers have looked at how these forms of communication relate to people's subjective experiences of aging well (i.e., successful aging), their perceptions of their ability to cope with aging (i.e., efficacy about aging), their emotions when they think about aging (i.e., positive and negative affect about aging), and the uncertainty they feel related to aging. Researchers have also examined how these forms of communication relate to outcomes like health-related quality of life and alcohol consumption (for those who do consume it). In line with our arguments in previous chapters, the big-picture take-away from this work so far is that communication matters and is related to all these experiences related to successful aging. In this section, we briefly highlight some specifics from the studies that have been conducted to date.

As discussed in the Preface, the work addressing these connections has been grounded in the communicative ecology model of successful aging (CEMSA).[24] The premise of this model is that people have agency over their own experiences of aging and that they can exert that agency through how they communicate about issues related to age and aging. The name of the model comes from the argument that the way we communicate about age and aging creates "ecologies," or social environments, that can facilitate or hinder people's experiences of aging successfully.

The CEMSA lays out a set of relationships between uncertainty about aging, communication about aging (both our own and others), affect related to aging, efficacy related to aging, and finally, experiences of successful aging (see Figure 7.1). The model proposes that "environmental chatter" – that is, the messages about aging we encounter in our social world (for instance, through conversations with friends and family, role models, consumption of mass media content, or participation in social activities) – affects nearly all the other

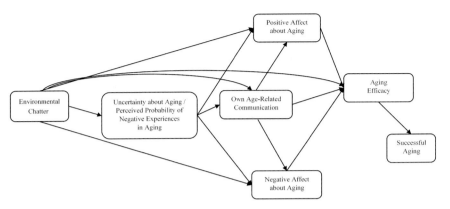

Figure 7.1 The Communicative Ecology Model of Successful Aging (CEMSA)[25]

variables in the model: our uncertainty about aging, our own communication, our affect related to aging, and our feelings of efficacy related to aging. These (theoretical) relationships highlight the importance of social interactions and social environments to people's experiences of growing older.

In turn, uncertainty related to aging is proposed to influence how we (ourselves) communicate about aging, as well as our affect (i.e., positive and negative emotions) and efficacy related to aging. Uncertainty can be thought of as taking two forms: first, it can be the gap, or discrepancy, between what we currently know about aging (and what our life will be when we get older), and what we wish we knew about this topic. Uncertainty can also be thought of as our *perceived probability of negative experiences* of aging – that is, our expectations that our future will involve negative (as opposed to positive) experiences.[26] Generally, the more we anticipate negative experiences in our future (and potentially, the larger the discrepancy between what we know and what we wish we knew), the more likely we are to communicate in ways that reflect or express uncertainty and negativity, experience higher levels of negative affect and lower levels of positive affect, and experience lower levels of efficacy related to aging.

The way we communicate (specifically, in terms of the domains outlined in the previous section) is also proposed to be related to our affect and efficacy. As one might guess, avoiding age-based self-categorization, expressing optimism about aging, managing being the recipient of agism, expressing healthy skepticism of negative age-based media messages, discussing care and end-of-life wishes, and embracing new technology are proposed to be associated with higher levels of positive affect and efficacy related to aging, and lower levels of negative affect. Positive and negative affect are also proposed to be related to efficacy, with higher levels of positive affect and lower levels of negative affect associated with higher levels of efficacy. Finally, efficacy is proposed to (directly) predict people's experiences of successful aging.[27]

Most studies guided by the CEMSA have looked at *profiles* of communication about aging, or the patterns of how people enact the different communicative behaviors we have outlined earlier in combination. Most consistently, three profiles of communication about aging have emerged: *engaged*, *disengaged*, and *bantering* profiles. People who have an *engaged* profile of communication behaviors – so named because they are actively engaged in managing their own communication related to aging – tend to avoid self-categorizing in terms of age and teasing others about age, express optimism and positivity about aging, seek to respond productively to agism when they encounter it, express skepticism about mass media's negative depictions of age, discuss care needs and wishes, and are open to the use of new technology to stay connected with people they care about.

People who have a *disengaged* profile of communication behaviors – so named because they appear to disengage from more or less all age-related talk – show comparatively low levels of the types of communication we have discussed. They generally do not self-categorize with respect to age, and they do not tease others about age. However, disengaged agers also tend to report lower levels of expressing optimism about aging, actively managing agism, and discussing care wishes with loved ones. They also tend to show a bit less enthusiasm for new technology than do engaged agers.

People with a *bantering* profile of communication behaviors exhibit a more varied mix of behaviors. They tend to express optimism about aging; however, they also tend to self-categorize with respect to age and categorize and tease others with respect to age. They do tend to try to actively manage agism (for example, they often have a comeback when someone makes an agist remark), but they do not engage in discussions about care wishes and needs to the same extent as people exhibiting an engaged profile. This group of people was labeled "bantering" because they tend to engage in a lot of the light, joking talk related to age (e.g., teasing, sending age-focused birthday cards, using age excuses), but do not necessarily address the more serious aspects of aging (reflected in less discussion of topics like future care needs).[28]

In a few studies, a profile that researchers have labeled *gloomy* has also emerged (though, we emphasize, it appears to be less common and appears less consistently than the three profiles we have just described). Gloomy agers tend to self-categorize in terms of age and show some tendencies toward managing agism in interaction and discussing care needs (though not to the same extent as engaged agers). However, they do not express optimism, tease or categorize others with respect to age, or engage with technology to stay connected with loved ones.[29]

When they looked at the associations between these different profiles of communication and experiences of aging, researchers found (as we might expect) that engaged agers often have the most positive experiences of aging, reflected in higher levels of self-reported successful aging and efficacy related to aging compared with disengaged or gloomy agers.[30] Engaged agers also tend to report more positive mental and physical health outcomes, including lower levels of alcohol use disorder symptoms (compared with gloomy agers), higher satisfaction with life (compared with disengaged agers), and healthier diets.[31] Disengaged or gloomy communication profiles have also been associated with higher levels of loneliness and depressive symptoms.[32] Interestingly, the findings associated with bantering agers are, like their communication, mixed: some research has found few differences between engaged and bantering agers' experiences of aging well,[33] while other work has found higher levels of stress in those with a bantering communication profile than in those with an engaged profile. It does appear that it is better to banter than to disengage – bantering agers reported higher satisfaction with life and better mental health than did disengaged agers.[34]

While most research has focused on profiles of communication, a few studies have examined each domain, or type, of communication separately. In such studies, expressing optimism about aging has had the strongest and most consistent relationships with successful aging and efficacy related to aging (see Chapter 8).[35] To date, nearly all the work that has been guided by the CEMSA has been quantitative in nature. Qualitative inquiries into the role of communication in successful aging (and its effects on other variables identified in the model, such as affect about aging and efficacy about aging), and particularly those that draw on naturalistic data, are an important direction for future work with this model. Additionally, nearly all published studies guided by the CEMSA have drawn on participants from the United States and New Zealand; more work is needed to determine whether and to what extent this model accurately captures the relationships between communication practices and successful aging in different cultural groups and subgroups who may have different communicative practices or norms around communication (see Chapter 8).

Finally, the studies we have summarized here investigated associations, or correlations, between communication and people's subjective experiences or attitudes toward aging. From the data alone, we cannot claim causality – that is, the evidence available does not explicitly show that communication is the *cause* of people's experiences and attitudes. Instead, it could be that having more positive (or negative) experiences of aging causes people to communicate in one or another of the ways we have described.

Recognizing that the world is a complex place, we suspect that reality is somewhere between these two causal extremes. Our experiences of aging likely affect our communication; for example, it is almost certainly easier to express optimism and positive emotions about aging when one is having a positive experience with the process of getting older. However, based on our knowledge of human communication, cognition, and social psychology, we also strongly believe that the way we communicate can and does affect our experiences of aging. So, while we cannot claim or promise that enacting an engaged profile of communication or expressing positive emotions and optimism about aging today will cause one to have more positive experiences of aging tomorrow, it may help, and almost certainly will not hurt.

Concluding Thoughts

In this chapter, we have argued for the importance of constructing and sustaining communication climates that collaboratively foster a more positive perspective on age and aging. In this way, we hope, readers can approach each life phase as an absorbing enterprise and challenge. We believe – and hope we have convinced readers – that older adulthood is a phase that should be embraced and enjoyed in-talk, rather than avoided, or begrudgingly accepted. Viewing old age as an adventure in communication has the potential to contribute to the psychological well-being of those who adopt this mantra.

Each of the seven elements of the communicative climate involves perspectives, skills, and practices that can be taught and learned at any age. Getting a better understanding of the effects of these different forms of communication, collectively and individually, will help us to target and tailor educational efforts, in addition to increasing our theoretical understanding of what contributes to successful aging, and by extension, psychological well-being for people across the lifespan. The research we have reviewed here has offered us a step toward understanding the relationship between different forms of communication and successful aging, but this work is arguably in its infancy. Additionally, as we have discussed throughout this book, there are a host of other factors that can affect both people's experiences of aging and their communication about it, such as people's race, ethnicity, sexual orientation, or socioeconomic status. Aging is a process that occurs in the context of a lifetime of experiences, and within larger social structures (see Chapter 3). In Chapter 8, we take a step back and examine successful aging in the context of these structures, and how it connects to other psychological processes, including resilience, hope, and empowerment.

Notes

1 Depp, C. A., & Jeste, D. V. (2006). Definitions and predictors of successful aging: A comprehensive review of larger quantitative studies. *The American Journal of Geriatric Psychiatry, 14*(1), 6–20. https://doi.org/10.1097/01.JGP.0000192501.03069.bc; see also: Phelan, F. A., & Larson, E. B. (2002). Successful aging: Where next? *Journal of the American Geriatrics Society, 50*(7), 1306–1308. https://doi.org/10.1046/j.1532-5415.2002.50324.x; Pruchno, R. A., Wilson-Genderson, M., & Cartwright, F. (2010). A two-factor model of successful aging. *Journals of Gerontology: Psychological Sciences, 65B*(6), 671–679. https://doi.org/10.1093/geronb/gbq051; Rowe, J. W., & Kahn, R. L. (1987). Human aging: Usual and successful. *Science, 237,* 143–149. https://doi.org/10.1126/science.3299702; Von Faber, M., et al. (2001). Successful aging in the oldest of old: Who can be characterized as successfully aged? *Archives of Internal Medicine, 161*(22), 2694–2700. https://doi.org/10.1001/archinte.161.22.2694; Wykle, M. L., Whitehouse, P. J., & Morris, D. L. (2005). *Successful aging through the lifespan: Intergenerational issues and health.* New York, NY: Springer.

2 Katz, S., & Calasanti, T. (2015). Critical perspectives on successful aging: Does it "appeal more than it illuminates"? *The Gerontologist, 55*(1), 26–33. https://doi.org/10.1093/geront/gnu027; Jensen, A., Claunch, K., Verdeja, M., Dungan, M., Goates, M., & Thacker, E. (2018). Successful aging: Cross-cultural comparison of older adults' lay perspectives. *Innovation in Aging, 2*(Suppl.1), 167. https://doi.org/10.1093/geroni/igy023.601; Nguyen, A. L., & Seal, D. W. (2014). Cross-cultural comparison of successful

aging definitions between Chinese and Hmong elders in the United States. *Journal of Cross-Cultural Gerontology, 29*(2), 153–171. https://doi.org/10.1007/s10823-014-9231-z

3 Depp, C. A., & Jeste, D. V. (2006). Definitions and predictors of successful aging: A comprehensive review of larger quantitative studies. *The American Journal of Geriatric Psychiatry, 14*(1), 6–20. https://doi.org/10.1097/01.JGP.0000192501.03069.bc

4 Depp, C. A., Vahia, I. V., & Jeste, D. V. (2012). Successful aging. In S. K. Whitbourne & M. J. Sliwinski (Eds.), *The Wiley-Blackwell handbook of adulthood and aging* (pp. 459–476). Chichester, UK: Wiley-Blackwell; see also: Montross, P., Depp, C., Daly, J., Reichstadt, J., Golshan, S., Moore, D., Sitzer, D., Dilip, D., & Jeste, V. (2006). Correlates of self-rated successful aging among community-dwelling older adults. *American Journal of Geriatric Psychiatry, 14*(1), 43–51. https://doi.org/10.1097/01.JGP.0000192489.43179.31

5 See pp. 144–145: Bieman-Copland, S., Ryan, E. B., & Cassano, J. (1998). Responding to the challenges of late life: Strategies for maintaining and enhancing competence. In D. Pushkar, W. Bukowski, A. Schwartzman, D. Stack & D. White (Eds.), *Improving competence across the lifespan* (pp. 141–157). New York, NY: Plenum Press.

6 See p. 842: Quinn, J. B. (1997). *Making the most of your money.* New York, NY: Simon & Schuster.

7 Neugarten, B. L., Havighurst, R. J., & Tobin, S. S. (1961). The measurement of life satisfaction. *Journal of Gerontology, 16*(2), 134–143. https://doi.org/10.1093/geronj/16.2.134

8 Beike, D. R., Markman, K. D., & Karadogan, F. (2009). What we regret most are lost opportunities: A theory of regret intensity. *Personality and Social Psychology Bulletin, 35*(3), 385–397. https://doi.org/10.1177%2F0146167208328329; Newall, N. E., Chipperfield, J. G., Daniels, L. M., Hladkyj, & Perry, R. P. (2009). Regret in later life: Exploring relationships between regret frequency, secondary interpretive control beliefs, and health in older individuals. *International Journal of Aging and Human Development, 68*(4), 261–288. https://doi.org/10.2190%2FAG.68.4.a

9 Bjälkebring, P., Västfjäll, D., & Johansson, B. (2013). Regulation of experienced and anticipated regret for daily decisions in younger and older adults in a Swedish one-week diary study. *GeroPsych: The Journal of Gerontopsychology and Geriatric Psychiatry, 26*(4), 233–241. https://doi.org/10.1024/1662-9647/a000102; Wrosch C., & Renaud J. (2011). Self-regulation of bitterness across the lifespan. In M. Linden & A. Maercker (Eds.), *Embitterment: Societal, psychological, and clinical perspectives* (pp. 129–141). Vienna, Austria: Springer.

10 See p. 42: Winerman, L. (2006). A healthy mind, a longer life. *Monitor on Psychology, 37*(10). Retrieved from: https://www.apa.org/monitor/nov06/healthy

11 See p. 164: Voorhees, R. (2002). *Old age is always 15 years older than I am.* Kansas City, MO: Andrew McMeel.

12 Rosenberg, T. (2012, August 12). For healthy aging, a late act in the footlights. *The New York Times.* Retrieved from: http://opinionator.blogs.nytimes.com/2012/08/15/for-healthy-aging-a-late-act-in-the-footlights/

13 For example, see: Pines, R., & Giles, H. (2020). Dancing while aging: A study on benefits of ballet for older women. *Anthropology & Aging, 41*(1), 83–94.

14 Cotten, S. R. (2017). Examining the roles of technology in aging and quality of life. *The Journals of Gerontology: Series B, 72*(5), 823–826. https://doi.org/10.1093/geronb/gbx109

15 Giles, H., & Coupland, N. (1992). *Language: Contexts and consequences.* Pacific Grove, CA: Brooks/Cole.

16 Myers, K. K., & Davis, C. W. (2012). Communication between generations. In H. Giles (Ed.), *The handbook of intergroup communication* (pp. 237–249). New York, NY: Routledge; see also Parker, K., & Igielnik, R. (2020, May 14). *On the cusp of adulthood and facing an uncertain future: What we know about Generation Z so far.* Pew Research Center: Social and Demographic Trends. Retrieved from: https://www.pewsocialtrends.org/essay/on-the-cusp-of-adulthood-and-facing-an-uncertain-future-what-we-know-about-gen-z-so-far/

17 Kalmijn, M. (2019). Contact and conflict between adult children and their parents in immigrant families: Is integration problematic for family relationships? *Journal of Ethnic and Migration Studies, 45*(9), 1419–1438. https://doi.org/10.1080/1369183X.2018.1522245

18 Vogels, E. A. (2019, September 9). *Millennials stand out for their technology use, but older generations also embrace digital life.* Pew Research Center: Fact Tank. Retrieved from: https://www.pewresearch.org/fact-tank/2019/09/09/us-generations-technology-use/

19 See also: Nussbaum, J. F. (1985). Successful aging: A communication model. *Communication Quarterly, 33*(4), 262–269. https://doi.org/10.1080/01463378509369606; Ryan, E. B., Meredith, S. D., MacLean, M. J., & Orange, J. B. (1995). Changing the way we talk with elders: Promoting health using the communication enhancement model. *International Journal of Aging and Human Development, 41*(2), 89–107. https://doi.org/10.2190%2FFP05-FM8V-0Y9F-53FX

20 For discussions of generativity, see: Nussbaum. J. F., Pecchioni, L. L., Robinson, J. D., & Thompson, T. L. (2000). *Communication and aging* (2nd ed.). Mahwah, NJ: Erlbaum; Cheng, S-T. (2009). Generativity in later life: Perceived respect from younger generations as a determinant of goal disengagement and psychological well-being. *Journal of Gerontology: Psychological Sciences, 64B*, 45–54. https://doi.org/10.1093/geronb/gbn027

21 Pecchioni, L. L. (2001). Implicit decision-making in family caregiving. *Journal of Social and Personal Relationships, 18*(2), 219–237. https://doi.org/10.1177%2F0265407501182004

22 Giles, H., Thai, C., & Prestin, A. (2014). End-of-life interactions. In J. F. Nussbaum (Ed.), *The handbook of lifespan communication* (pp. 405–423). New York, NY: Peter Lang; for a related discussion on future planning more generally, see: Prenda, K. M., & Lachman, M. E. (2001). Planning for the future: A life management strategy for increasing control and life satisfaction in adulthood. *Psychology and Aging, 16*(2), 206–216. https://doi.org/10.1037/0882-7974.16.2.206

23 Giles, L. C., Glonek, G. F. V., Luszcz, M. A., & Andrews, G. R. (2005). Effect of social networks on 10 year survival in very old Australians: The Australian longitudinal study of aging. *Journal of Epidemiology and Community Health, 59*(7), 574–579. https://doi.org/10.1136/jech.2004.025429

24 Fowler, C., Gasiorek, J., & Giles, H. (2015). The role of communication in aging well: Introducing the communicative ecology model of successful aging. *Communication Monographs, 82*(4), 431–457. https://doi.org/10.1080/03637751.2015.1024701

25 Adapted from: Gasiorek, J., Fowler, C., & Giles, H. (2016). Communication and successful aging. In J. Nussbaum (Ed.), *Communication across the lifespan* (pp. 35–50). New York, NY: Peter Lang. https://doi.org/10.3726/978-1-4539-1701-5

26 Gasiorek, J., Fowler, C., & Giles, H. (2019). Communication and successful aging: Testing alternative conceptualizations of uncertainty. *Communication Monographs, 86*(2), 229–250. https://doi.org/10.1080/03637751.2018.1538561

27 Fowler, C., Gasiorek, J., & Giles, H. (2015). The role of communication in aging well: Introducing the communicative ecology model of successful aging. *Communication Monographs, 82*(4), 431–457. https://doi.org/10.1080/03637751.2015.1024701; Gasiorek, J., Fowler, C., & Giles, H. (2016). Communication and successful aging. In J. Nussbaum (Ed.), *Communication across the lifespan* (pp. 35–50). New York, NY: Peter Lang. https://doi.org/10.3726/978-1-4539-1701-5; Gasiorek, J., Fowler, C., & Giles, H. (2019). Communication and successful aging: Testing alternative conceptualizations of uncertainty, *Communication Monographs, 86*(2), 229–250. https://doi.org/10.1080/03637751.2018.1538561

28 See: Gasiorek, J., Fowler, C., & Giles, H. (2015). What does successful aging sound like? Profiling communication about aging. *Human Communication Research, 41*(4), 577–602. https://doi.org/10.1111/hcre.12060; see also Gasiorek, J., Fowler, C., & Giles, H. (2016).

Communication and successful aging. In J. Nussbaum (Ed.), *Communication across the lifespan* (pp. 35–50). New York, NY: Peter Lang. https://doi.org/10.3726/978-1-4539-1701-5

29 Bernhold, Q., Gasiorek, J., & Giles, H. (2020). Communicative predictors of older adults' successful aging, mental health, and alcohol use. *International Journal of Aging and Human Development, 90*(2), 107–134. https://doi.org/10.1177/0091415018784715; Bernhold, Q. S. (2020). Patterns of age-related communication in families: A three-generation study. *Language and Communication, 72*(May), 79–92. https://doi.org/10.1016/j.langcom.2020.02.004

30 Gasiorek, J., Fowler, C., & Giles, H. (2015). What does successful aging sound like? Profiling communication about aging. *Human Communication Research, 41*(4), 577–602. https://doi.org/10.1111/hcre.12060

31 Bernhold, Q., Gasiorek, J., & Giles, H. (2020). Communicative predictors of older adults' successful aging, mental health, and alcohol use. *International Journal of Aging and Human Development, 90*(2), 107–134. https://doi.org/10.1177/0091415018784715; Bernhold, Q. S., & Giles, H. (2020). Older adults' age-related communication and routine dietary habits. *Health Communication, 35*(12), 1556–1564. https://doi.org/10.1080/10410236.2019.1652391

32 Bernhold, Q., Gasiorek, J., & Giles, H. (2020). Communicative predictors of older adults' successful aging, mental health, and alcohol use. *International Journal of Aging and Human Development, 90*(2), 107–134. https://doi.org/10.1177/0091415018784715

33 Fowler, C., Gasiorek, J., & Giles, H. (2015). The role of communication in aging well: Introducing the communicative ecology model of successful aging. *Communication Monographs, 82*(4), 431–457. https://doi.org/10.1080/03637751.2015.1024701

34 Gasiorek, J., & Barile, J. P. (2018). Associations between profiles of communication about aging and quality of life for middle-aged and older American adults. *International Journal of Aging and Human Development, 87*(2), 141–155. https://doi.org/10.1177/0091415017724546

35 Fowler, C., Gasiorek, J., & Giles, H. (2015). The role of communication in aging well: Introducing the communicative ecology model of successful aging. *Communication Monographs, 82*(4), 431–457. https://doi.org/10.1080/03637751.2015.1024701; Gasiorek, J., & Fowler, C. (2020). Effects of "environmental chatter" about age and aging on middle-aged and older adults' communication and perceptions of aging efficacy. *Western Journal of Communication, 84*(1), 98–122. https://doi.org/10.1080/10570314.2019.1637930

8 Conclusions and Vistas
Communicating Resilience, Hope, and Empowerment

Across this book, we have addressed distinct but related dimensions of aging, focusing on the role of communication in shaping these dimensions, and people's experiences of them. In the first edition of this book, we concluded with a discussion of the various ways that older adults can successfully age (now addressed in Chapter 7). For this volume, we have endeavored to think more critically about aging, and these efforts have been informed by the context in which we have been writing: the global COVID-19 pandemic and the economic crisis that has followed, as well as the racial reckoning that came to a head in the United States in the summer of 2020.

A critical aspect of successful aging that we have not yet addressed – and that has not received nearly as much attention as it should – is resilience. Over the lifespan, individuals come to experience the increasing specter and fear of time passing, searching for the existential "meaning of life," and knowing that there is an end to life.[1] Yet, people need to find ways to cope and live with these very challenges, and age successfully (or not). We suggest that resilience, along with the related concepts of hope[2] and empowerment, may help people "bounce back" and manage uncertainties, difficulties, and stresses, some of which are beyond their immediate control, as they age. More specifically, we will argue that resilience, hope, and empowerment affect and reinforce one another, and acquire much of their potency and impact on successful aging through *communicative* practices.

Our emphasis on these constructs stems from the recognition that people exist within larger social structures and systems. One of the major critiques of extant work on successful aging is that it positions successful aging as an individual accomplishment,[3] without necessarily recognizing the broader social context in which people live their lives. In addition to being individuals, people also belong to social categories (privileging and marginalizing) *beyond* those of age – see our discussion of intersectionality in Chapter 3 – that can enable or constrain their ability to engage in behaviors that are associated with successful aging. In this chapter, we will argue that within these larger systems and structures, people may build resilience over time and learn how to withstand challenges to their ability to age successfully, locate ways to feel empowered, and continue to have hope.

DOI: 10.4324/9780429330681-8

Lastly, in the final part of this epilogue, we will briefly overview the preceding chapters, drawing out how they have acknowledged that aging is dictated by culture, is a lifespan endeavor, and has applied implications for personal growth. Throughout this discussion, we will provide suggestions for future research. In so doing, we attempt to contribute in some modest way to the World Health Organization's call for 2020–2030 to be a decade for promoting healthy aging.[4]

Communicating Resilience, Hope, and Empowerment

Resilience has been defined as "the process of adapting well in the face of adversity, trauma, tragedy, threats or significant sources of stress."[5] We suggest that the benefits of adapting well may come, in part, from the responses that we get from others, such as admiration and respect, for such adaptive actions. Resilience has been studied internationally and across academic disciplines[6] (including social gerontology[7] and communication[8]) and has been invoked across a wide array of situations, including surviving and dealing with natural disasters, wars and violence, career setbacks, financial turmoil, family conflicts, and bereavement.[9] It has also been implicated as a factor in aging successfully.[10] While some scholars have looked at resilience as a personal trait that individuals are either born with (that is, *resiliency*) or acquired through socialization, there is also a significant body of work that approaches and conceptualizes resilience as a management *process*.[11]

Resilience has been studied across the lifespan as different risks, challenges, tests, and trials emerge at different ages.[12] Because people face different issues at different points in time, and people in different situations experience different challenges, there is no one-size-fits-all prescription for resilience. Rather, being resilient involves and manifests in different ways of coping across diverse sectors of society, especially when people are faced with social stigmas associated with being members of particular racial, ethnic, gender, and sexually oriented groups, to name but a few. In addition, there is a large body of literature that has demonstrated positive outcomes for those elders who possess high resilience. More specifically, research has shown, for older adults, that resilience has been associated with the social, psychological, and health benefits listed as follows (among others).[13]

- Positive emotions
- Social support
- Involvement and volunteering in the community
- Adaptive coping styles
- Hope
- Decreased depression
- Physical activity
- Healthy nutrition
- Longevity
- Successful aging

As the associations cataloged suggest, resilience is also a correlate of successful aging. Whether it is a causal factor, mediator, or outcome of successful aging – or perhaps all of these – has not been definitively established. However, some scholars have suggested "that achieving resilience should be *the focus* of aging, rather than striving for the traditional definition of successful aging"[14] (emphasis added). Some researchers have focused on the protective resources available through high resilience, developed across the lifespan, that give rise to what can be called *resilience repertoires*.[15] We think there is good potential for interventions focused on building and strengthening resilience (for instance, by helping people develop such repertoires). However, to date, few such interventions have been robustly designed or rigorously evaluated.[16] Interestingly, one intervention that was tested, and turned out to be successful, involved asking people to make journal entries of their expressions of gratitude to others.[17] Rather than advocate for individual-level interventions, however, we prefer to encourage efforts toward cultivating a sense of *collective* resilience. Here, we envision communities, networks, and institutions creating and sustaining *cultures* that communicate aging resilience[18] and that are accommodative and responsive to the unique demands of local and diverse communities.[19] In this sense, we see the potential for resilience to become an integral, systemic ingredient in different age groups' ways of thinking and operating in managing people's experiences of intersectionality.

As we discussed in Chapters 3 and 7, people in different social positions – which may be defined in terms of gender, race, ethnicity, socioeconomic status, or other factors – can have markedly different life experiences. This can include different degrees of exposure to discrimination and prejudice, different educational experiences and opportunities, different employment situations, and differential treatment by institutions like healthcare systems.[20] While largely context- and time-specific, the following situations offer some illustrations of the challenges older adults face because of their racial and ethnic background. In 2020–2021, older Asian Americans have been the targets of an increase in verbal and physical attacks, hate crimes, and discrimination that stem from people's ideas about the origin and spread of COVID-19.[21] These are, undeniably, racist responses to the devastating effects of the pandemic, being compounded by the racist and xenophobic references to COVID-19 as the "Kungflu" and "China virus" fueled by former President Donald Trump. For those older Asians who were, as Japanese American children, interned in camps for years during the 1940s in World War II, the current hate crimes are even more galling and frightening.[22]

In parallel, older Black Americans have had to contend with a lifetime of anti-Black racism, yet they had to face a further threat - the COVID-19 pandemic. These intersections of age and race came to a head in 2020–2021 as many Black elders were disproportionately dying from the virus due to race-based health disparities that made them more susceptible to contracting the virus. In addition, they experienced disparities in medical treatment where Black patients were denied ventilators, facetime with the doctors, or even a bed in intensive care units. It is also important to note that there were many older adults (of color) who could not afford to retire and, thus, were forced to continue working during pandemic lockdowns. Indeed, there were many whose work hours decreased significantly, and who suffered unthinkable economic hardship as a result. Experiences such as these can affect how people experience the process of aging psychologically, physically, and socially. As these two examples highlight, successful aging across the lifespan can be much more of a challenge for older people from disenfranchised groups than it is for white and/or wealthy Americans and, as such, may demand different forms of resilience.

In some cases, and for various psychological reasons, people can experience or express "identity denial," in which they reject certain social categorizations imposed on them by others (including age-based categorizations).[23] It is possible that, under certain circumstances, identity denial for older people of color can be seen to constitute its own form of resilience. Gratifyingly for future research, there are now tools for assessing linguistic indicators in texts that can allow us to make inferences about which group membership is salient for speakers in a given moment.[24]

For us, an important correlate of resilience is hope. At least one study guided by the communicative ecology model of successful aging (CEMSA) suggests that hope may be linked to successful aging;[25] in addition, hope has long been regarded as critical for adapting to ill-health, as well as to transcending many of the challenges of aging.[26] Hope has been defined as "expectancies that one can achieve goals through the combination of goal-directed planning and motivation."[27] Interestingly, much work emerging from hope theory,[28] unlike some work on resilience, relies on measuring hope as a trait-like disposition. Those high in hope believe they can plan at least one concrete way to achieve their goals and often contend they can generate multiple ways to achieve if a first plan fails.[29] People with high levels of dispositional hope also seem to devote less cognitive effort to processing discouraging and sad messages (as well as messages relating to negative aspects of aging) than those with lower levels of hope.[30] Hence, alongside a culture of resilience, it would seem that encouraging a hopeful disposition, in general, may prove helpful for navigating the challenges that people face across their lives (and more specifically, as we indicated in Chapter 6, for those enduring acute health threats). Cultivating hope also allows for a mindset that can form optimistic planning strategies as well as buffer some of the difficulties and inclinations toward unsuccessful aging people may experience. In addition to hope's role in helping people to orient toward less destructive thoughts and feelings about aging, we propose that the communicated *discourses* of hope and optimistic future prospects might also play a powerful role in managing the process of aging, both cognitively and affectively.

Moving to our final component of the communicated resilience-hope-empowerment triad, there has been much interest across the disciplines in the construct and process of empowerment.[31] In the discipline of communication, empowerment has not generated the same kind of attention as the other elements of this triad,[32] although it does appear as a central component in the

132 Conclusions and Vistas

so-called, *communication enhancement model of aging*.[33] This framework proposed (in tandem with social psychological theories of intergroup communication[34]) that if people interact with older people by first trying to discern individuating, rather than age-group-related, cues and accommodating to these personal characteristics, *both* younger and older can be "empowered." While empowerment has been defined in different ways, we favor the following conceptualization, which also is the foundation for a theoretical model:[35]

> [Empowerment is] ... an iterative process in which a person who lacks power sets a personally meaningful goal oriented toward increasing power, takes action toward that goal, and observes and reflects on the impact of this action, drawing on the person's evolving self-efficacy, knowledge and competence, related to the goal.

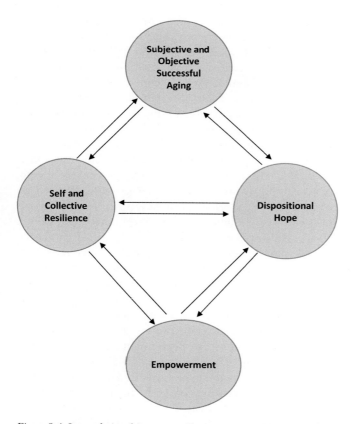

Figure 8.1 Interrelationships among Empowerment, Hope, Resilience, and Successful Aging

Furthermore, this conceptualization meshes well with CEMSA's featuring efficacy as a central component in managing aging successfully. We would also contend that power-oriented goals can be not only focused on enhancing the self's ability to successfully age but can also be oriented toward actively giving others more power in this process. By so doing, people can encourage their significant others to better understand and help plan for the personal and collective dilemmas relating to the aging process and its consequences.[36] Relatedly, scholars have argued that "knowledge (about the future is *empowering*)" and that "knowledge of what's going on with you *health-wise* is the most *empowering* thing you've got" (emphasis added).[37] In other words, having knowledge of your current and future health status gives one a psychological asset in terms of controlling a valued facet of one's destiny.

In Figure 8.1, we present a heuristic model that captures the potential interrelationships between resilience, empowerment, and hope that we suggest are deserving of further conceptual and theoretical development. Among the theoretical and empirical questions that can be raised on the basis of this framework are: When, how, and to whom are the discourses of resilience, hope, and empowerment (and the converses of them) introduced into older adults' conversations? What affective health and social consequences arise, and why?

Looking Back and Looking Ahead

In the opening chapter of this book, age demographics and other disciplines' analyses of aging, and the theories they avow, were explored. However, we also emphasized (and emphasize again here) the notion that age is not so much a chronological number, nor how old people think or feel that they are. Rather, we propose that *you are as old as you communicate and are communicated to and about*. Hopefully, those who have waded through this book will now find some solace in, and even encouragement by, this proposition. Relatedly, we hope the goals of promoting personhood and academic understanding of aging issues introduced in Chapter 1 have now been largely met and may have excited some readers to pose further questions of their own, in addition to those that we suggest later as directions for future research addressing communication and successful aging.

In Chapter 1, the rich heterogeneity of what comprises "older people" in any society was expounded in a discussion of the variable manifestations of humiliation and privilege that accompany aging, as well as the notion that different cultures have their own, unique social perspectives on what constitutes aging. We presented an alternative to the stance that aging is an inevitable decremental process associated with inherent deficits and stigmas. In its place, we outlined a healthier position in which aging across *all* points along the lifespan could be anticipated and envisaged as venturesome, bold, and audacious and that expressions of these would provide savoring narratives to both people constructing these messages, and those encountering them.[38]

Chapter 2 addressed agism and age stereotypes, highlighting the various ways that people think about old age and older adults. We noted the prevalence of agism in both Western and East Asian cultures and the extent to which age affects how people are treated across the lifespan. The balance of the chapter described the content and nature of age-based stereotypes, which have both positive and negative elements, and their consequences for communication and social interaction. We outlined a range of age-based stereotype "subtypes" – that is, collections of stereotypic traits that are often clustered in people's minds, creating different "personas" or "types" – of older adults identified by (predominantly) white Americans. We also noted that people can sometimes *self*-stereotype and that this can have negative consequences for their behavior, health, and longevity when the stereotypes they internalize and apply to themselves are negative.

There are several directions that future research could take to engage issues raised and discussed in Chapter 2. Researchers could investigate how (if at all) stereotypes of older adults change over time as people are living and working longer. Further investigation could also be directed to explore whether and to what extent the "subtypes" of older adults identified in previous American research extend to other cultural contexts. Finally, empirical work could be devised to explore how people of all ages address and/or communicatively manage agism in interaction in productive, positive ways, and whether effective strategies differ for members of various social groups or communities, including those of traditionally underrepresented groups in the United States (e.g., non-white racial and ethnic groups, sexual minorities).

Chapter 3 introduced the concept of age identity and discussed age as one of *multiple* social identity groups of which people are members; those social identities include race, gender, sexuality, and socioeconomic status (to name a few). We argued that age is the foremost identity that informs how individuals make sense of themselves and others. We also highlighted that individuals' age intersects with other identities that are both oppressed and privileged, a phenomenon formally conceptualized as *intersectionality*. Due to the differences that arise from people's intersectional identities, some older adults confront agism *as well as* other societal inequities and injustice that stem from additional oppressed social identities. This can mean that aging can be a particularly difficult process for subpopulations of older adults. With that said, various triggers make one's (older) age salient; we advanced six specific triggers in this chapter that ranged from (seemingly well-intentioned) honorifics to birthday cards. We then turned to the communication predicament of the aging model to consider the consequences (e.g., personal, relational, and health-related) of age salience, particularly during intergenerational encounters. Fortunately, older adults have the agency to enact various tactics that enable them to negotiate their age identity; for instance, they can cognitively reframe how they view old age, change how others view old age, or even attempt to disassociate themselves from their age group altogether.

There are several directions future research could take to engage issues raised and discussed in Chapter 3. Researchers could investigate how older adults are leveraging social media and virtual, online spaces to employ tactics that enable them to negotiate their age identity. Further investigation could also be undertaken exploring how the communication predicament model of aging translates to the communities of color in which disrespect to elders is not tolerated according to pervasive cultural traditions and values. Relatedly, future empirical work could explore how the model translates to the communities of color in which the physical signs of aging among older adults are less prevalent and/or detectable.

In Chapter 4, we explored intergenerational communication and introduced concepts from communication accommodation theory as tools for explaining and predicting what happens in intergenerational interactions. We discussed how negative stereotypes of older adults can lead younger people to speak to them in a patronizing way; we also noted, however, that older people can patronize younger adults as well, generally based on those older adults' stereotypes of younger adults. We also addressed the phenomenon of painful self-disclosures, in which older adults unexpectedly disclose about difficult or painful topics including illness and death, and how they affect interaction. We concluded with suggestions for improving the quality of intergenerational interaction, drawing on research in intergroup contact.

There are several directions future research could take to engage issues raised and discussed in Chapter 4. Researchers could investigate how new technology (e.g., mainstream videoconferencing applications, social media) will influence the quantity and quality of intergenerational communication that older adults will experience in the years ahead, compared with previous decades. Further investigation could also examine what kinds of interventions can be developed to improve the quality of intergenerational interactions. Finally, empirical work could be devised to explore how and to what extent younger adults underaccommodate older adults, and whether this looks the same across different communities, cultures, and subgroups.

In Chapter 5, we examined media images and representations of older people, highlighting their relative infrequency vis-à-vis other age groups. We argued that this (lack of) representation can implicitly convey messages about the value (or lack of it) societies place on these later life phases. Moreover, and across different genres and cultures, when images of older folk are apparent, they are often portrayed negatively, or as *exceptions* if the portrayal is positive. We suggested that for favorable images of older adults in mass media to change people's beliefs or attitudes about this group, these images somehow need to convey that these older people are actually *prototypical* of that target age group. Positioning positive images as prototypical can help prevent people from subtyping them into some kind of separate minority group. Relatedly, we also discussed the potential ramifications of mass media promoting a youth-oriented culture where tantalizing and persuasive anti-aging – and even so-called *de*-aging – cosmetics and surgeries are pervasively advertised (and often promoted by celebrity role models). We argued that this industry can have damaging effects on many older people (as well as younger) if they buy into these psychologically corrosive messages.

There are several directions future research could take to engage issues raised and discussed in Chapter 5. Researchers could investigate how to engage entertainment and marketing media to become more sensitive to the pernicious ways in which older (and often younger) age stages are portrayed; they could also examine ways to ameliorate these issues. Further investigation could also aim to determine how to induce people across the lifespan to become more media literate about the ways aging is represented, while still allowing for constructive and meaningful ways of enjoying and processing mass media content. Finally, empirical work could be devised for exploring at what life stages anti-aging products and procedures (whether explicitly labeled as such, or not) could be beneficial for whom, how, and why this is the case.

Chapter 6 dealt with communicative messages about death and dying in the latter phase of life – albeit far from being the only age stage where mortality happens. We discussed how different cultures and social groups manage death and bereavement in different ways. Much of the chapter focused on Western societies where talk about death can be fear-provoking, if not terrifying, and be considered "off-limits" when conversing with older people, people with terminal conditions, and the bereaved. We also addressed the ways in which medical personnel's disclosure, or not, of death-related information can be misplaced and/or problematic. Despite these issues, we emphasized the many ways in which talk – if sensitively designed and strategically engineered in certain social contexts – can hold a range of positive functions (e.g., a sense of personal control and a reduced sense of uncertainty about the future) for people of most ages, as can the communicative rituals associated with funerals. In sum, we argued for empowering benefits that can arise from addressing death and dying in conversation when appropriately administered and/or sensitively and empathically designed. In this, we noted particular benefits for planning and discursively confronting the issues attending particular kinds of deaths and the inevitably different trajectories of dying.

There are several directions future research could take to engage issues raised and discussed in Chapter 6. Researchers could investigate how, when, and why a person acquires a history of successfully managing death issues, and how this can be effectively resourced. Further investigation could also be directed at determining how, on the other side of the coin, death-related information and narratives from significant others can be managed, appreciated, and reconciled by recipients of them, and how this process can be optimized. Finally, empirical work could be devised for exploring how, when, and by whom death and dying issues can be timely and successfully introduced into young peoples' socialization processes and their media.

In Chapter 7, we addressed successful aging. We first reviewed different approaches to defining this concept and then provided our preferred definition, which treats successful aging as an individualized, subjective experience. We then reviewed three age ideologies, or ways of approaching life as we age, that we suggested could contribute to successful aging. The balance of the chapter reviewed research on communication and successful aging. Seven different domains of communication were highlighted that have the potential to affect people's experiences of aging. We also outlined the key variables and relationships comprising the CEMSA as a theoretical model that describes how these forms of communication are associated with experiences of successful aging. Finally, we reviewed extant research using the CEMSA, discussing both the approaches these studies have taken and their major findings.

There are several directions future research could take to engage issues raised and discussed in Chapter 7. Researchers could investigate the extent to which relationships outlined in the CEMSA extend to different cultural groups and subgroups who may have different communicative practices or norms around communication. Further efforts could also be directed at developing interventions to help people communicate about age and aging in more productive ways and examining whether these actually influence their experiences of successful aging. Finally, empirical work could be devised to explore when and how people, across the lifespan, develop the patterns of communication about age and aging that we see in older adulthood, and whether there are key points or opportunities to influence this development.

Three Overarching Themes

We move now to a consideration of the substance of this book as a whole from three interrelated and important angles: the lifespan, cultural variability in a broad sense, and applied implications that emerge. First, from the outset in Chapter 1, we made the case that we would be discussing successful aging from a *lifespan* perspective. This in the sense that whether one veers more toward more successful or unsuccessful experiences of aging often depends on the communicative experiences apparent earlier – and sometimes much earlier – in life. This is most vividly shown in a hand-crafted birthday card from a young boy to his middle-aged father we found while re-discovering old files (shown here). (How the particular father would have dealt with this visualized metaphor is anyone's conjecture in the light of the preceding chapters).

Nonetheless, lifespan issues have emerged throughout the chapters of the book. For example:

- We develop ideas of what aging is and "means" across the lifespan, and these cognitive maps inform our own experiences of (successful) aging in older adulthood;
- Generations within a society can constitute different cultures, which are often not appreciated as such, and can give rise to intergenerational misattributions, misunderstandings, and miscommunications;

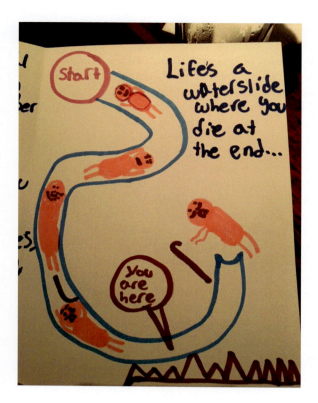

- The media can be an active (and sometimes, albeit hardly of course on all occasions, maleficent) instrument in creating and perpetuating agism against people of different ages (e.g., adolescents, tweens, middle-aged, and elderly);
- Death and dying, and people's subjective control of these, can appropriately be construed as an evolving episode in their lives as they discursively deal with it for others and themselves.

Second, in Chapter 1, we also made the case that much research and theory on communication and aging can be *culture-dependent*, with racial and ethnic heritages affecting the way aging is objectively and subjectively experienced. Such cultural variability is evident, for example, in different ways in:

- Age boundaries regarding the onset and end of young, middle-age, and older adulthood;
- Normative expectations for the nature of intergenerational communication and interaction more generally;

- Approaches to death and dying (which can range from fear to ritualistic celebration) and the institutional ways different people are communicatively "put to rest";
- People's progression through the lifespan and experiences as an older adult, which can vary considerably as a function of membership in other social identity groups such as their socioeconomic status, race, and sexuality.

Third and finally, implicit in the CEMSA model outlined in Chapter 7 is a range of personal and collective recommendations. Selected examples include our suggestions that people:

- Avoid conveying negative messages – face-to-face or in mediated channels –about the process of aging, as these messages can be affectively and cognitively destructive at any age and, especially so later in life;
- Listen when talking to others who are bereaved; avoid clichés and platitudes; do not recommend feelings, thoughts, and actions; and be supportive and offer resources;
- Avoid holding older adults to pervasive, age-related stereotypes that can lead to negative, problematic interactions, and instead accommodate the unique, individual characteristics of older adults during interactions;
- Express positivity and optimism about the experience of aging, accepting one's current place in the lifespan while looking forward to new opportunities, challenges, and experiences that each coming life stage will bring.

Concluding Thoughts

Needless to say, we wish readers hope, resilience, empowerment, and enjoyment as they age in their own unique personal and social circumstances. Even further, we echo the words of 98-year-old Norman Lear, a producer and TV writer, who remarked when accepting an honor at the 2021 Golden Globes Awards that "laughter adds time to one's own life!" It was our intent that this book would enhance readers' (scholarly as well as experiential) understanding of the relationships between communication and aging. We also hoped that this book would provide some modest practical assistance in the successful aging process, moving as we are into the Decade of Healthy Aging promoted by the World Health Organization. Certainly, our theoretical position on communication and successful aging is consistent with recent work emphasizing that brain cells – in addition to knowledge, subjective experiences, and psychological perspectives – can continue to develop and be activated throughout the lifespan.[39] We contend that the communicative resources highlighted in this book, together with being mindful about societally institutionalized constraints placed on certain people in underserved groups, offer ways to promote healthy and ongoing development at all levels—neural, person, and social.

Examining and reflecting on how people age, and the social factors that affect experiences of aging, is particularly timely as the frontiers of longevity become ever more elastic (with the attending personal and societal challenges). This matter was provocatively depicted on a cover of *Time Magazine* (February 12, 2015) that read, "This baby could live to be 142 years old." While there will doubtless be challenges as longevity increases and life trajectories change, we also see that in addressing such issues, there are opportunities for thoughtful (and even visionary) social policymaking, academic research, and interpersonal interactions. In all of this, we see the overarching goal to be making experiences of, and communications about, aging more positive for individuals across the lifespan.

Notes

1 Baars, J., & Visser, H. (Eds.). (2007). *Aging and time: Multidisciplinary perspectives*. Amityville, NY: Baywood; Tsuji, Y. (2005); Time is not up: Temporal complexity of older Americans' lives. *International Journal of Aging and Human Development, 20*, 3–26. Retrieved from https://doi.org/10.1007/s10823-005-3794-7; see also: Steger, M. F. (2009). Meaning in life. In S. J. Lopez (Ed.), *Oxford handbook of positive psychology* (2nd ed., pp. 679–687). Oxford, UK: Oxford University Press.
2 See, for example: Gooding, P. A., Hurst, A., Johnson, J., & Tarrier, N. (2012). Psychological resilience in younger and older adults. *International Journal of Geriatric Psychiatry, 27*(2), 262–270. https://doi.org/10.1002/gps.2712
3 See, for example: Calasanti, T., & King, N. (2020). Beyond successful aging 2.0: Inequalities, agism, and the case for normalizing old ages. *The Journals of Gerontology: Series B*. Advance Online: https://doi.org/10.1093/geronb/gbaa037
4 See: World Health Organization. *UN decade of health aging. 2021-2030*. Retrieved from: https://www.who.int/initiatives/decade-of-healthy-ageing
5 American Psychological Association. (2014). *The road to resilience*. Retrieved from: https://advising.unc.edu/wp-content/uploads/sites/341/2020/07/The-Road-to-Resiliency.pdf; see also: Southwick, S. M., Bonanno, G. A., Masten, A. S., Panter-Brick, C., & Yehuda, R. (2014). Resilience definitions, theory, and challenges: Interdisciplinary perspectives. *European Journal of Psychotraumatology, 5*(1). https://doi.org/10.3402/ejpt.v5.25338
6 de Terte, I., & Stephens, C. (2014). Psychological resilience of workers in high-risk organizations. *Stress and Health, 30*(5), 353–355. https://doi.org/10.1002/smi.2627; Carver, C., S. (1998). Resilience and thriving: Issues, models, and linkages. *Journal of Social Issues, 54*(2), 245–266. https://doi.org/10.1111/j.1540-4560.1998.tb01217.x
7 See book review of four major contributions to resilience: Perkins, M. M. (2014). Resilience in later life: Emerging trends and future directions. *The Gerontologist, 54*(1), 138–142. https://doi.org/10.1093/geront/gnt159
8 Afifi, T. D., Merrill, A. F., & Davis, S. M. (2016). The theory of resilience and relational load. *Personal Relationships, 23*(4), 663–683. https://doi.org/10.1111/pere.12159; Buzzanell, P. M., & Houston, J. B. (Eds.). (2018). Communication and resilience: Multilevel applications and insights. Special Issue of the *Journal of Applied Communication, 46*(1), 1–134. https://doi.org/10.1080/00909882.2017.1412086
9 See, for example: Walsh, F. (2007). Traumatic loss and major disasters: Strengthening family and community resilience. *Family Process, 46*(2), 207–227. https://doi.org/10.1111/j.1545-5300.2007.00205.x
10 See, for example: Jeste D. V., Slva, G. N., & Thompson et al. (2013). Older age is associated with more successful aging: Role of resilience and depression. *American Journal of Psychiatry, 170*(2), 188–196. https://doi.org/10.1176/appi.ajp.2012.12030386

11 Jacelon, C. S. (1997). The trait and process of resilience. *Journal of Advanced Nursing, 25*(1), 123–129. https://doi.org/10.1046/j.1365-2648.1997.1997025123.x; Windle, G. (2011). What is resilience? A review and concept analysis. *Reviews in Clinical Gerontology, 21*(02), 152–169. https://doi.org/10.1017/S0959259810000420

12 American Psychological Association. (2014). *The road to resilience*. Retrieved from: https://advising.unc.edu/wp-content/uploads/sites/341/2020/07/The-Road-to-Resiliency.pdf; Buzzanell, P. M., & Houston, J. B. (Eds.). (2018). Communication and resilience: Multilevel applications and insights. *Journal of Applied Communication, 46*(1), 1–4. https://doi.org/10.1080/00909882.2017.1412086

13 For examples, see: MacLeod, S., Musich, S., Hawkins, K., Alsgaard, K., & Wicker, E. R. (2016). The impact of resilience among older adults. *Geriatric Nursing, 37*(4), 266–272. https://doi.org/10.1016/j.gerinurse.2016.02.014; da Silva-Sauer, L., Lima, T. R. G., da Fonsêca, de la Torre-Luque, Yu, Fernández-Calvo. (2021). Psychological resilience moderates the effect of perceived stress on late-life depression in community-dwelling older adults. *Trends in Psychology*. Advance online: https://doi.org/10.1007/s43076-021-00073-3

14 Harris, P. B. (2008). Another wrinkle in the debate about successful aging: The undervalued concept of resilience and the lived experience of dementia. *International Journal of gaining & Human Development, 67*(1), 43–61. https://doi.org/10.2190/AG.67.1.c

15 Clark, P. G., Burbank, P. M., Greene, G., Owens, N. & Riebe, D. (2011). What do we know about resilience in older adults? An exploration of some facts, factors, and facets In B. Resnick, L. P. Gwyther, & K. A. Roberto (Eds.), *Resilience in aging: Concepts, research, and outcomes* (pp. 51–61). New York, NY: Springer.

16 See again: Perkins, M. M. (2014). Resilience in later life: Emerging trends and future directions. *The Gerontologist, 54*(1), 138–142. https://doi.org/10.1093/geront/gnt159

17 Lyubomirsky, S., & Della Porta, M. D. (2010). Boosting happiness, buttressing resilience: Results from cognitive and behavioral interventions. In J. W. Reich, A. J. Zautra, & J. Hall (Eds.), *Handbook of adult resilience: Concepts, methods, and applications* (pp. 450–464). New York, NY: Guildford.

18 Hill, S., & Giles, H. (2019). Resilience as a department cultural initiative: Sustaining wellness. *Police Chief* Online, May 29. Retrieved from: http://www.policechiefmagazine.org/resilience-as-a-department-cultural-initiative/

19 See, for example: Fredriksen-Goldsen, K. I., Emlet, C. A., Kim, H.-J., Muraco, A., Erosheva, E. A., Goldsen, J., & Hoy-Ellis, C. P. (2013). The physical and mental health of lesbian, gay male, and bisexual (LGB) older adults: The role of key health indicators and risk and protective factors. *The Gerontologist, 53*(4), 664–675. https://doi.org/1093/geront/gns123

20 Gilleard, C., & Higgs, P. (2020). *Social division and later life: Difference, diversity, and inequality*. Bristol: Bristol Policy Press.

21 Soldati, S. K. (2021). My anxiety at being Asian has morphed into fear. *Los Angeles Times*, March 3, A.11; see also: FACT SHEET: Anti-Asian Prejudice March 2020 – Center for the Study of Hate & Extremism. Retrieved from: https://www.csusb.edu/sites/default/files/FACT%20SHEET-%20Anti-Asian%20Hate%202020%203.2.21.pdf

22 Takei, G., Eisinger, J. Scott, S., & Becker, H. (2020). *They called us enemy: Expanded edition*. New York, NY: Penguin Random House.

23 Cárdenas, D., Verkuyten, M., & Fleischmann, F. (2021). "You are too ethnic, you are too national": Dual identity denial and dual identification. *International Journal of Intercultural Relations, 81*(1), 193–203. https://doi.org/10.1016/j.ijintrel.2021.01.011; See also: Louw-Potgeiter, J., & Giles, H. Louw-Potgeiter, J. & Giles, H. (1987). Imposed identity and linguistic strategies. *Journal of Language and Social Psychology, 7*(3–4), 261–286. https://doi.org/10.1177/0261927X8763008

24 Koschate, M., Naserian, E., Dickens, L., Stuart, A., Russo, A., & Levine, M. (2021). ASIA: Automated Social Identity Assessment using linguistic style. *Behavior Research Methods*. Advance Online: https://doi.org/10.3758/s13428-020-01511-3

25 Bernhold, Q. S., & Giles, H. (2019). Older adults' recalled memorable messages about aging and their associations with successful aging. *Human Communication Research, 45*, 474–507, 2019. https://doi.org/10.1093/hcr/hqz011

26 Forbes, S. B. (1994). Hope: An essential human need in the elderly. *Journal of Gerontological Nursing, 20*(6), 5–10. https://doi.org/10.3928/0098-9134-19940601-04; see also: Thompson, T. L. (2011). Hope and the act of informed dialogue: A delicate balance of end-of-life. *Journal of Language and Social Psychology, 30*(2), 177–192. https://doi.org/10.1177/0261927X10397150

27 Feldman, D. B., & Kubota, M. (2015). Hope, self-efficacy, optimism, and academic achievement: Distinguishing constructs and levels of specificity in predicting college grade-point average. *Learning and Individual Differences, 37*(January), 210–216. https://doi.org/10.1016/j.lindif.2014.11.022

28 Snyder, C. R. (2002). Hope theory: Rainbows in the mind. *Psychological Inquiry, 13*(4), 249–275. https://doi.org/10.1207/S15327965PLI1304_01

29 Cheavens, J. S., Feldman, D. B., Gum, A., Michael, S. T., & Snyder, C. R. (2006). Hope theory in a community sample: A pilot investigation. *Social Indicators Research, 77*(1), 61–78. https://doi.org/10.1007/s11205-005-5553-0

30 Snyder, C. R., LaPointe, A. B., Crowson, J. J., & Early, S. (1998). Preferences of high- and low-hope people for self-referential input. *Cognition and Emotion, 12*(6), 807–823. https://doi.org/10.1080/026999398379448

31 Mechanic, D. (1991). Adolescents at risk: New directions. *Journal of Adolescent Health, 12*, 638–643. https://doi.org/10.1016/1054-139X(91)90012-M; Rappaport, J. (1995). Empowerment meets narrative: Listening to stories and creating settings. *American Journal of Community Psychology, 23*(5), 795–807. https://doi.org/10.1007/BF02506992; Zimmerman, M. A. (2000). Empowerment theory: Psychological, organizational, and community levels of analysis. In J. Rappaport & E. Sedman (Eds.), *Handbook of community psychology* (pp. 43–63). New York, NY: Kluwer Academic/Plenum.

32 White, R. A. (2008). Communication strategies for empowerment. In W. Donsbach (Ed.), *International encyclopedia of communication* (Vol. 3, pp. 821–825). New York, NY: Wiley/Blackwell.

33 Ryan, E. B., Meredith, S. D., MacLean, M. J., & Orange, J. B. (1995). Changing the way we talk with elders: Promoting health using the Communication Enhancement Model. *International Journal of Aging and Human Development, 41*(2), 87–105. https://doi.org/10.2190/FP05-FM8V-0Y9F-53FX

34 Greenway, K. H., Gallois, C., & Haslam, S. A. (2018). Social psychological approaches to intergroup communication. In H. Giles & J. Harwood, Eds.), *The Oxford encyclopedia of intergroup communication* (Vol. 2., pp. 367–379). New York, NY: Oxford University Press.

35 See the schematic model of: Cattaneo, L. B., & Chapman, A. R. (2010). The process of empowerment: A model for use in research and practice. *American Psychologist, 65*(7), 646–659. https://doi.org/10.1037/a0018854; see also: Brodsky, A. E., & Cattaneo, L. B. (2013). A transconceptual model of empowerment and resilience: Divergence, convergence and interactions in kindred community concepts. *American Journal of Community Psychology, 52*(3–4), 333–346. https://doi.org/10.1007/s10464-013-9599-x; Cattaneo, L. B., Calton, J. M., & Brodsky, A. E. (2014). Status quo versus status quake: Putting the power back in empowerment. *Journal of Community Psychology, 42*(4), 433–446. https://doi.org/10.1002/jcop.21619

36 For a discussion of power in relationships, see: Dunbar, N. E., Lane, B. L., & Abra, G. (2017). Power in close relationships: A dyadic power theory perspective. In J. A. Samp (Ed.), *Communicating interpersonal conflict in close relationships: Contexts, challenges, and opportunities* (pp. 75–92). New York, NY: Routledge.

37 Although the quotes (see p. 618) relate to the endurance of brutal health conditions, we see their relevance for coping with health issues in general: Curtis, J. R., Engelberg, R., Young, J. P., Vig, L. K. Reinke, L. F., Wenrich, M. D., McGrath, B., McCown, E., & Back, A. L. (2008). An approach to understanding the interaction of hope and desire for

explicit prognostic information among individuals with severe chronic obstructive pulmonary disease or advanced cancer. *Journal of Palliative Medicine, 11*(4), 610–620. https://doi.org/10.1089/jpm.2007.0209

38 Pitts, M. J. (2019). The language and social psychology of savoring: Advancing the Communication Savoring Model. *Journal of Language and Social Psychology, 38*(2), 237–259. https://doi.org/10.1177/0261927X18821404

39 Gupta, S. (2021). *Keep sharper: Build a better brain at any age*. New York, NY: Simon & Schuster.

Index

Note: Page numbers in *italics* indicate figures and page numbers **bold** indicate tables

AARP *see* American Association of Retired Persons (AARP)
abuse: elder 13; younger 9
accidents 63, 93
accommodation: CAT 56, 135; CPA model 52; deflecting 67; despondent 29; nonaccommodation 57; overaccommodation 57, 59, 63, 67; perfect grandparent 29; underaccommodation 57, 59, 67; younger generations 52, 63, 67; *see also* patronizing talk
activities of daily living 32
activity theory 5
adults: age boundaries **12**; age identity 38–40, 49–52; agism 20, 22; age prejudice and discriminatory 21; age stereotyping 24–28; aging efficacy 11; ASIM 48–49; comedic portrayals 75; communication deficits 6; communication technology 119–120; consequences of stereotyping 28–31; COVID-19 130; despondent 29; elderspeak 57; end-of-life needs with family 118–119; expressive skills **29**; freedom from disability 109; gender transition 39; good death 90; health-related mistreatment 40; independent life trajectory 113; inevitable recipient of agism 117–118; lifespan 7–11, 111; memory failure **30**; modernization 23; negative stereotypes 25; negative stereotypes 28, 48; non-listening **62**; nonverbal patronizing talk **58**; normal adult speech 48; nursing homes 61; older, actively categorizing, teasing, and reacting 116–117; open-mindedness 63; overaccommodate 67; overprotective **62**; painful self-disclosure 57, 67; patronizing talk 57, **58**, 61, *63*; perfect grandparent 29; positive emotions and optimism 117; positive media messages 81–84; receptive skills **29**; sandwich generation 56; self-categorizing with respect to age 116; self-disclosures 64–66; senior discounts 20; social groups 26; socially engaged 5; stress test 22; subtypes **26**, 26–27; third-party talk 59; underaccommodate 67; underaccommodate 67; verbal patronizing talk **58**; Westernization 23; young, age boundaries **12**; youth disapproving **62**; *see also* accommodation; communication; death; health care; middle age
advertising: age-defying pillowcases 78; anti-aging products 118; anti-aging surgeries 73; de-aging cosmetics and surgeries 135; health-related products 78; magazine 83; prime-time TV shows 74; print 72; television 83; thick anti-age cushioning 78
age/aging: (dis)abilities 41; age-defying 79; agist images 73–78; barriers 39; Black lesbians and Black gay men 39; CEMSA 131–133; changes 86; chronological 40, 51, 111, 133; communication-centered approach 115–120; coping mechanisms 84; COVID-19 pandemic 128; crisis 76; cross-cultural and generational differences 11–13; de-aging 79; demographics of 2–4; disciplinary perspectives 4–7; effective 1, 49, 52, 108; empower 1, 90; experiences 38–39; identity 38–40, 49–52; ideologies 110–115; illness 4; images 118; institutions

5; intergenerational similarities and differences 66–68; lifespan social and communicative construction 7–11; negotiation and management 49–52; positive 1; privileges 23; productive 1; pyramid 3, *5*; robust 1; salience 40–42, 46–49; self-stereotyping 31–32; stereotyping 24–27, 46, 139; subtypes 26–27; successful 108–110, 120–123, 128; talk–sho 122; triggers of age identity 42–46; unsuccessful 131; *see also* anti-aging; fear of aging; health care
age discrimination 21–22, 39; eastern European countries 11; lawsuits 22; social prejudice 8
agency: age identity 49; CEMSA 120; older adults 48, 134
age stereotypes in interaction model (ASIM) 48
agism: communicative construction 14; cross-cultural and generational differences 11–13; inevitable recipient of 117–118; mass media 118; prevalence 21–24; senior discounts 20; social construction 14; *see also* adults; housing
air traffic controllers, mandatory retirement 21
American Association of Retired Persons (AARP) 46, 76
Amiel, Henri Frédéric 4
Anan, Kofi 4
ancient ivory 74
anti-aging: agism in media 84–85; agist images in media 73–78; cult of youth 78–81; positive media messages 81–84; products 80, 118, 136; surgeries 80; *see also* media
anti-Black racism 130
Asian-Americans pandemics 14, 130
ASIM *see* age stereotypes in interaction model (ASIM)
assertive response 60
assisted suicide 101
attitudes, agist: individualistic communities 11; intergenerational 85; negative 8, 20, 24, 29, 31; positive 60; stereotyping 24–31

Baby Boomers 73, **114**
bad news 93
behaviors: age-based self-categorization 65, 122; children's 43; communicative 12, 122; nonverbal 58; older people 60; physical rigor 51; prototypical 39, 59; rational 65; stereotype 27–28; verbal 58; younger people's 20
Black Americans 44; COVID-19 pandemic 130; stereotypes 26
Black family life 74
Black lesbians 39
Boomers burden 76

caregiver 83
CAT *see* communication accommodation theory (CAT)
categorization, age-based: Abbies 73; Golden Ager 28; memorable messages 10; patronizing 62–63; self-categorizing 116–122; social 38–39, 128, 131; tween girls 73; Twixters 73
CEMSA *see* communicative ecology model of successful aging (CEMSA)
children: age stereotypes 23; cross-cultural and generational differences 11–13; education 23; first-generation immigrants 115; Japanese American 130; memorable messages 10; TikTok 50; TV interviews 43
China virus 130
chronological age 40, 51, 111, 133
commercial airline pilots, mandatory retirement 21
communication: age salience 46–49; age stereotypes 29; CEMSA 131–132; centered approach 6; construction 7–10; CPA model 49; disciplines *5*; empowerment 129–133; end of life 95–98, 118–119; hope 129–133; lifespan 1; objective and subjective health *2*; patronizing 48; predicament model of aging 134; resilience 129–133; scholars 23; self-categorizing with respect 116; stay connected 119–120; to successful aging 1, 120–123; *see also* intergenerational communication; language
communication accommodation theory (CAT) 56, 135
communicative ecology model of successful aging (CEMSA) 120, *121*, 131
communicative predicament model of aging (CPA) 47
community: extraordinary gang violence 92; festivities at cemetery 91; institutional settings 58; organizations 112
competence: incompetence 61; mental 30; stereotypes 25–27

conflicts 62, 115, 129
Confucian value of filial piety 23
continuity theory 5
coping: age-related coping mechanisms 84; resilience 129; social creativity 50; terminal illness 94
COVID-19: China virus 130; economic crisis 128; ICU 97; Kungflu 130; older age 40; social distancing 101; videotaped message 99
CPA *see* communicative predicament model of aging (CPA)
cremation, pre-paid 92
cross-cultural differences 11–13, 23

death: accessibility 28; accidents 93; Asian cultures 91; cafes 102; Chinese cultures 91; communicative messages 136; COVID-19 3; Day of the Dead 91; emotional repression 90; end of life 92–98, 118–119; feelings of control 98–102; good 90, 103; hospice care 93; longterm illness 93; mortality salience 28; in Muslim societies 90; protective buffering 94; successful dying 103; sudden illness 93; *see also* emotions; funerals
Death with Dignity Act 101
decline: age excuses 30; cognitive 10, 66; memory 29; mental 4, 7, 65; physiological 7, 10, 49, 67, 78; stereotypes of aging 116
dementia 60
demography: of aging 1–4; time bomb 76
derogation of older people 24
discrimination *see* age discrimination
disengagement theory 5
dyad 96
dying *see* death; end of life; family; lifespan; terminal illness

emotions: communication at end of life 95–98; CRS 10; distress 49; instrumental support 51; negative 26, 62; positive 26, 117, 123; repression 90; resources 50; *see also* age/aging; fear of aging
empathy 65, 93–94, 115
end of life: communication 92–98; feelings of control over death 98–102; needs with family 118–119
entertainment: icons 85; industry 74; TV 76
environmental chatter 120
ethnicity: experiences of aging 124; groups 26, 134; stereotype 27

excuses, age 30–31
exemplar 76, 85; traits **26**

family: Black family life 74; communication 93; conflicts 129; endeavors 14; end-of-life needs with 118–119; exemplar traits **26**; funerals, as expensive occasions 92; grandparent role 40; needs 11, 24; personal lives 7; positive stereotypes 25; proud 75; social support 4; structure and intergenerational 4, 23; talking to dying and bereaved person **97**; videotaped message 99; visit 90; *see also* terminal illness
fear of aging: age-based discrimination 22; death and dying 96, 139; lack of ability 15; meaning of life 128; physical deficiencies 6; protective buffering 94; provoking 136; psychology deficiencies 6; *see also* death
filial piety 23–24
forces: of agism 84–85; societal 14
funerals: age salient 40; communicative rituals 136; COVID-19 pandemic 101; expensive occasions 92; Nine Nights 92; service 99

gender: assigned-at-birth 101; based honorifics 44; differences 8; social identity 38–40; social variable 14; stereotype 27; transition 39
Generation X **114**, 115
geriatrics 21
goodbye 96–97
grandparent: perfect **26**, 29; roles 40, 83

healing, of relationship 95
health care: age ideologies 110–115; COVID-19 130; cult of youth 78–81; diets 123; lifespan social and communicative construction 7–10; nurses 97; objective and subjective 2; painful self-disclosures 63–66; physical 1, 5, 109; psychological 1, 5, 132; settings 24; sociological 5; status of patient 59; successful aging 120–123; treatment plans 40; vision checks 21; workers 97; *see also* medical care
heterosexism 39
heterosexual marriage 101
housing, older people: senior discounts 20; tax advantages 20

identity balance theory 6
impairments **26**, 32, 48, 51, 59, 92, 118

148 Index

interdependent systems of oppression/ privilege 39
intergenerational communication: painful self-disclosures 63–66; patronizing talk 57–63; similarities and differences 66–68
It's a Beautiful Thing (Mazzio) 92

judges, mandatory retirement 21

Kungflu 130

labeling: Abbies 73; Baby Boomers 73; bantering 122; de-aging 79; patronizing talk 62; positive stereotyping of older people 25; successful aging 108; tween girls 73; Twixters 73
language: agist 74; communication deficits 6; people's aging process 46
lawsuits, age discrimination 22
lifespan: age boundaries **12**; age ideologies 110; agism 20; communication 1; continuity theory 5; development 1; end of life 92–98; interculturing process 113; issues 137; mental and physiological decline 7; resilience 129–130; social and communicative construction 7–10; successful aging 128, 131

magazines: advertising 83; portrayals of older adults 72; public forums 118
mandatory retirement 21
media: agism in 84–85, 118; agist images in 73–78; communication 5, 119–120; CPA model 49; cult of youth 78; digital 7; Facebook 115; industry 72; Instagram 115; magazines 72; mass media messages 10; negative stereotypes 32, 121; social media 72, 115; TikTok 50; TV shows 72; Twitter 115
medical care: anti-aging surgeries 80; appointment 59; painful self-disclosures 63–66, 136; patronizing talk 59; professionals 22, 40; settings 59; specialties 21; treatment 130; visits 59; workers 3
memory: age excuses 30–31; communication capacities 29; failure, excuses types **30**; negative stereotypes 32; social support 4
Merry Cemetery 100
military precision 99
Miracle Man (Ryan) 83
mortality salience 28; *see also* death
motivated acceptance 110–111

Nine Nights 92
nonaccommodation 57; *see also* accommodation
non-patronizing talk 62
nursing homes (NH) 58, 61, 109; *see also* well-being

overaccommodation 57, 59, 63, 67; *see also* accommodation

painful self-disclosures 63–66
patronizing talk 57–63; agist 116; elderspeak 57; negative stereotypes 68; older-to-younger adult **62**, *63*
personal trait 129
physicians: assistance 101; medical appointment 59; *see also* health care; medical care
positive media messages 81–84
prejudice: age 21; age stereotypes 68; social 8
pre-paid cremation 92
print advertising 72

race: social class 39; social group 38, 75
racism: anti-Black 130; intersecting oppressions 39
Red Hatters 32, 50
resilience 129–133
retirement: feeling older 41; mandatory 21; pandemic lockdowns 131; party 43; successful aging 109
routine talk 96

sandwich generation 56
secondary baby talk 58
selective optimization with compensation theory 6
self-categorization: age-based 65, 121; gloomy agers 122; with respect to age 116, 122
self-esteem 6, 38, 48, 52, 75, 96
self-image 96
self-report: life satisfaction 52; successful aging 122
senior centers 51
senior discounts 20
SeniorNet 51
sensory decrements 63
sexuality 39, 40, 75, 134, 139
shifting belief systems 96
silent revolution 4
social creativity 50

social identity theory (SIT) 38–39, 49–52, 80; of intergroup contact 85
social media: developments 113; Facebook 115; Generation Z 115; Instagram 115; portrayals of older adults 72; smartphone 115; TikTok 50; Twitter 115
social mobility 49
Social Security benefits 76
socioeconomic status 38, 124, 130, 134, 139
socioemotional selectivity theory 6
speech: loud **58**; nonverbal communication 61; normal adult 48; patronizing 60; slow 57, **58**; verbal communication 61; *see also* language
stereotypes 27–28; age salience 46–49; agist language 74; ASIM 48; consequences 28–31; embodiment 46; incompetence 61; intergenerational conversations 66; in media 84–85; middle age 25; negative age 7, 44, 51, 60, 68, 82, 118; non-stereotypes 83; older people 20, 75, 138; patronizing talk 68; positive 25, 49; positive media messages 81–84; self 31–32, 40, 65, 134; threat 46; traits 134; *see also* age stereotypes; decline
stigmatization 39, 50, 129, 133
successful aging 108–110; communication-centered approach 115–120; communicative ecology model 120, *121*; health care 120–123; labeling 108; lifespan 128, 131; retirement 109; self-report 122; steps 120–123
suicide, assisted 101
Supreme Court Justices, on age discrimination 22

technology: communication 115, 119–120; digital 63; mainstream videoconferencing applications 135; *see also* social media

television: age salience 41; American 74, 83; Nielsen-rated 74; prime-time 72; Saturday morning 72; shows 75, 83
terminal illness 93–96, 101–103; videotaped message 99
terror management theory 28

uncertainty reduction theory 98
underaccommodation 57, 59, 67; *see also* accommodation

video: conferencing 120, 135; events 43; family 43; games 90, 115; message 99
voice: cues 9–10; media 5; perturbations 9; shaky 75; terminal illness 94

walking stick, negative traits 25
well-being: nursing homes 61; psychological 46, 110–111, 117
women: American Black 26; feeling older 41; feeling younger 41; Latina 39; media messages 80; natural aging 80; painful self-disclosures 63; portrayals of white 74; positive reactions to elder 9; Red Hatters 32; white 39
workers: healthcare 97; hospice 95, 103; medical 3; middle-aged 25; nurses 97; older 22, 25
workplace: age stereotyping 27; middle-aged people 8; older people in 60

young adult: age boundaries **12**; age stereotyping 24; financially independent 23; social demands 63; underaccommodate 67